HEATHENS

CRADLEY HEATH SPEEDWAY

1977-1996

HEATHENS

CRADLEY HEATH SPEEDWAY

1977-1996

Peter Foster

TEMPUS

First published 2003

PUBLISHED IN THE UNITED KINGDOM BY:
Tempus Publishing Ltd
The Mill, Brimscombe Port
Stroud, Gloucestershire GL5 2QG

PUBLISHED IN THE UNITED STATES OF AMERICA BY:
Tempus Publishing Inc.
2 Cumberland Street
Charleston, SC 29401

British Library Cataloguing in Publication Data.
A catalogue record for this book is available from the British Library.

ISBN 0 7524 2738 5

Typesetting and origination by Tempus Publishing.
Printed in Great Britain by Midway Colour Print, Wiltshire

CONTENTS

INTRODUCTION

Cradley Heathens went through a period in the doldrums during the early 1970s and were tagged 'The Great Unfashionables'. It ended only with the arrival of promoters Dan McCormick and Derek Pugh in 1977, which began a golden era at Dudley Wood that was to set Cradley on a roller-coaster ride of success – and nobody deserved it more than the long-suffering Heathens supporters.

The fairy tale had begun. As Cradley improved year by year, young Bruce Penhall was brought over to Dudley Wood from the States, and had a bigger impact on the sport than any rider before him. In 1979, Cradley won the KO Cup and the Inter-league Cup. The following year, the club won the KO Cup and the Midland Cup and in 1981, with McCormick long gone, they became British League Champions for the first time ever. To top it all, Penhall, in that same year, became the Heathens' first ever World Champion. Cradley was the most talked-about club in the sport of speedway.

The year 1982 brought further success with victory in the KO Cup and League Cup, and Penhall successfully defended his World Championship before announcing his retirement on the rostrum, leaving Cradley high and dry for the rest of the season. Such a blow would have had a devastating effect on most clubs, but at Cradley it was 'business as usual' and other riders were brought in to replace the American.

In 1983 Cradley assembled perhaps the best speedway team of all time, when they once again became League Champions, and added the Midland Cup and the KO Cup to the silverware. Not only that, but they seemed to have another prospective World Champion waiting in the wings – Eric Gundersen. The young Dane had begun at Dudley Wood riding in the second half and progressed to become a timely successor to Penhall. He did in fact become Cradley's next World Champion, lifting the crown in 1984 and 1985, and leading the Heathens to further honours in the process.

In 1987 the Heathens began a trio of KO Cup victories that put them in the record books as the most successful KO Cup team ever. Gundersen helped himself to another World Championship in 1988, and was firmly established as one of the all-time greats of speedway before a near-fatal accident in 1989 ended his career.

It was another terrific blow for Cradley, but there were other stars at Dudley Wood such as Jan O. Pedersen and Simon Cross to soldier on. Pedersen proved himself to be a worthy successor to Gundersen. The minute Dane took the World Championship himself in 1991, and by that time he was established as one of the most accomplished riders of his day.

Injuries had always figured largely in the Heathens' history, but the early 1990s were a nightmare. Cross broke his back, but made a successful return to the sport, and Pedersen broke his too – but didn't. Injuries no doubt robbed Cradley of success over this period, but, even though they had lost the World Champion, the Heathens had two future World Champions in their camp in Greg Hancock and Billy Hamill. Dudley Wood was truly the breeding ground of World Champions.

In the mid-1990s, Cradley were just getting over 'the injury years' and re-forming the squad, when the owners of the stadium pulled the plug. Cradley Heath had always been one of the best-supported teams in speedway, and, over the last twenty years, had also been one of the most successful, but greed is a powerful enemy, and with property developers waving wads of notes under the owners' noses, the Heathens were chucked out. 1995 saw the end of a fairy tale that had seen a rags-to-riches speedway team take the name of Cradley Heath all around the world.

ACKNOWLEDGEMENTS

There are many people to thank for their help in writing this book. Unsung heroes Les Pottinger and Mr and Mrs Derek Pugh were the first people contacted, and they gave me permission to reproduce the Cradley programme covers in the book.

All of the Cradley Heath programmes were pored over for hours to try and ensure that any details included in 'The Heathens' were correct, and all of the programme compilers and contributors over the years deserve thanks for their input.

Photographs are an important part of all non-fiction journals, and I would like to thank John Hall, John Hipkiss and Mike Patrick for their contributions. I would also like to pay tribute to the *Speedway Star* for allowing me to use some of their archive photographs. Photographer John Hall was especially helpful, giving me access to his entire collection of photos, and, over the weeks, he spent many hours in his loft sorting through his negatives for anything that he thought may be of any use to me.

A special mention should go to Paul at Willow Print company – who currently produce programmes for many speedway tracks.

My appreciation is also given to Phil and Steve Johnson who run the excellent Cradley website at www.cradleyspeedway.co.uk. They have been associates for many years and, with regard to information, never fail me in my hour of need.

Finally, may I thank every single Heathen that has ever graced Dudley Wood. The hours of pleasure that they have given to me and their thousands of supporters over the years is immeasurable and unforgettable.

Every effort has been made to make sure that the information given in the book is authentic and accurate. If any inaccuracies are present, then my apologies go out to any person concerned, or to the huge band of speedway statisticians that exist throughout the land. I can only hope that any such inaccuracies do not spoil anyone's enjoyment of the book.

1

DAN, DAN
THE SPEEDWAY MAN
1977

The year 1977 saw the end of Cradley Heath as the 'Great Unfashionables' of speedway. It was to be a turning point in the club's history, and it was started by one man – Dan McCormick.

The winter had seen a change of regime at Dudley Wood. The promotion was taken over by Dan and a Shrewsbury businessman, Derek Pugh, and Bob Wasley was named as team manager. McCormick had been involved in the sport as early as 1960 when he was part of the stadium management at Newcastle, and he had also been stadium manager at Wolverhampton. He was outspoken about the sport that he loved, and frequently made the headlines with his innovative, and sometimes radical, point of view. Dan arrived at Dudley Wood making the proclamation that he already had the best supporters in the world, and it was his intention to give them the best team in the world. He claimed that within three years, Cradley would be League Champions. He certainly made all the right noises, and won many fans when he decided that there would be no more 'United crap'. It would be Cradley Heathens – period.

Dan intended to make a start with virtually the same team as 1976, with just one signing – Bob Valentine. Bob was a 37-year-old Australian who had come to England in 1970 to ride for Workington in the National League. He graduated into the BL and rode for Sheffield, Coventry and Birmingham before signing for the Heathens. With Nigel Wasley dropping back into the second halves, the line-up was complete – so Dan thought. He had talked Bernie Persson into returning, newly-married Dave Perks was back, so were Price and Bastable, and Bruce Cribb was to be the new skipper. McCormick had spoken to John Boulger at the end of 1976, and the Aussie had pledged his allegiance to Cradley, but, as the 1977 season approached, it began to look doubtful that John would take his place in the Heathens' line-up.

Leicester offered a reported £12,000 plus Illa Teromma for John, but were told that it was not cash that Cradley wanted – it was Boulger. Dan huffed and puffed and shouted indignations, but it was to no avail, and Boulger lined up with the Lions for the 1977 season.

The new Cradley management had decided to adopt a youth policy, and had established promotional ties with National League Ellesmere Port in an effort to have their own breeding ground for prospective Heathens. Prior to the season, Cradley had been running weekly practice sessions, and Ellesmere youngster Phil Collins (brother of World Champion Peter) had been clocking up some amazing times, and his name went into Dan's book, along with Manchester's 17-year-old John Hack. Another new signing was James Timu Te Kere Herini Moore. James, like Bruce Cribb, was a Maori, and came highly recommended by the legendary Ronnie Moore. Dan signed him up with the intention of him serving his apprenticeship with Ellesmere Port, putting in second-half appearances at Dudley Wood, and taking up the reserve berth, if the opportunity arose.

Even so, with such an abundance of young talent, the Heathens were still lacking a star rider. Typically, McCormick went straight to the top. He had promised action, and by God, he was going to provide it. He announced that Cradley had agreed terms with Anders Michanek, and that the Swede would be flying into Britain in time for the first League match. Michanek had said all along that he had no intention of riding in the British League in 1977, so the news was sensational, to say the least.

Anders Michanek was truly one of the superstars of World Speedway. The 34-year-old Scandinavian was one of the most convincing winners ever of the World Championship, when he won the title in 1974. He began riding in Britain for Long Eaton in 1967, and immediately made an impact in the BL. He moved with the rest of the team to Leicester, before becoming the undisputed number one at Newcastle and Reading, before electing to ride solely on the Continent in 1976. Anders had won every honour in speedway and was now on his way to Cradley Heath – eventually.

Cradley Heath Speedway had never seen the likes of Dan McCormick before, and even before the gates opened on the season, there was an excited buzz about the place. Here was a no-nonsense aggressive businessman, who would stop at nothing to get his own way, and if he got his own way, then Cradley were going places.

The Heathens began with four challenge matches, all against their local rivals. They began at Monmore in mid-March and won by 16 points. Nigel Wasley had hastily been drafted back into the side and scored a creditable 5 points, but the star of the night was Steve Bastable, who, paired with Persson, scored a superb maximum. Perks was also super, scoring 9 points. Wolverhampton tracked their new Danish signing Hans Nielsen, but he failed to score. The following night at Dudley Wood in their opening match of the season, Cradley repeated the dose, Perks once again riding impressively.

One week later, the Heathens played host to Birmingham, and due to a dazzling display by the Brummies' Alan Grahame, Cradley could only manage a 3-point win. When Cribb returned to the pits after finishing second in heat 11, the Birmingham riders protested that his silencer had worked loose. The protest was upheld, and Bruce's points were deducted – so much for 'friendlies'. Two nights later at Birmingham, the Brummies were winners by 4 points, but Persson scored a brilliant 15-point maximum.

The Michanek affair had taken a turn for the worse, however. Anders' last club, Reading, had jumped in at the last moment and had demanded a transfer fee of £12,000. McCormick was having none of that and offered £2,000 to cover administration costs and the like. He argued that he would never have allowed Boulger to move to Leicester if he had been made aware of these demands at the start of his negotiations.

The League programme began in April, when Cradley were trounced at Belle Vue. Michanek was not in the line-up, but the supporters were assured that he was on his way. Cradley thrashed Halifax in their first home League match, in which a vintage Persson scorched to an 18-point maximum, and was well supported by Perks and Bastable. But the question everyone was asking was 'Where's Mich?'

In all fairness, he was trying to get to Britain, but his efforts were being thwarted by the British Airways strike. After a 48-hour drive, Anders arrived at Dudley Wood in time to take his place against Swindon on 9 April. He scored 7 points on his debut, looking tired and jaded on a bike that lacked power. Persson could only fare one better, and he was top scorer as the Heathens lost 36-42.

Mich had two days to recover before Cradley met Sheffield in a challenge match at Dudley Wood. Persson opened proceedings by setting a new track record of 65.9 seconds in the opening race, and went on to score a fine maximum. Not to be outdone, Anders was also unbeaten, scoring 12 points as the Swedes led Cradley to a 16-point victory.

Michanek was again unbeaten when the Heathens played host to Wimbledon in the League and won 48-30. The outstanding feature of the match was the Michanek/Price pairing. Three times they were paired together, and three times they scored 5-1.

Mich predictably led the Cradley assault at Reading, when the Heathens lost by just 2 points, and, once again, the Swede was unbeaten. He finished the month by winning

Cradley Heath, 1977. From left to right, back row: Dan McCormick (promoter), Dave Perks, Bernt Persson, Steve Bastable, Anders Michanek, Bob Wasley (manager). Front row: Bob Valentine, Bruce Cribb, Arthur Price. (Hipkiss)

the Midland Riders qualifying round at Wolverhampton, and the Cradley fans rejoiced in having one of the world's true speedway superstars at Dudley Wood.

In Cradley's first match in May, at Swindon, Anders took on the Robins virtually on his own. Persson was away in Sweden, and after finishing behind Martin Ashby in his first race, Michanek went on to record six heat wins, and scored 20 of the Heathens' points as they lost 37-41.

Cradley's next match was at Dudley Wood, against King's Lynn, and Anders was again unbeaten by the opposition, and thanks to some solid support from Persson and Perks, the Heathens were comfortable winners. Michanek had joined Cradley on the understanding that he had to honour the Continental bookings that he had already taken, and he missed the next five matches.

The first was a hard-fought duel at Sheffield, when not even a maximum by Bernie could prevent the Tigers from winning 42-36. The next one hurt – a 2-point defeat at Dudley Wood at the hands of Wolverhampton. The Heathens lost on a technicality, as Persson crossed the line first in heat 1, only to be disqualified on the grounds that his silencer had worked loose. Cradley gained swift revenge the following Friday when they won at Monmore by 5 points. Bastable led the fray with 10 points, and young Phil Collins made his debut for the Heathens, scoring 5 points.

Bastable maintained his good form when he dropped just 1 point at Cradley, as the Heathens beat White City the following night. Two nights later, Cradley visited Birmingham without either Michanek or Persson. They had been allowed Jim McMillan and Keith White as guest riders, but just before the start of the match, McMillan withdrew, after a dispute between the Cradley and Wolverhampton managements. The Heathens lost their remaining guest, White, in a heat 8 crash, but led by a Stevie B. maximum, they rode their hearts out to win the match, against all odds, by 2 points.

Michanek decided to grace Cradley with his presence for a couple of matches at the end of May, and the Heathens took a full-strength team to Hackney. Cradley produced an awesome display, beating the Hawks 53-25 on their own track. Mich was unbeaten by the opposition, scoring 11 points, Valentine 10, Bastable 9, Cribb 8, Persson 8, Perks 6 and Price 1. Unfortunately, in the second half, Perks fell and injured his shoulder and hand, causing him to miss the next six meetings.

Cradley saw out the month with a victory over Exeter at Dudley Wood, but the eagerly-awaited clash between Michanek and Mauger never materialised as the Kiwi was absent through injury. May had been good to the Heathens – they had scored four consecutive League wins, and had moved up into third place in the British League – but as they moved into June, Anders was off on his travels again.

In the Challenge match that was an opener for the month at Dudley Wood, in which Cradley beat Belle Vue, Nigel Wasley was recalled to cover for Perks. Arthur Price turned up at the match, and, much to everyone's amazement, announced that he had got married! The next two matches saw Hull knock the Heathens out of the KO Cup on aggregate. Persson was missing from both matches, having joined Michanek to represent Sweden in a qualifying round of the World Pairs Championship.

The next few matches saw the two Swedes playing 'ducks and drakes' with all concerned. Cradley lost at Ipswich – Persson in, Michanek out. Cradley thrashed Poole at Dudley Wood – Michanek in, Persson out. Cradley beat Birmingham at Dudley Wood – Persson in, Michanek out. Michanek was out for the next three matches.

The Heathens took just six riders to National League Newcastle, and won by 10 points to progress into the next round of the Inter-League KO Cup, Persson scoring an immaculate 15-point maximum. Perks made his comeback at Coventry at the end of the month, but it was premature, and the Heathens lost by 6 points. Dave went back on the injured list for another two weeks.

The beginning of July brought about the World Pairs final, that featured Michanek and Persson riding for Sweden. As luck would have it, the event was to be staged at Belle Vue, Manchester, thereby ensuring that the pair of them would be in England at the same time. One hoped that they might put in some appearances for their club, timetables allowing, of course. England's Peter Collins and Malcolm Simmons beat the Swedes into second place.

Cradley travelled to Bristol with both their Swedes, but without Perks and Valentine, Bob being ill. Richie Cauldwell was given his debut at reserve, but understandably found the going a little tough, as Cradley crashed 48-30.

Bob Valentine was the hero, scoring 10 points, in the Heathens' next match at Dudley Wood, when Cradley just scraped home by 2 points against Coventry in a League match. The Swedes both had a poor match, Persson suffering with a sick motor. Olsen took full advantage for the Bees and he reigned supreme, lowering the track record to 65.4 seconds in heat 1, and remaining unbeaten by a Heathen all night.

Bernie was still having motor problems two nights later when the Heathens thrashed Sheffield at Cradley, but again Valentine top-scored alongside Michanek with 11 points apiece. With Bastable and Cribb scoring well, it was one-way traffic all the way. John Williams made his debut at reserve and scored 1 point, and one could not help but think how much greater Cradley's 50-28 win would have been had Perks been fit.

With a full team, the Heathens were a formidable outfit, but it was over before they realised it – Anders Michanek had ridden his last race for Cradley Heath. Perks made his comeback in the middle of July in a Midland Cup match at Leicester, but the Heathens had only six riders – Michanek was missing, without any explanation. The lads all pulled together, and even with Persson managing a paltry 4 points, they managed a 2-point win over a poor Leicester side. Ex-Heathen Boulger dropped only 1 point to a Cradley rider, and that was Stevie Bastable.

McCormick had had enough, and announced that Michanek had been officially released. Dan had originally agreed to the Swede's request to fulfil his Continental engagements, but Anders' absences had gone far beyond what the Cradley promoter had been led to expect. The split was as amicable as it could be under the circumstances, and Michanek was even invited to take part in the prestigious 'Golden Hammer', but that was later in July.

Cradley moved into the next round of the Midland Cup when they trounced Leicester at Dudley Wood, inspired by a classy Bastable display, but they lost their next three League matches at Exeter, at home to Belle Vue, and at eventual League winners White City. Bastable was now challenging Persson for the top spot, and, although he still

Anders Michanek. (Hall)

had the odd 'dog' of a match, Steve was rapidly becoming a class act and had surpassed everyone's expectations so far in 1977.

Cribb and Valentine were performing heroics, never giving up although not always getting their just rewards, but Arthur Price had not progressed as the Heathens had hoped, and, more often than not, he found himself under the 5-point mark. Michanek's departure had left a void that was almost impossible to fill, although, God knows, Cradley had had enough practice during his many Continental excursions.

1977 was the inaugural year of the 'Golden Hammer'. It was a meeting that brought together one of the best possible line-ups in world speedway. Every rider was truly a world-class competitor – no lemons in sight. Ole Olsen was the first ever winner, after a run-off with John Boulger. Bastable and Michanek finished joint fifth on 10 points and, with the meeting being sponsored by the *Daily Mirror*, Cradley Heath seemed to have arrived on the world speedway scene – just as Dan said it would.

The Heathens finished July with a win at Dudley Wood against Reading, and began their August League campaign with a win at Poole, without Persson. Bastable was top scorer and beat Malcolm Simmons in the process. Meanwhile, at the beginning of the month, Cradley were involved in a three-team tournament with Wolverhampton and Birmingham, one leg to be run at each of the tracks. The Heathens finished first in every leg and won the trophy sponsored by the *Express and Star*. During the tournament, one couldn't help but notice how much Wolves' Hans Nielsen had improved in the few short weeks that he had been in the country – why, he looked almost as good as Stevie B!

Bob Valentine. (Hall)

Cradley's next match at Dudley Wood was a great embarrassment to Dan McCormick. The Heathens were to face League leaders White City in the first ever BL match to be covered by ITV – and they lost 33½-44½. Persson was in Sweden winning the Swedish Riders Championship, and guest Jimmy McMillan could only manage 6 points in a match that Cradley could have won, but for a spate of machine failures. But Dan had done it again. In July alone, small town Cradley Heath had been frequently mentioned in the *Daily Mirror*, and now the bloody speedway team was on the telly!

The next night, Cradley visited Halifax, and although they brought in Nigel Wasley, and Persson was back, they found themselves with only six riders again – Dave Perks had retired. He was totally brassed off with the way that the season had gone for him, and now he wanted to live the life of a normal human being. The Heathens seemed to thrive on these 'backs to the wall' situations, and with fabulous performances by Persson, Bastable, and Valentine, they won by 6 points.

Four nights later at Wimbledon, Person was missing from the Heathens line-up again – but Perks wasn't. Four days of being a normal human being was quite enough for Dave and he was back to face the Dons, and to see the rest of the season out. Cribb fought a one-man battle, scoring 13 of Cradley's points in a match that saw him with very scant support.

The Heathens ended the month still without Persson, but they caused a few raised eyebrows when they won at highly-rated King's Lynn, and then thrashed Wolves 51-27 in the Midland Cup semi-final at Dudley Wood, Tony Davey and Larry Ross both being excellent guests in their respective matches.

Persson had been give permission to miss the King's Lynn match, in order to take his place in the World Final practice session in Gothenburg, on the understanding that he would return for the match against Wolverhampton. After all, Wolves' Finn Thomsen was booked on the same flight, and he had ridden in the meeting. McCormick was not amused and 'looked forward to seeing Persson' upon his return from the World Final.

The Heathens actually rode on World Final night, and lost by 2 points at Monmore Green, but they went into the Midland Cup final comfortably on aggregate. Bob Valentine was not so comfortable however, withdrawing from the meeting with a badly gashed arm sustained in his first outing.

While all of this was going on, Ivan Mauger was winning his fifth World Championship, equalling Ove Fundin's record. Unlucky Peter Collins had been injured prior to the final, but still did England proud, finishing in second place, in front of Ole Olsen. Michanek had also injured his foot a couple of weeks earlier, and he had to be satisfied with 8 points and eighth place; Persson finished three places behind him with 6 points.

Some could have argued that Cradley had two riders in the final. Some could have argued that Cradley had none. Michanek had definitely gone, and Persson's future at Dudley Wood was looking in some doubt, to say the least. McCormick had already disposed of one Swedish 'prima donna', and was not about to suffer another. Besides, Bernie was not the 'golden boy' any more – Bastable was.

Steve had everything going for him – he was not yet 21, and had a whole career ahead of him, whereas Persson was ten years older. Steve also turned up for all of the matches, and this was a quality in a rider that Dan was beginning to hold dear. Talent-wise, Bernie probably still had the edge on Steve, but it was a matter for conjecture how many more fruitful years the Scandinavian had left in him. McCormick was betting that it wasn't many and issued an ultimatum: come back and ride in the rest of the fixtures, or be put on the transfer list and be fined £200.

Cradley rode all through September without Persson. They rode in four League matches, winning three at home and beating Leicester at Blackbird Road. Bastable and Cribb bore the brunt of the scoring, but Perks and Valentine could not be faulted for their efforts, and even John Hack put in an appearance and scored an impressive 5 points. The end of the month saw the Heathens lose at home and away to Coventry in the Midland Cup final, guests Larry Ross and Les Collins having poor meetings.

Cradley began October by beating Hull at Dudley Wood, only to be told afterwards that Persson had been taken off the transfer market, his £200 fine had been waived, and he was on his way back. He made his comeback on 5 October at Hull and scored 5 points as the Heathens lost 34-44. If the Cradley fans were looking forward to see him again, they were about to be disappointed, because as quickly as he came, he went – never to return again as a Heathen.

Bernt Persson had been a good servant for Cradley Heath Speedway and had

Anders Michanek. (Hall)

15

given them some dignity in the bad years, but the way he conducted his business in his final year lost him a lot of respect. It was a great pity really, for he was, after all's said and done, Cradley's first world-class star.

The Heathens' next fixture was a double-header at Dudley Wood, and they seemed to be momentarily thrown out of gear by all the comings and goings, as they were beaten by Ipswich. Fortunately, they got their act together for the second match, and beat Hull to secure a place in the Inter-League Cup final.

Stevie Bastable, no doubt revelling in his new role as 'numero uno' won a brand-new car (the richest prize ever in British speedway up till then) when he took the Second City Trophy from a first-class field at Birmingham. He continued his great form at Dudley Wood in the first leg of the Dudley/Wolves Trophy, but the Heathens were without flu-ridden Bob Valentine and could only manage a 2-point win. Two nights later, Wolves capitalised on this small deficit and easily took the trophy, Nielsen dropping only 1 point to Bastable. The Heathens won their last League match at Cradley, against Bristol, before losing the Inter-League Cup final on aggregate to Ipswich.

Dan McCormick had had his problems in his debut year at Dudley Wood. He had lost his top man before the season had started, had found another and then he had lost him, as well as losing the number two!

Michanek finished with a tremendous 10.35 average for his eleven matches, and Persson 8.34 for his twenty-two matches, but now they were gone, and if Dan was to keep his promise, then he certainly had some re-building to do. Already he was talking about Phil Herne and Alan Grahame, but he would no doubt go into 1978 a wiser man, being wary of riders' promises.

For all that, it had been Cradley's most successful year ever in the British League. They finished seventh in a league of nineteen and boasted one of the best young riders in the British League. Who knew what McCormick had in store for the Heathens fans in '78? Only one thing was sure – it wouldn't be boring.

1977 programme.

2

THE TIMES THEY ARE
A-CHANGING
1978

Before the beginning of the 1978 season, it looked as though Dan's promise was already on shaky ground. Bob Valentine had announced his retirement from the sport, and Cradley found themselves with only four riders as the start of the season loomed. Bastable, Cribb, Perks and Price were all down as starters, but three more riders had to be found to complete the squad. It was hardly the start Dan wanted, but, in effect, 1978 was to be one of the most significant years in Cradley's transformation.

Before the season began, McCormick had established managerial ties with National League Oxford, where youngsters like John Hack and James Moore could gain experience at team level instead of just managing with second-half rides at Dudley Wood, but while this was expected to bear fruit in the future, Dan needed experienced riders immediately.

McCormick went to the Control Board but they were unsympathetic, and he realised that he would have to get himself out of the predicament with no help whatsoever from them. He had not been idle in the winter months and had been keen to sign John Titman, Phil Herne and Birmingham's Alan Grahame. He also maintained his policy of going to the top when he approached Ivan Mauger. Ivan ultimately signed for Hull, Titman went to Leicester and Herne ended up at Birmingham, but Dan did get 24-year-old Brummie Grahame.

With five down and two to go, young Australian Les Sawyer was Dan's next signing, along with a 17-year-old Finn who had showed up well at Ole Olsen's winter training school at Dudley Wood – Pekka Hautamaji. There were still holes to fill, however, and McCormick was heard to say that he might have been hasty regarding Michanek, but Persson – no way!

On the eve of the season, Dan went on a signing spree. Czechoslovakian Zdenek Kudrna was signed, and also Danish Kristian Praestbro. Praestbro proved to be an inspired signing. Whether or not McCormick signed him out of desperation as the season approached is a matter of speculation but, in effect, the 23-year-old Dane became a natural successor to Bob Valentine. He had spent two unsuccessful years at Belle Vue, but in just one season at Dudley Wood he would double his average and also prove instrumental in bringing one of Cradley's best-ever riders to Dudley Wood.

McCormick finally completed his squad as the curtain went up on the 1978 season. The Cradley patrons were told that Dan had managed to secure the services of one

John Hack. (Hipkiss)

Bruce Lee Penhall, but at the expense of Kudrna, Cradley having used up all their foreign rider permits. Penhall was a much sought-after American, whose only appearance in Britain was in the previous year's Intercontinental Final when, frankly, he looked unimpressive. He had, however, had an impressive test series against the Rest of the World side in the States in the early part of the year and, at 20 years old, was reckoned to be a star of the future.

Bruce had lost his mother and father in an air crash some three years earlier and, despite having to help run the family construction business, he had ridden with some success in Israel, New Zealand and Australia, as well as finishing twice in the top three in the United States National Championship. To say that Penhall was an inspired signing would be an understatement, for neither Dan, nor anybody else for that matter, could have possibly foreseen the impact that the American would have on the sport.

Cradley began the season with matches for the *Sandwell Mail* Trophy, an event between the Heathens, Wolves and Birmingham, the opening match being at Dudley Wood against Wolverhampton. Penhall was not due to arrive until April, so the trophy was contested without him. Cradley won the first match easily, Cribb and Bastable both claiming maximums and new boy Grahame looking impressive with 8 points. Perky and Price both scored 5 points, while Praestbro and Hautamaji scored 3 and 1 respectively.

Cradley ended March with the last match in the tournament at Wolverhampton and, despite maximums from Wolves' Nielsen and McMillan and a night of engine problems for Bastable, the Heathens lost by only 1 point, Praestbro topping the scorechart with 9 points.

Bruce Penhall arrived on 3 April. Praestbro was fulfilling a booking on the continent, so that solved the problem of who to leave out. Bruce arrived amidst a blaze of publicity. He was Cradley's first American rider and Dudley Wood had never seen anything quite like him. Sure, there were already Americans in the BL – indeed, Scott Autrey was already an established world-class rider – but the arrival of Penhall heralded the emergence of a new breed of flamboyant, extrovert Yankees whom the British would come to love. Bruce was tanned, with blue eyes and blond hair, and had the looks of a film star rather than a speedway rider. He was the first true pin-up of speedway (although John Davis would probably disagree).

Penhall made his debut at Dudley Wood in a challenge match against Sheffield and scored 1 point. Despite a sick bike, he tried hard – maybe a little too hard – and was visibly upset with his poor return, but he certainly put himself around the track, and a solid display from the rest of the team saved the match.

Cradley then re-embarked on their League programme and played host to Wimbledon. With Praestbro back, young Pekka was pulled out and dropped back into the second halves. Penhall came good and scored 9 points, and the Heathens, led by another Bastable maximum, won by 8 points. Steve seemed content to let the American take the spotlight, while he continued with the job of becoming one of the top riders in the sport. His recent efforts had been rewarded with a place in the England side to face the Australasians.

Bruce settled down to middle-order scoring for the rest of the month, as the Heathens began to take on the look of a very compact outfit. Bastable was the undisputed number one, with Grahame, Cribb and Praestbro all scoring well. Perks was having a quiet time, but Price was looking jaded and lost his place to Hautamaji at the end of April. Arthur put in a transfer request and subsequently dropped back into the National League with Workington.

Bastable won the semi-final of the Midland Riders Championship at Cradley, but it was Penhall that everyone was talking about. He was the darling of the media: photogenic, articulate and witty. In one interview on local radio, he was heard to say that the English tracks were so big that you could eat a cheese sandwich going down the back straight! He was the promoter's dream. The girls loved him for his looks and the boys loved him for his grit and determination. He was quickly becoming a draw wherever he went and, in short, he brought the fans through the turnstiles. Dan was seen to have a big smile on his face – and why not? At the end of April, after just a handful of meetings to his name, Bruce was given an invitation to ride in the prestigious Superama at Hackney, and finished fifth in a top-class field with 10 points. Cradley won all their home matches in April, but lost at Swindon and Coventry by just 3 points in each match.

May saw Penhall down in the reserve spot – and he made the most of it. As Cradley beat Wolves, he scored 8, and in the next match at Hull, he top-scored with 13 points, although a Cradley defeat was inevitable when Bastable retired after two races with a foot injury.

The Heathens travelled to Ellesmere Port for the first round of the Inter-League KO Cup and, despite a spate of machine troubles that saw the team reduced to three bikes by the end of the match, Cradley were comfortable winners, Bastable and Penhall remaining unbeaten by the opposition. It was victory at a price, however, as Alan Grahame chipped a bone in his ankle in his second ride, but the Brummie showed that he was made of stern stuff and missed only one match as a result of the injury.

Bastable and Penhall, meanwhile, were getting their fair share of open meetings and Bruce finished fourth in the Olympique at Wolverhampton, and Steve took second place behind Gordon Kennett in the Yorkshire Bank Trophy at Sheffield. Not to be out-done, Alan Grahame, despite his painful ankle injury, won the VW Grand Prix qualifying round at Dudley Wood.

Cradley continued through the month beating White City at home and taking the points at Hackney, led by Bastable and Penhall with 12 points apiece. Penhall again top-scored as the Heathens were well beaten at Exeter, but Bruce was a man on a mission and did what he went to the County Ground to do when he beat fellow-countryman Scott Autrey in the last race.

Bastable led the Heathens into June with some brilliant performances that again saw them win all of their home matches, but they failed to pick up any further away points. Cradley were unlucky to lose at Halifax when manager Bob Wasley paired Steve and Bruce together – they scored three 5-1s and looked certain to score a fourth when Penhall's ignition box packed up. Bastable eclipsed the month by qualifying, along with Grahame, for the British Final and finishing fourth in the Midland Riders Championship at Coventry.

June began poorly for the Heathens. Penhall was upset by the news that the American Motorcycle Association had nominated Scott Autrey and Steve Gresham to appear in the Inter-Continental Final, and so Bruce's World Final hopes had been dashed without him having a chance to race for it.

Cradley lost by 2 points at Bristol and made their exit from the Inter-League KO Cup in a match that caused Wasley to call referee Mel Price one of the worst referees he had ever seen. The Heathens had their revenge the very next night as they thrashed Bristol by 50-28 in a League match at Dudley Wood.

Two nights later, Cradley made their debut in the KO Cup at Reading and came away with a 4-point lead, which was just as well because in the second leg at Dudley Wood they lost by 2 points and lost Penhall into the bargain. A terrifying heat 9 crash saw Reading's Steve Clarke seriously injured and Penhall sustain a dislocated ankle. The crash put paid to the starting-gate mechanism and the rest of the races were started on the green light, but Cradley progressed to the next round on aggregate.

Meanwhile, back at Dudley Wood, although McCormick was puffing his chest out at his new-look Heathens, he generally acknowledged that the stadium was a dump. It was his intention to do something about that and he made a start by installing £12,000-worth of lighting equipment. With Penhall missing, the Heathens brought in James Moore to fill the team at Wimbledon (where they lost) and John Hack at Cradley (when they beat Poole) but the youngsters found the points hard to come by.

July saw much activity at Dudley Wood. Bruce Cribb put in a shock transfer request and the Cradley skipper moved to Bristol for £5,000. McCormick then moved into the market to clinch a deal that some said was pure lunacy. He paid Ellesmere Port a reported £15,000 for British junior champion Phil Collins. In those days that figure was enormous, and Dan was accused by the powers that be of setting a precedent that would financially ruin the sport. In essence, Phil was a bonny battler, but he was, after all is said and done, a National League rider and as such was unproven in the British League. In his favour, his pedigree was of the highest calibre and if he could do half as well as his brother Peter, then Cradley would be quids in. And, at 18 years old, he must surely have many years ahead of him. The idea was that he should stay on at Ellesmere for the rest of the season and become a fully-fledged Heathen in 1979.

Phil actually found that he was put straight into the team to fill the gap left by Cribb. He made his debut as Penhall made his comeback at Leicester and the Heathens forced a draw in the third round of the KO Cup. Collins battled hard for his 4 points, while Bruce top-scored with 10 points.

The next match saw Penhall score his first paid maximum against the high-flying Belle Vue Aces at Cradley Heath. It was only the third time that the Manchester outfit had been beaten in 1978, as the Heathens won 43-34. Bruce continued to have a great month, finishing third in the Strongbow Trophy at Hull, sixth in the Jubilee Trophy at Reading and joint third with Bastable in the Littlechild Trophy at King's Lynn. He was indeed in great demand, but he failed to make an impact in the Golden Hammer at Dudley Wood, scoring only 7 points as fellow-countryman Autrey took the prize in a meeting that saw Mike Lee equal the track record.

Cradley won the last two matches in July at home to Exeter and Leicester, the last match putting them into the semi-final of the KO Cup. Bastable had been injured in the Golden Hammer and missed the Leicester match, but the six remaining Heathens all responded, headed by Penhall 12, Grahame 11, Collins 8, Praestbro 6, Perks 6 and Hautamaji 5.

Perhaps the most significant event in July was Kristian Praestbro bringing a Danish youngster over for a holiday. Erik Gundersen practised at Leicester, Wolverhampton, Birmingham and Cradley and, although the 18-year-old looked a little wild, Dan liked what he saw and signed the youngster up for the 1979 season.

Victorious Heathens with the Sandwell Trophy, 1978. From left to right, back row: Dan McCormick (promoter), Dave Perks, Pekka Hautamaji, Arthur Price, Steve Bastable. Front row: Kristian Praestbro, Bruce Cribb, Alan Grahame. (Hipkiss)

Kristian Praestbro. (Hipkiss)   *Pekka Hautamaji. (Hipkiss)*

Bastable came back battered and bruised in August, but looked far from comfortable as he scored only 2 points at Bristol. The rest of the team fared little better, Collins and Praestbro top-scoring with 7 points each. The Heathens brought in 20-year-old Australian Dave Shields at reserve. He had been one of the Oxford riders that Cradley had featured regularly in their second-half races and looked a fine prospect, but his hard-earned 4 points could not save the Heathens.

Cradley's next match at Dudley Wood found them facing Reading without Hautamaji, Praestbro and Collins. Once more, the Cradley management relied on the Oxford connection and drafted in Shields, John Hack and Pip Lamb. To add to their problems, the Heathens lost Dave Perks in heat 8, when he fell and broke his collarbone. With Bastable suffering from gastro-enteritis, Cradley leaned heavily on Penhall and he responded with a faultless maximum and, with Shields proving a revelation by scoring 8 points, the Heathens scraped home by 2 points. Praestbro had been busy competing in the Danish Championship and had finished as runner-up to Hans Nielsen, but the really exciting news was that young Gundersen had finished third.

One the home front, Bastable had finished in fifth position in the British Final and had clinched a World Final place, albeit as reserve. No such luck for Alan Grahame, who managed only 4 points and fell by the wayside.

Cradley were forced to visit Leicester for the first leg of the Midland Cup semi-final without Penhall and Perks, and were soundly thrashed 52-26. Three nights later, they rode at Wolverhampton in the first leg of the Dudley/Wolves Trophy and, although

Bastable, Penhall and Grahame all scored well, they lost the match by 6 points. Moore, Hack and, to a lesser extent, Hautamaji proving to be a weak tail end. The following night, the Heathens brought in Shields and Collins to take the trophy 81-75 on aggregate at Dudley Wood.

Although Cradley lost their next match at King's Lynn, Penhall scored an incredible 15-point maximum, beating British Champion Michael Lee twice in the process. He followed this the very next night by winning the Skol Masters Trophy at Birmingham from Ole Olsen and Chris Morton. The next three matches were all at Dudley Wood and the Heathens won them all easily, with maximums from Bastable and Penhall and another fine performance from Dave Shields. They finished off the month by drawing at White City.

On 2 September, Ole Olsen joined the illustrious band of riders who have won the World Final three times, Gordon Kennett was a surprise runner-up and Scott Autrey third – poor old Steve never had an outing. A couple of weeks later, Ole was celebrating again as Denmark won their first ever World Team Cup final in Landshut, West Germany, giving the first ominous signs that Denmark were emerging as a forceful speedway nation.

Cradley's September started off with two cup matches at Dudley Wood. They failed to pull back the large deficit incurred at Leicester and, although they won the match by 10 points led by a Grahame maximum, it was the Lions who went through to the Midland Cup final.

Bruce Penhall leads Mike Lee. (Hall)

1978 programme.

In the first leg of the KO Cup semi-final, despite a paid maximum from Penhall, Cradley only managed a 2-point win over Ipswich and their chances of a place in the final looked slim. The next night in the return at Ipswich, the Heathens featured guests Bruce Cribb and Arthur Price, but they were not the answer and with Bastable and Penhall failing to click, Cradley lost the match by 10 points and failed to reach the final.

Back in league action, the Heathens lost by only two points at Belle Vue and gave Birmingham an unmerciful drubbing at Dudley Wood, Bastable equalling the track record in the first heat. Grahame, Bastable, Penhall and Collins were all unbeaten by a Brummie and, with Hautamaji scoring 8 points, they scored a 57-20 win. Two nights later Cradley completed the double by beating the Brummies by 2 points on their own track.

Only a maximum by Hans Nielsen and the absence of Phil Collins prevented the Heathens from taking the points at Wolverhampton as the Wolves won 40-38 in Cradley's last match of September. Bastable, Penhall, Grahame and Praestbro were all fighting valiantly, but with Collins not always being available and Perks being out for almost two months, the Heathens tail end was suspect and it was full credit to the top four that Cradley had been getting the results that they had.

The Heathens opened October by beating Coventry at Dudley Wood and delayed the Bees celebrating winning the league. They followed this with a fine away win at Leicester, but lost at Sheffield. On 19 October, Cradley staged the Dudley Rotary Club Best Pairs, won by Steve Bastable and Alan Grahame. But the star of the night was Bruce Penhall, who stole the show with 17 points, which somehow seemed fair, as it was his last appearance of the season. Bruce had been called back to America to compete in the qualifying rounds of the '79 World Championship and certainly went out on a high note.

The Heathens completed their last two league matches without Bruce and even pulled off a win at Reading before losing at Ipswich. Bastable made it a successful month by winning the Daily Mirror Midlands Classic at Dudley Wood, finishing a very creditable third in the BLRC behind Ole Olsen, after losing a run-off with Peter Collins for second spot, and by lowering the Cradley track record to 63.0 seconds.

The last match of the season at Dudley Wood featured Cradley against a 'Supporters Select' side. The Heathens won with ease, but the main point of interest was the inclusion of Erik Gundersen, who managed only 1 point for Cradley, but gave a hint of things to come.

Cradley had nudged up the league table another two notches from 1977 and finished in fifth place. Bastable had topped the averages with 9.52 and, incredibly, Penhall was just behind him on 9.26. The American had made himself the most talked about rider in speedway in just one season.

Dan McCormick's promise of two years ago suddenly looked on the cards.

3

EXPERIENCING THE POINTS LIMIT
1979

As the 1979 season approached, Dan McCormick experienced none of the problems that he had in the close season prior to the 1978 term, when he had been told to 'get off his ass' and sign his own riders. He named his squad as early as January, and it was as follows: Steve Bastable, Alan Grahame, Phil Collins, Bruce Penhall, Kristian Praestbro, Pekka Hautamaji, Bobby Schwartz, Eric Gundersen and Dave Perks – nine in all!

Not only had he retained the squad of 1978, but also he had added to it by signing the winner of the American round of the World Championship, Bobby Schwartz. The 22-year-old was already an established star in the USA, and as early as the end of the previous year, his good friend Bruce Penhall had persuaded Bobby to throw in his lot with the Heathens for the '79 season. So as early as January, Cradley already had one rider through to the Inter-Continental Final – but only one. As Schwartz had won the qualifying round, so Penhall, after an engine failure and a fall, had failed, much to the disappointment of just about every speedway fan in England.

As the weeks ticked by, McCormick, as well as maintaining his interest at National League Oxford, also became co-promoter at the newly-formed Nottingham club, also in the NL. Dave Perks was sent in to lead the team, and Dan was down to eight riders. Just before the start of the season, Pekka Hautamaji was transferred to Belle Vue – and then there were seven.

Bastable, Collins and Grahame had all featured in the England 7-0 whitewash of Australia in the winter, and had come back with a wealth of experience to take them into the 1979 campaign. Grahame thought that the experience had made him worth more money than McCormick was offering, and for a short time it looked as though a transfer would be the only solution. Fortunately, a compromise was reached, and Alan, along with skipper Steve and Phil, all signed up for the oncoming season.

A 50-point limit had been imposed on all British League teams, and this was opposed vehemently by Dan at every opportunity, his viewpoint being that we should be striving to make teams better, rather than worse. When it was pointed out the Cradley were above the limit, he argued that there had been two teams in the BL in 1978 that had been allowed a 52-point total average, only to be told that these particular teams had built up their own resources. McCormick asked the Control Board just what they thought he'd done when they had told him to get off his ass twelve months before! He further argued that Gundersen and Schwartz were coming in on an assessed average of 6 points and that they were an unknown quantity. Dan was then accused of chequebook speedway! He answered his critics by pointing out that the money he had paid for Collins, Grahame, Valentine and Praestbro was less than the money that he had received for Boulger, Cribb and Persson, and in anybody's language that was good business. He was keeping his riders by hook or by crook!

Although McCormick had his riders, he did not have an easy passage into the 1979 season, but he was determined to keep his squad together at any cost. A date of 21 April was decided upon for the first 'green sheets' of the season to be produced and the team's averages examined. (The green sheets were the official sheets on which the current average of every rider in the League was reported.)

If Schwartz was as good as his reputation, and Gundersen turned out to be as good as he was expected to be, Mac knew that he had a bloody good team, and so did everyone else in the League. After all was said and done, if Dan was to maintain his promise, the Heathens had to win the League this year. If necessary, in order to keep his seven riders, McCormick said that he would form a pool and alternate the riders, and add perhaps one National League rider, but nobody would be released!

The Americans arrived early, and were both present to take place in Cradley's opener on 23 March, a challenge match between Bastable's English Select and Penhall's Overseas Select. All eyes were on Bobby Schwartz and he exceeded all expectations,

Cradley Heath, 1979. From left to right: Alan Grahame, Phil Collins, Bob Wasley (manager), Bruce Penhall, Dave Perks, Bobby Schwartz. Kneeling: Kristian Praestbro, Erik Gundersen. (Hall)

Dave Perks. (Hipkiss)

top-scoring for the Overseas team with 11 points, including a win over Bastable from the back, which was the only point that Steve dropped all night. Bobby dropped his only point to Steve, as did Penhall. With Collins and Grahame scoring 9 and 8 points respectively for the English, the match ended in a draw, but it was all academic as McCormick left the pits with a smug smile on his face. Schwartz, as it turned out, was a kind of Bruce Penhall clone – shoulder-length hair, very polite and with just as much charisma as Bruce. Dan indeed had cause to smile. The Cradley Gremlin had turned into a Fairy Godmother.

The following Friday, the Heathens faced Wolves in a challenge match at Monmore Green, by which time Praestbro and Gundersen had arrived, and they duly took their place in the team. Schwartz was 'dropped', and John Hack from nursery club Oxford was brought in at reserve. Cradley came away with a 10-point win, with young Phil Collins scoring a paid maximum from the other reserve berth. With Bastable and Penhall both scoring 10 points and Gundersen making his debut with 5 points, the match was in the bag and Dan's smile became a little broader.

McCormick continued his strategy for Cradley's first League match at Halifax, replacing Gundersen with Schwartz, but the American failed to come to terms with the Shay and scored only 1 point, as the Heathens lost 31-46. Phil Collins was the next rider to 'take a rest' as Cradley just managed to hold Belle Vue to a draw at Dudley Wood in the first match of April. A few nights later, Stevie B. managed to grab a bit of the spotlight when he was joint winner of the Midland Riders semi-final with Ole Olsen at Wolverhampton.

Cradley faced Reading in their home League debut without Praestbro and Gundersen, and called in Dave Perks and Oxford's Les Rumsey. Perks was a revelation, top-scoring with 10 points, as the Heathens won by 2 points. He was kept in the team alongside Rumsey the next night, as Cradley stole the points at Eastbourne, led by Bastable aided and abetted by Penhall and Schwartz. Bruce was being offered many invitations to open meetings and finished fourth in the *Daily Express* Spring Classic at Wimbledon.

Meanwhile, back at Dudley Wood, Praestbro had returned to face Leicester in a challenge match, but Gundersen had carried on to Poland to ride for the Danish Under-21 team. A 10-point Heathen victory was capped by an Alan Grahame maximum.

On 21 April, the day that the green sheets were compiled, Cradley lost by 6 points at Coventry, and, lo and behold, when the team average was calculated, it was 49.09 points! Dan was home and dry, and whether it was sheer luck, good management or a calculator that was responsible, he had his squad for 1979.

Two nights later at Dudley Wood, Cradley fielded their full-strength team for the first time in a challenge match against Wolverhampton. The Wolves opened with a 5-1 as Bastable blew his engine, and then Cradley ran riot. Only Hans Nielsen could match the Heathens as, even without Bastable, they won the match 50-27. Penhall led the rout with 10 points, Schwartz 9, Gundersen 9, Grahame 8, Collins 8, and Praestbro 6. If Dan's grin had got any bigger, he would have been the first one of the season on the injured list when the top of his head fell off! Three nights later, without Praestbro, the Heathens beat Ipswich 45-33 in the League at Foxhall Heath, Bruce scoring a maximum and Steve dropping only 1 point to the opposition.

Penhall began May by winning the Cradley round of the VW Grand Prix, with Bastable taking third place behind Scott Autrey. Cradley began the month by beating Leicester in another challenge, and followed this by facing Belle Vue in a League match at Dudley Wood. Against the Aces, Penhall and Bastable both had a poor match, but the rest of the team responded. Gundersen top-scored with 9 points and beat Peter Collins while he was at it (this was only Eric's seventh match, remember). Praestbro, Schwartz and Grahame all did their bit towards the 14-point win.

The next few matches saw Praestbro away on one of his many Continental excursions, but the Heathens easily progressed into the next round of the Inter-League KO Cup with a comprehensive win at Peterborough, before taking 2 more League points from Eastbourne at Dudley Wood. They approached the end of the month by losing at Exeter and, when back at full strength, thrashing Hull by 32 points at Cradley.

On an individual basis in May, Schwartz and Collins finished second and third respectively in the Midland Riders Championship, following a run-off with the eventual winner, Hans Nielsen, after they all finished on 12 points. Steve Bastable won the VW Grand Prix round at Ipswich and qualified for the British Final, and Penhall was runner-up in the Olympique at Wolverhampton, with Schwartz finishing fourth.

Cradley saw the month out by beating Leicester at Blackbird Road by 28 points in the first round of the KO Cup. It was a fabulous all-round team performance by the Heathens, all except Steve Bastable – he had fallen in the first heat and had dislocated and broken his ankle. It was an injury that kept him out of the sport for many weeks, and robbed him of the chance to progress in the World Championship competition.

Penhall took on the captain's role as the Heathens began June by thrashing Coventry. Using rider replacement for Steve, the skipper was hardly missed – but worse was to come. Later in the week, Cradley visited Wolverhampton in a Midland Cup match and, on a deep track, they lost Collins and Gundersen in a first-heat crash. The Heathens battled on gamely with only five riders and in five races had only one representative, so a 1-point defeat was a credit to the boys – but the news was not good. Collins had got away with a shaking, but Gundersen had broken his leg. It was a tragedy for the young Dane,

Bobby Schwartz. (Hipkiss)

Steve Bastable. (Hipkiss)

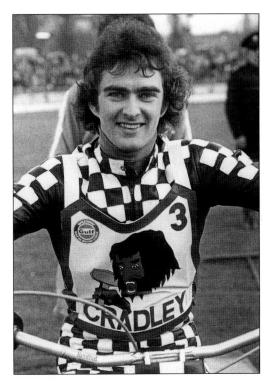

who already had one maximum under his belt after just a handful of meetings and, in the matter of a few days, McCormick had lost two of the squad he had fought tooth and nail to keep together.

Cradley were undeterred and took the round on aggregate the next night at Dudley Wood. Two days later they recalled Perks to the squad and took the League points at Birmingham and added Dave's Nottingham team-mate, Mike Sampson, to beat Leicester on aggregate and move into the next round of the KO Cup. Incidentally, Dave had established himself as one of the top boys in the NL and was currently second in the NL averages. Meanwhile, Kristian Praestbro had managed to get himself on the injured list and Dan was looking at four riders only.

Cradley's next fixture was at home to Hackney and they were to face the Hawks without the three injured riders and also Penhall, who was on World Pairs duty. They retained Perks and brought in Oxford's Les Rumsey and, led by brilliant performances by Grahame and Collins, plus an impressive six points from Rumsey, recorded an incredible 50 points to Hackney's 25.

Bruce returned to lead the Heathens to a resounding win over Wolves in the last match of the month at Dudley Wood, but it had not been a good period for Cradley on the World Championship front. Bastable's place in the British Final had been taken by first reserve Alan Grahame and he had failed to progress, scoring only 3 points, and Bobby Schwartz managed to score only 2 points in the Inter-Continental Final.

June was an important month for the Heathens. If they were to maintain their challenge for the promised League Championship, then they would have to survive the month with just four regulars. They used a succession of Oxford and Nottingham riders to fill in the gaps, but only Rumsey and Mike Sampson made any significant contribution. They began at Belle Vue, where a blistering display by Phil Collins, scoring 13 points, could not prevent a 6-point defeat. Young Pekka Hautamaji put one over on Cradley by beating Penhall, but Phil was looking worth his hefty transfer fee. He top-scored again at Sheffield with 10 points, but point-less returns from Perks, Sampson and Ian Gledhill caused Cradley to lose by 10 points.

Two days later, at Dudley Wood, 6 points by Mike Sampson and a paid maximum by Bruce gave the Heathens their first win of the month as they crushed Birmingham, but

Phil Collins, Bruce Penhall, Alan Grahame, Bobby Schwartz. (Hall)

they lost their next match at Poole by just 4 points, despite an incredible 11 points from 23-year-old Les Rumsey.

Cradley finished off the month with home wins over Sheffield and high-flying Hull, when Bobby Schwartz was the only Heathen to lower Ivan Mauger's colours. The match marked the comeback of Praestbro, and Cradley were beginning to rebuild.

July saw the third staging of the Golden Hammer and Bobby Schwartz was the surprise winner after a run-off with Hans Nielsen – no mean feat for a rider with just four months' experience of BL racing under his belt. Phil Collins and Bruce Penhall filled the third and fourth places respectively, giving Cradley a fair representation in a top-class field.

Gundersen returned at the beginning of August, but as he did, Penhall took off to compete in, and win, the Master of Speedway tournament in Vojens, Denmark. Alan Grahame, so often the unsung hero of Dudley Wood, also enjoyed success early in the month by finishing second in the Superama at Hackney.

As for the Heathens, they began with a defeat at Coventry in the first leg of the Midland Cup semi-final and followed that with a comfortable win at Cradley Heath against Poole. Penhall made his return for the next match at Reading and immediately made his presence felt as he, Collins and Grahame all scored 10 points and Cradley won the match by an incredible 14 points. Even a 10-point win at Cradley was not enough to stop Coventry going through to the Midland Cup final on aggregate, and Olsen showed that although Cradley had a stable of young stars, he was still one of the sport's top riders as he raced to 17 brilliant points.

Gundersen had found the going a little tough since his comeback and was understandably tentative. If he had not been injured, he would probably have been scoring double figures regularly by now but, as it was, Cradley had to be satisfied with him finding his confidence in his own time, which he undoubtedly would.

August was to be an eventful month for the Heathens and they put on a real power display when they lost by just 1 point at Wimbledon in the first leg of the KO Cup second round and obviously fancied their chances in the return. Schwartz was superb, scoring 15 points. He continued his good form as the Heathens won easily at Dudley Wood and drew at Wolverhampton to take the Dudley/Wolves Trophy.

On 18 August, Steve Bastable returned as skipper to lead the Heathens at home in a League match against Wimbledon. After some dreadful weather, the track was in a somewhat tricky state and, as the meeting got underway, riders from both teams questioned the wisdom of the match continuing. Bastable, representing the Cradley riders as their captain, asked for the referee to make a track inspection after heat 4. McCormick was angry at this move as he wanted the meeting to continue. The referee duly made his inspection and promptly called off the match, much to the frustration of the Cradley promoter and a fiery verbal exchange took place between Dan and Steve, after which McCormick stormed off to his office. A short time later, Bastable burst in and demanded a transfer, which was immediately granted.

Had circumstances been different, then a compromise may have been reached, but at Cradley Heath Steve was just one star among many. It was a bold move by Dan as Cradley were still in two cup competitions and still in with a shout for the League title, but he explained his actions by saying that any rider who didn't want to ride for Cradley would not ride for Cradley – and anyway Bastable was having a worse season than last year. Normally Steve's popularity would have been an influential factor, but Penhall, who had emerged as Cradley's new number one and, to a certain extent, Schwartz also, had surpassed him in popularity. Alan Grahame certainly had his share of fans with his never-say-die style of riding and then there was Phil Collins, whose tearaway tactics had made him a great favourite. And how about young Gundersen, who had quickly endeared himself to the Cradley public?

For any other team in the BL, Bastable's departure would have been a devastating blow, but at Cradley he was possibly a victim of the team's enormous popularity and potential, maybe he was even a victim of the points limit, or perhaps he had been subject to a shrewd managerial move by McCormick. At any rate, I hope he is remembered for being the shining light when the Heathens were falling apart some two years earlier.

Bastable in fact remained at Cradley for another month while negotiations took place over his transfer, which was to Birmingham for a reported £18,000. Steve made his debut for the Brummies in the middle of September with a maximum and stated in the press: 'If you are an Englishman at Cradley, you don't get a look-in.' After the Wimbledon match that sealed Bastable's fate, Cradley won three League matches at Dudley Wood and lost one at Leicester, but Gundersen had begun to find his confidence and was once again getting some good returns.

September began at Dudley Wood with the staging of the Badge of Courage Best Pairs Trophy, which was won, much to the delight of the crowd, by Penhall and Schwartz. It was a month that was rich in cup ties, and Cradley won them all.

The Heathens progressed into the quarter-finals of the KO Cup when, led by a full house from Alan Grahame, they beat Wimbledon by 49 points at Cradley, with Penhall equalling the track record in the process. Three days later they met the Dons at Plough Lane in the League and took full advantage of Wimbledon's abysmal luck when the Dons lost three riders during the match, coming away with a 6-point win. Led by Penhall and Gundersen, the Heathens easily beat Exeter at Dudley Wood in order to meet second-in-the-League Hull in the semi-final of the Inter-League Cup, in what was Steve Bastable's last match for the Heathens.

Penhall was second to Peter Collins in the Manpower Trophy at Reading and Phil Collins took second place to his elder brother Les in the Champion of Champions Trophy at Wolverhampton, Alan Grahame taking fourth place. Ivan Mauger placed himself in the speedway history books forever, when he, at almost 40, won the World Championship for a record-breaking sixth time. But amongst all the celebration, September turned out to be a black month for speedway. Former Heathen Nigel Wasley, son of Cradley manager Bob, was fatally injured riding for Nottingham and lost his life on 14 September.

Cradley recalled Dave Perks to replace Bastable, but even with him in the side, the team average was 51.42! They travelled to Wolverhampton for the first leg of the KO Cup quarter-final, and even though Praestbro and Gundersen arrived late, and the Heathens had only five riders to contest the first 10 heats, they won the match by 4 points despite a brilliant maximum by Nielsen. Three days later, Cradley coasted into the semis with an easy win in the return.

The Heathens finished the month with two home wins and an away defeat at Hull. They were currently third in the League, just behind the Vikings, so a 4-point defeat was no shame, and Penhall scored an immaculate 12-point maximum despite Hull fielding the new World Champion.

October started badly for Cradley as Schwartz was sidelined by injuries sustained in a fire at his workshop in Tamworth. They took John Hack with them to King's Lynn, but he was point-less and only Penhall resisted as the Heathens were comprehensively beaten. McCormick lost no time in plugging the gaps and signed Illa Teromaa, the 26-year-old Finn who had been with Leicester since 1975 – the only trouble was that Illa was cup-tied and so could not compete in Cradley's up-and-coming semi-finals. He did, however, feature in the Heathens' next League match, when they defeated Hackney at Waterden Road, and he scored 5 points.

The very next night, Cradley were beating Halifax 42-23 in the first leg of the KO Cup semi-final when the match was rained off after 11 heats and, when they won the return the next night by 10 points, led by 13 from Dave Perks, the Halifax management realistically waived the right to a first-leg re-run and the Heathens found themselves in the KO Cup final.

The other finalists were Hull Vikings and a classic final was in prospect. The first leg was at Cradley Heath on 13 October and saw Schwartz make his comeback but, despite brilliant displays from Mauger (14) and Bobby Beaton (13), Cradley's all-round strength won the day and they went into the second leg with a 16-point advantage. Three days later in the return at Hull, Cradley were robbed of victory in the KO Cup final. The

Vikings had not been beaten at home for two years, but certainly looked like being beaten when the Heathens came a-calling. Rain had fallen steadily since the start of the meeting, but the track had not worsened and was in good condition with fast times being registered and, after 7 heats, Cradley led 23-19. Ivan Mauger was beaten by Schwartz in his first race and was beaten from behind by Penhall in his second, and he called for the referee to inspect the track and meet both sides in the pits. As per the rules, he discussed the situation with the managers and captains. For Cradley, Bob Wasley and Penhall wanted to continue and for Hull, manager Ian Thomas also agreed, but his captain, Mauger, said that conditions were too dangerous and inexplicably referee Vic Harding came down on Mauger's side and called off the match. The Heathens were furious and stormed out of the pits, McCormick exchanging harsh words with the Hull management, but it was to no avail and a rematch was to take place.

Meanwhile, Bruce Penhall had been nominated as October's challenger for the Golden Helmet and was to face the holder, Phil Crump, in the first leg at Dudley Wood before Cradley took on King's Lynn in the first leg of the Inter-League Cup final. It was a successful night for the Heathens as Bruce took a 2-0 lead in the match race championship and Cradley took the first leg of the cup by 8 points. Two days later in the return at Saddlebow Road, Phil Collins paid back his transfer fee in full as he led the Heathens to a 6-point win with a blistering 12-point maximum to give Cradley their first major honour since the formation of the British League.

Although they lost their next League match by just 2 points at Swindon, the Heathens fans had plenty to cheer about, as Penhall again beat Crump 2-0 on the Aussie's home track to become the first American holder of the Golden Helmet. He only just missed

1979 programme.

out on winning the British League Riders Championship when a mistake let eventual winner John Louis through and Bruce had to settle for a very creditable second place.

Cradley slipped into top gear to end the season. Penhall stood down at Wolverhampton to make way for Teromaa as Cradley, led by 11 points from Gundersen, won by 12 points at Monmore Green, and the next night at Dudley Wood they thrashed Exeter 57-21. In their last home League match, the Heathens equalled the biggest ever BL win when they beat Halifax 64-14, with Erik Gundersen the only Cradley rider to be beaten!

Cradley's last match of the season was the rerun of the second leg of the KO Cup final at Hull, and if the Vikings thought they had won a reprieve when the match was previously rained off, they were very much mistaken. The Heathens started with a 5-1 from Schwartz and Penhall and finished with a 5-1 from the American pairing, winning the match by 8 points and winning the cup by 24 points on aggregate. The final meeting at Dudley Wood was the Nigel Wasley Memorial, a best pairs competition, which was won by Alan Grahame and new boy Illa Teromaa.

Dan McCormick had failed in his promise to bring the League title to Cradley within three years, but the Heathens had had a season that any team in the BL would have been proud of. They had finished third in the League behind Champions Coventry and Hull and finished up KO Cup winners – not once, but twice. There is no doubt that injuries hindered the Heathens in their bid for the League, but since Dan's arrival they had moved up two places in the League table every year and, if they continued that trend, next year would see them at the top.

McCormick had assembled a veritable stable of stars, but in ending the year with an average of 54 points, he finished the season as he had begun, with scathing remarks about paying the price for success as the points limit would undoubtedly force him to make changes.

He had made Cradley Heath the most attractive and talked-about club in the British League, a far cry from the early seventies. Penhall had emerged as a true world-class rider and was possibly the most popular speedway star in the country, while his fellow-countryman, Schwartz, was being hailed as the find of the season. The two Englishmen, Grahame and Collins, were far less flamboyant than the Americans, but just as important in Cradley's success. Both had been the match winners on many occasions, and seemed satisfied to play second fiddle to the Yanks and just get on with the business of scoring points and winning matches. Kristian Praestbro was very much in the same mould, a solid scorer who finished with a 7.54 average, just below Phil and Bobby. Bruce had topped the averages with 9.88 and ten maximums, which put him in ninth position in the League averages, followed by Alan on 8.34.

Erik Gundersen's average of 7.35 would have been much improved had it not been for that broken leg, but he came back better than ever and already, after just one season in the BL, the people in the know were talking of him as a future World Champion. Dave Perks, after 25 matches, finished the year on his best ever average with 6.84, but his contribution, although appreciated, was almost overshadowed alongside the exploits of Cradley's glittering stars.

4
CONTINENTAL EXCURSIONS
1980

The year began well for Cradley as Bruce Penhall qualified for the Inter-Continental Final by winning the American qualifying round, ahead of Scott Autrey, in the close season. Unfortunately Bobby Schwartz fell by the wayside, but joined Bruce on a tour of Australia and New Zealand in the winter.

Meanwhile, back in Britain, Dan McCormick was sweating it out, trying to form a squad that would fit into the 50-point limit. Kristian Praestbro had eased the problem somewhat by announcing that he was quitting Britain to race in Germany, but even so, he would be sorely missed at Dudley Wood, as he had so often been the cornerstone of a Cradley victory.

McCormick put forward the proposal that he would rotate his riders to enable the Heathens to retain their remaining team members, but he was told in no uncertain terms that this would 'violate the spirit of the rule' and would not be allowed. The battle raged during the winter months, but as the new term approached, it became obvious that either Schwartz or Alan Grahame, the only two riders not on a three-year contract, would be leaving Dudley Wood.

At the end of the day, it was Schwartz who was listed for transfer, much to the disgust of the Cradley promoter and the huge following that Bobby had built up in his short time at Cradley Heath. Upon his return from New Zealand, Schwartz retaliated by threatening not to return to the UK as Cradley was the only team that he wished to ride for, but Dan promised to keep his transfer fee down and get the best deal possible for him if he returned, so Bobby came back with Bruce Penhall.

McCormick had retained Penhall, Gundersen, Collins, Teromaa and Grahame, but one of his plans for reserve was squashed as the young South African Denzil Kent signed for Canterbury in the NL. Dan was justifiably upset, as he had featured Denzil many times at Oxford and Nottingham in 1979. He had even paid the youngster's fare back home, on the understanding that he would return to Cradley for 1980, but Dan did not think that a contract was necessary at that stage and was punished for his trust. It was no catastrophe, however, because Dan still had a wealth of talent in his NL sides, and Dave Perks and John Hack would feature regularly in the Heathens line-up throughout the year.

Cradley opened at Dudley Wood on 15 March with a challenge match against a British League Select side, and, with Penhall slipping quickly into the groove, they won by 3

Erik Gundersen and Bruce Penhall. (Hall)

points. Teromaa had yet to arrive, and a ferry strike in Finland in fact kept him out of Britain until the first week of April.

The next five matches were in the newly-formed Midland League, and a week later the Heathens faced Birmingham at Dudley Wood. As Schwartz's transfer had not been finalised, Cradley featured him in the line-up. Bobby broke all the fans' hearts as he looked better than ever, racing to an immaculate maximum, and with Penhall and Gundersen also being unbeaten and Grahame dropping only 1 point, the Heathens won the match 55-23. Afterwards, Bobby said his good-byes and left for Reading for an £8,000 transfer fee.

At the end of March, Cradley made their first signing of the season and bought Craig Featherby from King's Lynn. The 20-year-old from Norwich would be good back-up for Cradley when required and Dan immediately placed him at Nottingham. Craig's father Clive had of course been a Heathen before him.

Cradley's last two Midland League matches of the month were both at Dudley Wood, against Coventry and Wolverhampton. The Heathens won both, and Perks and Craig Featherby were effective at reserve against Wolves, but Nielsen looked ominously superb, scoring a magnificent 15-point maximum. The Heathens first defeat came when they put up a dismal display at Coventry in the Midland League at the beginning of April. They scored only 29 points, and skipper Penhall was responsible for 14 of those!

Another poor performance followed three nights later when the Heathens lost at home for the first time in three years to Leicester in the ML. Teromaa made his debut but managed only 2 points, but apart from a great performance by Hack, scoring 6 points, and Penhall, scoring 10 points, the Heathens were an uninspired bunch and suffered a 4-point defeat.

Cradley retained Perks and Hack for their first two League matches at Dudley Wood. Hull and Wimbledon both found themselves heavily defeated, and against the Dons, Perks scored a maximum from the reserve berth.

Before the next match, Penhall went to Ipswich and defended his Golden Helmet, winning the first leg 2-0 against John Louis. The following night, he led the Heathens to a sweet victory over Wolverhampton in the Midland League, but once again, he failed to get the better of Hans Nielsen. Gundersen and Grahame did though, and Cradley came out the winners by 14 points.

In the next match at home, the Heathens beat Reading (who were without Schwartz) in a challenge match, but the highlight of the night was at the beginning of the meeting when Penhall beat John Louis 2-0 in the Golden Helmet, and made his first successful defence of the Match Race Championship.

Illa Teromaa missed Cradley's next match, as he had gone to fulfil a Continental engagement, as did Penhall – in fact, the American missed the next three. It was a situation that became almost intolerable in 1980, not just for Cradley, but for almost every club in the BL.

Most of the top riders in the League were being offered very lucrative bookings on the Continent and naturally they accepted as many as they could. It was a bone of contention that these meetings sometimes clashed with British fixtures. The riders claimed that when they took these bookings originally, their clubs had no fixtures on these dates, but, as we all know, the British climate necessitates the alteration of fixtures, and on many occasions, fans felt let down when they attended matches, only to find that the top riders were not present.

As for Penhall, he had set himself an almost impossible schedule, jetting off every Saturday night to ride on the Continent and returning for Monday night meetings, whenever they arose. He also flew back to America more than the other Yanks, and at one point, he was begged by manager Wasley to 'slow down', Bob fearing that he would burn himself out. Bruce countered by saying that there were too many fixtures in England and that, apart from a 'warming-up' period at the beginning of the year, challenge matches and the like were a waste of time, and they only resulted in losing him money in Continental bookings.

The Heathens won at Birmingham in the ML without Bruce and Illa, but lost at Leicester by just 2 points in their final ML match and finished as runners-up to Coventry. A very depleted Cradley narrowly defeated Halifax in one of those damn challenge matches at Dudley Wood in their next encounter. The Finn had gone again, and the American had not yet returned, and the team was made up by the inclusion of Craig Featherby, Mike Sampson, Glen McDonald and Mark Collins. Even so, the Heathens won by 4 points, although young Kenny Carter impressed for the Dukes, beating Grahame and Gundersen.

Penhall returned (Teromaa didn't) to lead Cradley to victory at Swindon in the BL, but despite great performances from Bruce, Eric and Phil, the Heathens failed to repeat the dose at Belle Vue. The return at Dudley Wood was one of the finest matches seen for years, with Chris Morton and Les Collins leading the assault for the Aces, and Cradley winning by 6 points.

Alan Grahame was going through a particularly bad spell at this time. He was still out of luck as the Heathens were felled at Wimbledon, but Penhall was in magnificent form and defended his Golden Helmet again, this time against Reading's John Davis. Bruce also finished as runner-up to Dave Jessup in the Wimbledon Spring Classic, and won the Midland Riders semi-final at Dudley Wood. He was kept even busier leading the USA team to victory in their first ever Test series against England, averaging 14.8 points per match. Cradley in fact played host to the second Test match, which was the only match in the series that England won. It was a terrific achievement for the Yanks, who had only a handful of riders in England at that time, but they showed a team spirit that was to become legendary. Penhall and Scott Autrey were established stars, but with Schwartz, the Moran brothers, John Cook and Dennis Sigalos all up and coming, England not only had to look out for Denmark, but for the USA as well.

On 17 March Cradley visited Coventry, and became the first team to win at Brandon for three years, Teromaa scoring 10 points in his best match to date. The Heathens also featured a new face in their line-up – 20-year-old Hans Albert Klinge, the current Danish Junior Champion, who was taking a break from his studies to holiday in England. He finished the match with no points and a wealth of experience, having faced the likes of Ole Olsen, Tommy Knudsen and Mitch Shirra.

Penhall was riding in the aforementioned Test series when Cradley met Hackney in their next home match, but Gundersen took over the star role, leading the Heathens with 11 points. Collins and back-to-form Grahame supported well with 10 points each, but the highlight of the match was a brilliant 10 points from Dave Perks, giving the Heathens a 10-point win. Dave was on the crest of a wave at that time, having completed seven consecutive maximums for Oxford in the NL, for whom he currently held an average of 11.50!

The next night, Cradley began their defence of the KO Cup at King's Lynn, and although Mike Lee and Dave Jessup (who currently topped the BL averages) were in fine form, a good all-round performance saw the Heathens hold the Stars to an 8-point lead to bring to Dudley Wood in the return leg.

The Heathens finished May by beating Swindon at Cradley, and were again without Teromaa, but Perks stood in well, scoring 9 points to add to a Penhall maximum, which gave the Heathens a comfortable win.

June started unusually for Cradley with a match at NL Glasgow in the Inter-League Cup. They won by 10 points, but the Tigers' Steve Lawson brought the house down by inflicting Penhall's only defeat of the night in heat 1, and he broke the track record in so doing.

A large chunk of the month was taken up by the Inter-League Four-Team Tournament, which necessitated Cradley riding at Dudley Wood, Hackney, Coventry and Rye House. The Cradley leg was deemed to be a failure, pulling in only 2,500 punters (about half the usual amount), and it was the lowest turnout for years. However, the Heathens qualified on aggregate, and booked their place in the final at Monmore Green.

In the first leg of the Dudley/Wolves Trophy at Cradley, Wolverhampton had a handy guest in Bobby Schwartz. He scored a brilliant 16 points, but twice had to take second place to his mentor Penhall, as Bruce scored a maximum, broke the track record and led his team to an 8-point lead. With Teromaa absent, Oxford's Derek Harrison stepped in and did more than was expected of him, scoring 9 superb points.

The British League Management Committee constantly criticised McCormick for using riders from his NL tracks to fill in the lower end of the team, but he was equally critical of them. Dan was still seething over the Schwartz affair, and demanded to know how Hull were still retaining Ivan Mauger, who was only riding in selected meetings, but, when he did, the Vikings were over the 50-point limit. Hull's Manager Ian Thomas had flatly refused to let any of his riders go and the situation still continued. Also McCormick called their attention to Swindon, who had given leave to Phil Crump. He was on his way back, and upon his return, the Robins would also be above the limit.

Dan had constantly been at loggerheads with the 'powers that be' ever since his arrival at Dudley Wood, and sympathy for him was short on the ground – he was told to stop trying to run the sport and get on with running his own club. Such was the Cradley supremo's rage that, at one point, he even threatened to sue the Control Board, but it was to no avail, and Schwartz was to remain lost to the Heathens forever.

In the second leg of the Dudley/Wolves Trophy at Monmore, the Heathens were still without Teromaa and the tail-end was fearfully weak. Mark Collins, Mike Sampson, and guest Arthur Price scored only 1 point between them, but Grahame hit top form, and along with Gundersen, Penhall and Collins, they combined to win the match by 5 points and take the trophy back to Dudley Wood.

Derek Harrison and Illa Teromaa. (Hipkiss)

Earlier on in the month, Phil Collins had finished third in the British Final behind Dave Jessup and Michael Lee, but he failed in the Commonwealth Final at Wimbledon, leaving only Penhall to fly the Cradley flag in the remainder of the World Championship competition. The Midland Riders Championship was won by Scott Autrey, with Penhall second and Olsen third, but fourth place Gundersen was undoubtedly robbed of the title by an engine failure. Erik was continually proving that he was at home in any company, no matter how good.

July proved to be a very interesting month at Dudley Wood. It began ordinarily enough when Cradley had four straight home wins, beating Eastbourne and Birmingham in the League, Sheffield in the Inter-League Cup and King's Lynn in the third round of the KO Cup. John Hack was being given an extended run, and was producing some excellent speedway, and with Grahame back to his best, the Heathens were a formidable outfit. Penhall had won the qualifying round of the VW Grand Prix at Birmingham, and had broken the two-year-old track record three times during the meeting, which gives an indication as to how well he was riding. But a number of jolts were to hit Cradley.

In the Birmingham match, Phil Collins fell in the second half and broke his collarbone, and a couple of weeks later, Penhall lost his Golden Helmet to arch-Wolf Hans Nielsen. The Heathens lost their next three League matches at Hull, Sheffield and Leicester. At Hull, Sampson failed to turn up, and Teromaa was taken to hospital with concussion. Back in the saddle at Leicester, Illa blew two motors, making July a bad month for him, and the Heathens. They did register some success in the month, however, by winning the final of the Inter-League Four-Team Tournament, represented by Penhall, Grahame, Perks and Teromaa.

There was not a Heathen to be seen on the rostrum at the Golden Hammer. Chris Morton, Scott Autrey and Kelly Moran took the top three places, with Penhall finishing fifth, but Alan Grahame managed to lower the track record to 63.4 seconds in the first heat. After the meeting, a young American was trying out the Dudley Wood circuit. His name was Lance King and he had come highly recommended by Penhall. At the end of the night, McCormick swooped to sign him, only to be told that, as a 16-year-old, Lance could not

Alan Grahame. (Hall)

be granted a work permit and, furthermore, one could not be issued until he was 18, but at least when he was old enough to ride in Britain, it would be for Cradley. It was to be Dan's last signing.

Although Birmingham had enjoyed success in the National League, since their arrival in the British League in 1976 they had struggled. In July 1980, they threatened to fold, and McCormick stepped in to take over the promotional reins from Joe Thurley. It was pointed out to him that this would surely bring about a conflict of interests. Dan took the huff, saying that he wouldn't stay where he wasn't wanted and left Cradley as quickly as he had arrived! McCormick enjoyed the highest profile of any promoter in the League – he made sure of that. He was the master showman, who knew how to handle the press, and they loved him for it. If things were quiet at Cradley, then he would come out with some controversial statement that would put the Heathens straight back in the public eye. He always had something to say and, during his three-and-a-half years at Dudley Wood, although he had failed to produce a League-winning side, he had made Cradley the most talked about club in speedway – a far cry from the days before his arrival.

Much will remain unanswered about Dan – was he a genius or an egomaniac? Did he have great foresight, or was he plain lucky? Whatever people's opinions were, his achievements were there for all to see. Besides Cradley's cup successes, and their ascent up the League table, there were the riders to consider. He did the seemingly impossible and brought Anders Michanek to Dudley Wood. He brought Bruce Penhall, who had a bigger impact on the sport than any other rider before him or since. He brought Erik Gundersen, who would rise to even greater heights than Bruce. He brought Alan Grahame, who was to become one of the Heathens' greatest ever servants. He brought Phil Collins, who would repay a transfer fee that some had described as ludicrous. He brought, and was robbed of, Bobby Schwartz, who was to enjoy a highly distinguished career in the BL. And he had brought Kristian Praestbro, who had been given a new lease of life at Cradley. Was that luck – or had the man been inspired? It mattered not because the fact is that the Heathens were still enjoying the fruits of Dan's labours ten years after his departure, and into the bargain he had left them with a legacy – young Lance King.

Bob Wasley stayed on as team manager, with Derek Pugh taking over as sole promoter, so Dan took ex-Heathen and Cradley youth manager Mike Gardner with him to manage the Brummies. McCormick never again enjoyed the success that he had at Dudley Wood – but the Heathens did. He had instilled in them a will to win that stood them in good stead for many years to come. That is not to decry the efforts of any subsequent managers or promoters, but make no mistake, it all began with Dan in 1977.

Cradley received their last jolt of the month at Dan McCormick's Birmingham! Dave Perks, who was currently the leading rider in the National League, the Silver Helmet holder and second in the Heathens averages, fell in his second outing of the Midland Cup match and cracked his vertebrae. It was the end of the road for unlucky Dave in 1980.

Even without him, Penhall, Gundersen, Grahame and Teromaa had too much power for the Brummies and took the leg by an amazing 18 points. The following night at

Dudley Wood in the second leg, the Heathens completed the job and moved into the next round of the competition.

Cradley's top three were enjoying a consistency that was keeping the team afloat, despite the injuries, and early August saw Gundersen and Grahame also doing well in open meetings. In the Champion of Champions Trophy at Monmore, won by Schwartz, Grahame was second and Gundersen third, whilst in the Superama at Hackney, won by Dave Jessup, Gundersen was second and Grahame third.

Penhall meanwhile was competing in the Inter-Continental Final at White City. It proved to be a shock event as both Mauger and Olsen were eliminated, but Bruce made no such mistakes. Even though he lost a run-off with Chris Morton for first place, he was well pleased to take second place and book himself into his first ever World Final.

Bob Wasley made a positive start to the month by signing John Hack and Paul Bosley on a permanent basis. The Heathens also made a positive start by beating Coventry at Dudley Wood, and followed that with an incredible 2-point win at Reading in the first leg of the KO Cup quarter-final, despite a fighting 16 points from the Racers' Bobby Schwartz.

Penhall was missing from the next three League matches for one reason or another. In the first, at Cradley against Wolves, Nielsen, like Bruce, was absent on World Team Cup duty, and the match saw Phil Collins make his return with 10 battling points. Steve Lawson from Glasgow also put in an appearance for the Heathens, scoring an impressive 8 points, and Cradley had a comfortable win. Not so at Poole however, when they mustered only 30 points, and Cradley only just scraped a win at home against Leicester a couple of nights later, thanks to 12 points from Alan Grahame's brother Andy, who stood in as a guest. Erik Gundersen was missing from this one too, as he was busy taking second place in the Danish Final.

Penhall returned and was the Heathens' only challenger as they crashed out of the Inter-League KO Cup at King's Lynn. Bosley had yet to score in three matches, and an inspired move by Wasley saw Craig Featherby called in to ride on his former track at Lynn, which proved to be a successful tactic as he scored 5 points. Cradley were so poor that it made young Craig the second highest scorer to Penhall, and they lost the semi-final match 29-49.

In the quarter-final of the KO Cup, the Heathens must have cherished the 2-point lead that they had established at Reading, as they struggled against the Racers at Dudley Wood. They went into the last heat 2 points down on the night and level on aggregate, and only heroics by Penhall and Mike Sampson in the last heat got them the 4-2 that Cradley needed to get through to the semi-final of the competition. Reading were reckoned by many to be the best team in the League, and subsequently became the 1980 League Champions, so the Heathens had expected a fight, but the night belonged to one man – Reading's 'Heathen', Bobby Schwartz. He gave one of the most outstanding performances of any visiting rider to Dudley Wood as he clocked up a faultless 21-point maximum.

Bruce only managed to complete two rides in Cradley's next match against King's Lynn when he injured his shoulder, and only a 10-point score from Teromaa held them together for a 2-point win. Phil Collins was still suffering from his injuries, Gundersen and

Cradley Heath, 1980. From left to right: Alan Grahame, Erik Gundersen, Dave Perks, Bob Wasley (manager), Bruce Penhall, John Hack, Phil Collins, Illa Teromaa. (Hall)

Grahame were struggling with inconsistency and, apart from the odd match, Teromaa was only half the rider that he had been in previous seasons. The Heathens were looking an unlikely bet for the League, but at least they were still in with a chance of two cups.

At the end of August, Cradley featured in a two-leg challenge against local rivals Birmingham, and Penhall took the opportunity of resting his injured shoulder. Steve Lawson stepped in and once again impressed, as the Heathens won on aggregate.

Bruce returned to show his best form prior to the World Final, and stormed to a 12-point maximum as Cradley thrashed Sheffield 50-28 to close August. The month also saw a final split between co-promoters Pugh and McCormick, as Dan resigned from both Nottingham and Oxford.

The 1980 World Championship final took place at the Ullevi Stadium, Gothenburg, Sweden, on 5 September and Bruce Penhall, on his debut, was rider number one. He started as an outside favourite, but it was not to be Bruce's big night. He began well enough, winning a difficult heat 1 from John Davis and Hans Nielsen, but it was to be the American's only race win of the evening. He seemed to be tense and nervous all night and never looked the cool, relaxed rider that people were used to seeing. He did, however, have a good final, finishing in fifth place with 9 points, and now he knew what it was all about.

The World Championship in 1980 belonged to King's Lynn. The 21-year-old Michael Lee deservedly took the title, and his team-mate Dave Jessup was runner-up after a run-

1980 programme.

off with Australian Billy Sanders. Jan Andersson was the man who separated the top three from Bruce.

Penhall returned to a hero's welcome at Dudley Wood, and he celebrated with a stunning 12-point maximum, leading the Heathens to an emphatic 18-point win over Leicester in the first leg of the Midland Cup semi-final. Bruce was back – but then he was gone again, to compete in the World Longtrack final, and it was Gundersen who led the team to a comfortable win over Poole at Cradley.

The KO Cup semi-final was to be a local derby between the Heathens and the Brummies, and Birmingham hosted the first leg on 15 September. A close match saw the Brummies hold on to a 4-point win despite a 5-1 from Penhall and Gundersen in the last heat, which gave the Heathens an excellent chance of making it through to the final.

After losing at Ipswich, Cradley faced a glut of matches – three in four days – all without Penhall, who was otherwise engaged. Schwartz stepped in at Leicester to lead the Heathens into the final of the Midland Cup on aggregate, but without a guest at Eastbourne and Birmingham, Cradley failed at both venues.

October began at Dudley Wood with the Heathens gaining their revenge over Ipswich. Penhall had returned, and Steve Lawson was also included in the squad, and one had to say that when young Steve was in the side, Cradley had a very solid look about them. The Witches must have thought that too, as they were pounded 53-25. The same night, as part of a double-header, as expected, the Heathens cruised into the KO Cup final as Birmingham unsuccessfully contested the second leg of the semi-final.

As a very busy month continued, Cradley rode three League matches in as many days. They won at Hackney, beat Halifax at Dudley Wood and lost to the Dukes at the Shay by just 2 points. The young Englishman Kenny Carter was in brilliant form at Halifax, rattling off a superb 15-point maximum. Little Kenny, although being one of the toughest competitors in speedway, had been known to ruffle a few feathers in his short time in the sport. He was a blunt Yorkshireman who disliked the Danes, hated the Americans, and he hadn't got a good word to say for most of his England team-mates either! But most of all, he hated Bruce Penhall. A feud had begun that would far surpass the Brown/Mauger war in the early sixties.

The first leg of the Midland Cup final was at Coventry, and a thrilling match saw the Heathens come away with a 2-point lead. Penhall led by example with a brilliant 12-point maximum, but it was a fine all-round team performance that beat Olsen's merry men. The second leg was something of an anti-climax, with Cradley winning by 18 points and picking up their second piece of silverware to add to the Dudley/Wolves Trophy. Penhall was absent from the match – he had returned once again to America to win the American National Championship – but guest Schwartz dropped only 1 point to the opposition, and Collins and Gundersen were both unbeaten.

A couple of nights later, Cradley travelled to Belle Vue to defend their KO Cup, still without Penhall, in the first leg of the final, but the bottom three Heathens looked decidedly shaky. Hack, Lawson and Featherby only managed 2 points between them and, although Collins and Grahame fought bravely, Cradley came away with a 20-point deficit.

The following night at Wolverhampton, ironically, Kenny Carter guested for Penhall, and top-scored for the Heathens alongside Erik Gundersen with 11 points. Despite stout opposition from Nielsen, the Heathens won the match 43-34, but there were no celebrations. In heat 2, John Hack had fallen and was rushed to hospital in a critical condition with a broken leg and severe head injuries. The news was not good, and John began a fight for his life.

Three weeks into October saw the return of Cradley's American ace in a League match at table-topping Reading. Gundersen, Penhall and Grahame all gave stirring performances, but again a weak tail-end cost the Heathens the match, and they lost by just 2 points. The Racers were no match for Cradley in the return League match at Dudley Wood, however, and found themselves on the wrong end of a 'right drubbing'.

On 29 October, the second leg of the KO Cup final took place at Cradley Heath. Belle Vue, with a 26-point advantage, started as favourites, but the Heathens were the cup holders and defended it with pride. By heat 11 they had cancelled out the deficit, and over the remaining heats they built up a steady lead to win the match 75-33, retaining the cup by 16 points on aggregate. It was a tremendous display by all the team, led by Penhall with a 15-point maximum, Gundersen 13, Collins 12, Grahame 11, Andy Reid 9, Teromaa 8, Lawson 5 and Featherby 2.

The match was the curtain-closer at Dudley Wood, but Cradley still had one outstanding League match at King's Lynn on the last night of October. Penhall had already flown home and the Heathens lost heavily, but it had no bearing on the League position and they finished in fifth place.

The year finished on a happy note, when John Hack won the fight for his life and immediately announced his retirement. Hack had been a success in the Heathens line-up, and would no doubt have developed into a fine rider, but his brush with death understandably persuaded him to take up a quieter lifestyle.

Although Cradley had not managed to improve upon their 1979 League position (in fact they had dropped two places), it had still been a good season for them, as they had won just about everything else, apart from the Inter-League KO Cup.

It could have been better, but for two things. Poor old Perky was struck down whilst having his best season ever in the sport. As it was, only Penhall bettered his 8.96

Heathen average, but he had been lost to the team way back in July, and there was no doubt that further points would have been picked up but for his injury.

The other factor was those Continental excursions. Penhall had missed nine League matches and Teromaa six. Admittedly, in Bruce's case, sometimes he was absent due to World Pairs or World Team Cup duty, but League matches apart, there were also many challenge and four-team tournaments that he had not taken part in. Penhall had a fantastic season, topping the Heathens averages with 10.35 points and finishing fifth in the BL Riders averages. He was once again runner-up in the British League Riders Championship and had performed well in his first World Final.

Alan Grahame had finished third in the team averages, but there was nothing in it between him, Gundersen and Phil Collins. Alan had been Cradley's only ever-present and, like Collins, had been the Heathens' match-winner on many occasions. Young Gundersen was beginning to look something a wee bit special, and when he made one of his lightning gates, the opposition, no matter who they were, were finding him increasingly difficult to pass.

Teromaa had failed to supply the goods and finished the term with an average below five points, and the Finn's future at Cradley looked grim. Bob Wasley, who had so tragically lost his son Nigel the previous year, may have been influenced by the Hack incident and announced his retirement shortly before the end of the season.

5

CHAMPIONS AND CHAMPIONS
1981

As early as November 1980, Peter Adams had been named as Bob Wasley's successor. The university graduate with a BSc in civil engineering, brought quite a reputation with him to Dudley Wood. He began his career in speedway by running the Ole Olsen fan club, but the last three years had seen him as manager of Coventry, leading them to two League Championships.

Adams hit his first snag when Illa Teromaa informed him, as late as February, that he would not be returning to England, but would be riding in Germany instead. It was a blow to Peter, who knew that the Finn's 1980 average was well below what he was capable of, and in forming his 1981 squad within the 50-point limit, he had seen Illa as a possible trump card.

Phil Collins and Alan Grahame had enjoyed a good winter season with England in Australia; indeed, the recently married Grahame had finished second to Michael Lee in the Lions' averages, and both had agreed to ride for Cradley in 1981. Gundersen and Penhall had also pledged their allegiance, in fact, Erik returned as early as February to prepare four machines for the new campaign, showing an enthusiasm and professionalism that few in the sport could match.

The ACU ban on Lance King was still in force until August, so Adams dipped into the transfer market and came up with 23-year-old Dane Bent Rasmussen from King's Lynn. The deal was that Craig Featherby was transferred to the Stars for £3,000 and Rasmussen became a Heathen for £7,000. Adams' next signing was a clever one. He persuaded Aussie Dave Shields to end his three-year retirement and return to Dudley Wood full-time.

With days left before the start of the season, the new manager had another couple of problems to deal with. There was still the number seven spot to fill, and he took a chance with Arnold Haley from Belle Vue. Arnold had been a fine rider in his time, but at 38 he was way past his prime, and he knew it. So did Adams, and Haley joined the Heathens on the understanding that if he didn't settle down quickly and start scoring a few points, then he would be replaced.

The second problem was that Alan Grahame had turned down the terms offered to him and refused to sign on the eve of the season. This became a traditional tactic with Alan throughout almost his entire Cradley career, and in 1981 he signed just one hour before the first scheduled match.

British League Champions, 1981. From left to right, back row: Alan Grahame, Derek Pugh (promoter), Dave Shields, Phil Collins, John McNeil, Peter Adams (manager). Front row: Bent Rasmussen, Bruce Penhall, Erik Gundersen. (Hipkiss)

Peter had completed his squad. Unfortunately, there was no room for Dave Perks, whose 1980 average was too high to fit him into the team, so Dave went back to sister track Oxford in the National League. Another unfortunate thing about speedway at Cradley in 1981 was that there would be no titanic Cradley/Wolves clashes, as Wolverhampton had elected to move down to the National League.

Cradley began the season with League Cup matches, which were to be run on a 16-heat format. The opener, a win at Dudley Wood against Sheffield, saw Penhall, Grahame and Collins all score well, but Rasmussen was a revelation, scoring 10 points on his debut, and the Heathens looked to be on a winner with this one. Bent was staying with Erik in a flat at Wolverhampton, so maybe some of Gundersen's enthusiasm had rubbed off on him.

Further victories away at Birmingham, and at Dudley Wood against Leicester and Belle Vue followed, and the Heathens were looking an impressive outfit. Penhall had returned better than ever (he had dropped only 1 point in his last three matches and had lowered the Cradley track record to 64.0 seconds), and so were Grahame and Gundersen. Collins wasn't far behind them, and Rasmussen and Shields were grabbing the points too. The only Heathen not performing was Haley. He had scored only 1 point in the first four matches, and his future at Cradley already looked to be in jeopardy.

A trip to Belle Vue found Penhall away for the first time in the season and the Heathens lost. On his return, however, they were soon back to their winning ways, and overcame Birmingham and Coventry at Dudley Wood. Bruce, meanwhile, had secured a £25,000 sponsorship deal with Urban Cowboy Supplies, and received from them a Travel Cruiser, with three double beds, a cooker, fridge and shower, reported to be worth a cool £18,000.

The Heathens continued their League Cup campaign until the end of April, losing at Sheffield and winning at Leicester. The end of April also saw England beat America 4-1 in the annual Test series. Alan Grahame had three fine matches, and finished only behind Dave Jessup in the Lions' averages, with 13.33 points. This was even better than the USA skipper Penhall, who topped the Americans' averages with 13.00 points. Phil Collins was also selected by England for two matches and averaged 6.60 points.

The end of April also saw the end of Arnold Haley. He had failed to do what he had been brought in to do, and he was transferred to Oxford. Adams saw the 25-year-old Australian John McNeill as a much better bet. John was riding for Swindon, but owned his own contract, and as Cradley entered the League competition at the beginning of May, McNeill lined up as their number seven. Even without Penhall, the Heathens slaughtered a poor Hull side at Dudley Wood, and John had a fantastic debut, scoring 10 points in a match that saw Grahame and Collins undefeated.

Penhall returned with two 15-point maximums at Cradley and Hull, as the Heathens beat Halifax and the Vikings in further League Cup matches. They finished off the LC campaign with a win at Halifax, despite 17 sizzling points from Kenny Carter. He and Penhall beat each other once and the battle was hotting up. On the one hand, the blonde glamour boy who never seemed to say the wrong word, and on the other hand, a spit-and-sawdust fiery Yorkshireman who was forever putting his foot in it.

In a home match against Hackney, the Heathens were a very depleted side, with Penhall and Collins away riding longtrack, but Gundersen and Grahame did enough to earn Cradley a 2-point win. Collins was back for the next match at Cradley, when the Heathens beat Sheffield, but Penhall had moved on to ride in America. As he was winning the World Championship qualifying round in the States, Cradley completed their League Cup matches with a home win over Hull. The Heathens had lost only three matches in the competition but, even so, had finished Northern Section as runners-up to Coventry, and so it was the Bees who went into the final.

Cradley rode their first KO Cup match on 7 June, still without Bruce, and lost the first leg at Eastbourne by only 2 points, thanks to a brilliant Gundersen maximum. With the team back at full strength, Cradley lost by 6 points to Swindon at Blunsdon, and Adams hit the roof! Apart from Penhall and Gundersen, he blasted all the Heathens for being unprofessional and told them, in no uncertain terms, that this just would not do.

An instant response saw Birmingham thrashed at Dudley Wood (Birmingham had acquired the services of Hans Nielsen from Wolves) and then Bruce was off on his travels again – this time to Poland where he and partner Bobby Schwartz won the World Pairs Championship. He was hardly missed as the Heathens crushed Eastbourne in the second leg of the KO Cup to progress into the second round.

As Gundersen moved smoothly through the Nordic Final of the World Championship, Collins failed in the British Semi-final, and Grahame in the British Final, but Penhall finished in third place in the Overseas Final, despite being excluded in one race for allegedly bringing down his 'pal' Kenny Carter. That should have been an end to it, but Carter abused Penhall over the public address system and accused him of cheating – and the war raged on. Cradley's World Championship hopes now lay with the American and the Dane.

With Adams' words still ringing in their ears, the Heathens embarked on a phenomenal string of League victories that made them one of the most feared teams in the country. They saw out June beating Swindon at Dudley Wood and Reading at Smallmead. They went through July undefeated, Coventry, Poole, Belle Vue and Leicester all being beaten at Dudley Wood, and Sheffield, Hull and King's Lynn all receiving the same treatment at their own tracks. These results helped established the Heathens at the top of the British League.

At Sheffield, the Tigers seemed reluctant to ride on their own wet track, and sensing this, Adams instructed the Heathens to get changed and warm up their bikes, thus seizing the initiative and almost beating Sheffield before the match was even underway. The result was a 49-29 win for Cradley.

Penhall had established himself as the world's top rider, winning the Yorkshire Television Trophy at Hull, taking third place in Hackney's Superama, lowering the Cradley track record again to 62.9 seconds, and topping the British League averages. And guess who was second in those very same averages? The most improved rider in speedway – Erik Gundersen. Poor old Alan Grahame was riding better than ever, and in most teams in the BL he would have been the number one rider, but at Cradley Heath, he found himself well and truly in third place. The Heathens were indeed riding on the crest of a wave.

August began with one of the most amazing results of the season. Cradley had replaced Coventry at the top of the League, but when they visited Brandon, it looked as though the Heathens' unbeaten run might come to an end. On the contrary! On an unusually deep Coventry track, the Bees could muster only 26 points, as Penhall, Gundersen and Grahame were all unbeaten, and the Heathens stormed to a 26-point win on the home track of their nearest League rivals! Olsen and the young Danish whiz kid Tommy Knudsen just never knew what hit them.

Four nights later, Cradley were pulled up sharply at Dudley Wood when they met Ipswich in the first leg of the KO Cup quarter-final, and the Witches held them to a draw. Ipswich

Phil Collins. (Hipkiss)

Dave Shields. (Hipkiss)

were a good team who were themselves in the League title race, and, on the night, they had a more solid look about them. They were led by Penhall's cousin and friend Dennis Sigalos, another of the new breed of flamboyant Americans that had seemed to spring up overnight. Bruce scored a maximum, and Gundersen and Grahame both scored double figures, but the rest of the team were disappointing, and McNeill, whose form had slumped dramatically over the last few matches, failed to score.

But Cradley had cause for a double celebration, as two Heathens made it through to the World Final. Bruce Penhall was the new Intercontinental Champion, and the ever-improving Erik Gundersen was runner-up. Erik cashed in on his fabulous run of form by winning the Midland Riders Championship at Brandon, from Tommy Knudsen and Andy Grahame, while Penhall had to settle for fourth place. Bruce did, however, seem to have the Golden Hammer in his grasp when he was unbeaten in his first three rides, but the meeting was abandoned after 14 heats due to rain and was never restaged. In the Star of Anglia, at Ipswich, Bruce faced his fearsome rival Kenny Carter in a run-off for the title, but this time, the Yorkshireman got the better of the American, and Penhall had to settle for second spot. He did one better in the Blue Riband at Poole, however, taking the title with a 15-point maximum, and his August run-up to the World Championship seemed to be going to plan.

After more harsh words from Adams following the Ipswich match, Cradley continued their challenge for the League title, beating Hackney at Waterden Road and Hull at Dudley Wood, Penhall remaining unbeaten in both matches. He was at that time generally acknowledged as being the best rider in speedway and was the people's favourite for the World Championship.

The Heathens were knocked out of the KO Cup competition at Ipswich, losing by 12 points, but the result would undoubtedly have been different had Cradley not lost Gundersen in his first race with an injured foot. He shrugged off the injury to score a maximum two nights later as the Heathens continued to plunder the League with a huge win over Reading at Dudley Wood, followed by a 5-point win at Poole. To end the month Cradley visited Belle Vue, who were well placed in the League, and crushed them by an almighty 20 points.

1981 programme.

Cradley's top three were scoring consistently well, Collins was always capable of scoring double figures, and Shields and Rasmussen were scoring respectably in most matches. The Heathens were red-hot favourites for the League title, although Adams repeatedly refused to admit this at this stage of the game.

The start of September saw Cradley beat Swindon on aggregate to book their place in the Midland Cup final, and then on 5 September at Wembley Stadium, Bruce Penhall and Erik Gundersen took their place in the 1981 World Championship Final. The meeting itself is reckoned to be probably the best World Final ever. It had everything – tension, excitement, great racing – and the right result.

The support for the Cradley boys was nothing short of phenomenal, and they responded. They were both out together in heat 3, and Penhall won from Gundersen, who had taken Mike Lee from the back. With Bruce out of the way, Erik consolidated his position and won heat 6, breaking the track record into the bargain. The next heat was one of the best ever seen in a World Final as Penhall chased Ole Olsen for four laps, before taking him on the last bend to win by a tyre. Heat 9 saw the American take another 3 points, and he was looking good to take the title.

Heat 12 was a tragedy for Gundersen. It was his easiest race on paper, but machine problems put him in last place and seemed to have ended his chances. A lesser man in his World Final debut may have crumbled – indeed, Erik's temperament on the big occasions had been suspect in the past – but this was the night that the boy became a man, and young Gundersen was far from finished.

No such misfortunes befell Penhall, however, and his next heart-stopping race saw him ride the fence around Tommy Knudsen on the last bend to take another 3 points. Four rides – four wins. His only worry was that arch rival Carter had only dropped 1 point in three outings, and Bruce was to meet him in the very last race.

The next race was significant for the Cradley fans, not just because Gundersen got his act back together and notched up another win, at the expense of Olsen, but because in that very same race, Carter suffered an engine failure and dropped 3 valuable points. Erik finished his programmed rides in heat 17 with a win over Hans Nielsen and finished the meeting with 10 points. Olsen and Knudsen won the next two heats, putting them on 12 points each, and Penhall went into his last race knowing that third place would be enough to give him the World Crown. When Carter made the gate, Penhall did not let his heart rule his head and settled into second place, giving Kenny plenty of room and taking no chances with the fiery Englishman. As Bruce did a wheelie across the finishing line, the stadium erupted. It may have been the most popular World Championship win of all time. If there were any impartial fans at Wembley, he had won them over with his daredevil riding on the night, and they celebrated along with the new World Speedway Champion.

In the run-off for second place, the master beat the pupil, as Ole Olsen led Tommy Knudsen from the gate to the finishing line. Poor old Erik had to settle for fourth place, along with Carter, but it was an incredible performance on his World Final debut. If only it hadn't been for that bloody bike, Cradley may have been celebrating the world's number one and number two! As it was, they had their first ever World Champion – and rightly so – Penhall was simply the best rider in the world. Cradley's dynamic duo were soon back in action, four nights later in the Brandonapolis at Coventry, when Penhall took first place and Gundersen finished third, Mitch Shirra splitting them.

They returned to Dudley Wood on 12 September. Bruce arrived by helicopter (as you do) and the two heroes were paraded around Dudley Wood to rapturous applause. Unfortunately, the programmed match against King's Lynn was called off due to rain, but not before Bruce had received a telegram from the President of the United States, Ronald Reagan, congratulating him (thanks to Peter Adams pulling more strings than a puppeteer!).

Back to the League rampage, and Cradley took the points at Leicester and then hammered King's Lynn, Halifax and Ipswich at Dudley Wood. Their next match at Wimbledon would have secured the League Championship had they won, but the Heathens only managed to draw and the champagne was put on ice.

It was not to be for long, however, as three nights later at Eastbourne on 4 October, Cradley won by 8 points and became British League Champions for the first time in the club's history. Typically, Penhall and Gundersen led the assault with 11 points apiece, Shields excelled with 8, Collins 6, Grahame 5, Rasmussen 2, and McNeill failed to score.

Further into October, the rout continued, even though Penhall had returned home to win the American National Championship. He returned to challenge Kenny Carter for his Golden Helmet, but the jet-lagged American was not up to the task and Carter revelled in the win.

Coventry gained their revenge for the humiliating home defeat when they forced a draw at Dudley Wood in the first leg of the Midland Cup final and then secured the win at Brandon, but at that stage the League Champions were all burnt out. They lost their last two away matches at Halifax and Ipswich, but by then the hard work had been done and the title had been won.

It had been a fabulous year for the Heathens. Apart from winning the League title by a clear 7 points, they had the World Champion in their camp. Penhall had topped the League averages with 11.08 points, and Gundersen had finished fourth behind 20-year old Kenny Carter and Mike Lee with 10.26 points. Grahame had 9.26, Collins 7.26, Shields 6.12, Rasmussen 4.70, and McNeill 3.61. In their League campaign, the Heathens had lost only three matches and had enjoyed an incredible run of twenty-six matches without a defeat.

It is true that Adams had inherited most of his championship-winning team, but he balanced it up beautifully with Shields and Rasmussen. Every winner has to have luck, and indeed Cradley had it in '81, for not only did they escape injuries, but their top three maintained a consistency that was unprecedented. It was almost as if unfashionable Cradley Heath had become the speedway centre of the world, which was no more than their faithful supporters deserved.

Penhall had truly arrived as the superstar of speedway, but success comes with a price, and the supporters and his other team members paid for it with Bruce's constant trips abroad. He ended the season on a slightly sour note, when he returned home five days early, as a tour of the Black Country on an open-topped bus had been arranged for the Heathens, terminating at Dudley Council House, where they were presented with the Championship Cup by the Mayor of Dudley.

The event drew hundreds of people, and one couldn't help but think that even though he was World Champion, Bruce was going to have to watch it in the popularity stakes, because the ever-accessible and friendly Gundersen was rapidly becoming the people's favourite.

6

HOLLYWOOD CALLING
1982

Cradley was to have an incident-packed year in 1982. It could have been the greatest year in the club's history, but although it was by no means a failure, it ended with supporters and management alike feeling bitter and cheated. It was a year that saw Bruce Penhall commit a series of misdemeanours that tarnished his tremendous popularity, and also saw the end of the Americans as the blue-eyed boys of speedway.

It all began as early as the winter when Penhall, who was touring Australia and New Zealand, was reported as saying on Australian television that if he won the world title in 1982 then he would retire. When questioned about this statement later, his management denied this and Peter Adams was given assurances that this would not happen.

This year also saw the World Final being held in the United States for the first time ever, at the Los Angeles Coliseum, and this was to have a bearing on the events that were to happen at Dudley Wood in the forthcoming season.

Adams was determined to fit Lance King into the new squad, and Alan Grahame, who was enjoying another fine season in Australia, was informed in a telephone call from one of his relatives that he had been transfer-listed. He returned to England furious, and demanded a showdown with Adams. In Alan's absence, Adams had received a flood of letters from supporters protesting that he was getting rid of one of the most consistent scorers in the BL – and an Englishman to boot.

Meanwhile, he set about forming a squad within the 50-point limit. Bent Rasmussen had retired from speedway, as his girlfriend had secured a post as a warden in an open prison in Denmark and the appointment carried a salary that was far greater than Bent's speedway earnings, so he moved back to Denmark and got a job as a mechanic.

Dave Shields had failed to reach the required 6-point average for an overseas rider, and was therefore unable to compete in the BL in '82, so he too hung up his leathers and stayed home in Australia. John McNeill wanted Cradley to buy his contract if he returned, but Adams reckoned that he was asking too much money, so John appeared to be out of the frame.

The 23-year-old Ian Gledhill from Mildenhall had been the National League Riders Champion in 1979, and although he had not made the expected progress since, he had been an impressive guest for the Heathens a couple of times in the past, and he was Cradley's first signing in February. The next was 25-year-old Andy Reid from Glasgow, leaving room for Alan Grahame to fit in the squad, alongside Penhall, Gundersen Collins and King.

The side was a little top-heavy for Adams' liking, but with Grahame reinstated, there was no room to manoeuvre. With just days to go before the tapes went up on the new season, Peter began a signing spree in the National League. Joe Owen was signed as Cradley's number eight and was loaned out to Newcastle, Graham Drury was signed as number nine and was loaned out to Oxford, along with Ashley Pullen, the number ten. Finally, Wayne Jackson was signed from Workington and was also sent to Cowley.

The season began on 20 March with the first leg of the Premiership, a new cup introduced to feature the League winners against the KO Cup winners from the previous season. Cradley's opponents in the cup were KO Cup winners Ipswich, and at Dudley Wood, the four feet added to the width of the track in the winter certainly seemed to suit Phil Collins. He led the Heathens' scorers with 10 points and they established an 8-point lead to take into the second leg. Penhall, who also scored 10 points, was paired with young King, and the new American looked to be a future champion, scoring paid 10 points. For the Witches, John 'Cowboy' Cook, beaten only by Collins, scored 14 points, and it looked as though the English had yet another flamboyant American to deal with in the oncoming Test matches.

Five nights later, Cradley won their first piece of silverware for the season, when, again led by Collins, they beat Ipswich at Foxhall Heath to win the first ever Premiership. King was, again, highly impressive dropping only 1 point to the Witches, but there was a price to pay as Andy Reid, who had done well in the first leg, fell in his first outing and broke his thumb, putting him on the sidelines for a number of weeks.

Meanwhile, there were rumblings from the Penhall camp. Bruce claimed that his contract had not yet been sorted out, and unless Cradley met his terms, he would withdraw his services from the Heathens and immediately fly back to the States. It was a harder line than we had ever seen the American take before, but he was, after all's said and done, World Champion – a commodity that Cradley had not had to deal with in the past. Following a meeting with Adams, Bruce signed his contract the night before the Heathens began their League title defence at Dudley Wood against Wimbledon.

Penhall responded with a brilliant maximum, and with Gundersen and Grahame also scoring well, the Dons were well beaten. Wayne Jackson was brought in to replace Reid and impressed with 3 points, but as the Heathens moved into April, Adams signed 21-year-old Aussie Bill Barrett, who was also loaned to Oxford.

Cradley began their League Cup campaign impressively, beating Sheffield at home and away, drawing at Birmingham, and beating the Brummies at Dudley Wood. Penhall, Gundersen and Grahame had settled down quickly, and King, after his dramatic start, had slowed down somewhat, but Phil Collins had become a cause for concern. Never the best of gaters, Phil was famous for his exciting surges from the back, but they were becoming few and far between as on many occasions he was starting last and finishing last. Gledhill was doing as well as could be expected, and the number-seven spot had become a lottery. Jackson, Barrett, Pullen and the impressive 16-year-old Simon Cross all had a stab at it in the first few matches, and just as Jackson was looking to be the best bet, he injured his leg and was out for some weeks.

The Heathens continued in the League Cup, losing at Coventry by 10 points. Penhall was away, riding in America, but Andy Grahame proved to be an excellent choice of

Cradley, Heath, 1982. From left to right: Erik Gundersen, Lance King, Bruce Penhall, Andy Reid, Phil Collins, Peter Adams (manager). Kneeling: Ian Gledhill, Alan Grahame. (Hipkiss)

guest, scoring 14 points. The problem had been that King and Collins could only muster 1 point each.

Joe Owen scored 9 points as he guested for Bruce in Cradley's next League Cup match at Dudley Wood against Halifax. A Gundersen maximum led the Heathens to victory, but the public was robbed of another Penhall/Carter showdown. Bruce was due to return the next day to take his place in the return at the Shay – in fact the Dukes had even put back their starting time to accommodate him – but he elected to stay in America, and although Cradley forced a draw, Penhall dropped a few more popularity points.

He arrived back in time for the next match at Dudley Wood, when the Heathens beat Belle Vue, but it was amidst more controversy. Bruce announced that he did not wish to ride for America in the forthcoming Test series against England, as it would cost him too much in loss of earnings in Continental bookings. The press made a meal out of it, and Penhall defended himself saying that he was not unpatriotic, and if it had been the World Team Cup, for example, then that would be fine. He went on to say that he regarded the Test matches as nothing more than open meetings, and if he was expected to ride, then he would require a sum of £1,500 to cover his losses. The Americans had a very good team, but without their top star they would become a 'just above average' team, and as the matches were being covered by national television, to maintain the sport's credibility, the BSPA agreed to pay him. Penhall tried to rationalise the situation by pointing out that the money was only the equivalent of 150 extra punters coming through the turnstiles, and he was sure that he would draw more than that, however, the fact remains that Bruce mugged the BSPA. The whole incident was very unsavoury, and last year's 'Personality of the Year' was already looking to be out of the '82 contest, with only one month of the season gone.

Just three nights later at Belle Vue, he was soundly booed, when the Aces lost Louis Carr as he fell following a brush with Bruce in the opening heat. The incident may have cost the Aces the match, as Cradley romped home by 4 points to put the pressure on Coventry at the top of the Northern League Cup table.

Further wins at Leicester and at home to King's Lynn found the Heathens looking favourite to qualify from the Northern section – until leaders Coventry visited Dudley Wood on 3 May and ended Cradley's two-year unbeaten home record, winning by 9 points. Kevin Hawkins was the Bees' star, scoring 11½ points from the reserve berth. Adams was furious and called the riders to his office after the match, where they were given the pleasure of his company until after midnight. He called their team-riding disgraceful and their basic machine errors unprofessional. It had been a successful tactic the previous year, and he no doubt hoped that it would have the same effect in 1982.

In their next match at Cradley, the Heathens faced Leicester without Gundersen, who was away winning the Danish round of the World Championship, but even so, they won by 18 points. Phil Collins, who many believed to have born the brunt of Adams' criticism, put up his best performance for many weeks, scoring 12 points.

Left: Jan Verner. (Hipkiss) Right: Bruce Penhall, the 1982 World Champion. (Hipkiss)

Phil had acquired a reputation as a 'high flyer', enjoying the nightlife and even being seen out with a page three girl on his arm for some time. Nothing wrong with that, but he had been a shadow of his former self so far in 1982, and Adams was not content to sit back and let Phil's immense talent go to waste. His contribution in the Leicester match booked Cradley a place in the League Cup final.

Penhall meanwhile led the USA to victory in the Test series against England. With the score at two matches each after four Tests, he set himself an almost impossible schedule to make the final match at Poole. A few days before, he had jetted out to America for yet another business meeting, to return via Herxheim, Germany, to attend the official practice session for the World Longtrack final, and fly into Britain the later on the same day, to ride in the final Test, that same night!

His German trip was cut short and he arrived in the Poole Stadium, by helicopter, to lead the Americans to a series win. Upon his return to Germany the following day, he paid the price as his untried equipment let him down and put him out of the Longtrack Championship. It was a meeting that perhaps Bruce should have cancelled when he agreed to ride in the Test series, but that was his business, and at least he had honoured his agreement with the BSPA. A couple of weeks into May, he led the Americans to a 2-1 series win in Sweden.

On the home front, Alan Grahame won the Birmingham British Semi-final, and with Collins finishing in third place, Heathens fans had two riders to cheer in the British Final. Cradley ended May by beating Sheffield on aggregate to move into the next round of the KO Cup, and just managed to beat Reading at Dudley Wood to take 2 more League points.

Early June saw Alan Grahame finish in second place to surprise winner brother Andy in the British Final at Coventry, and with Collins also scoring well, both Heathens moved on to the Overseas Final. Cradley began the month by taking League points at Wimbledon, and at home against Hackney, but just as their campaign seemed to be going well, news came through that Lance King had broken his collarbone riding in America. With the League Cup final just two weeks away (in which time Cradley had no matches), Adams moved swiftly to cover King and signed three of the top National League boys on a five-match basis. Simon Wigg from Weymouth, Steve Lawson from Glasgow and John Barker from Exeter were the aforementioned riders.

The last two matches had seen the welcome return of Andy Reid, but Adams was still not satisfied with the reserve situation, and after discussions with Gledhill, he signed Jan Verner, the 31-year-old Czechoslovakian from Swindon, to replace Ian. Verner was unable to ride in the first leg of the final at Dudley Wood against Ipswich, so young Simon Cross was brought in, and what a fine job he did too, scoring 5 points. Lawson was Adams' choice from his NL men, and although he scored only 2 points, Cradley's big guns did enough to ensure a 6-point victory. In the return leg at Foxhall Heath, Verner made a point-less debut, but NL Simon Wigg proved to be a wise choice, scoring 6 points and helping the Heathens to a 4-point win, and their second piece of silverware. Maybe prematurely, people were talking about Cradley doing the Grand Slam.

In the Midland Riders Semi-final at Birmingham, Alan Grahame once more showed his liking for the track, winning the meeting after a run-off with brother Andy. Gundersen

Simon Wigg advises a young Simon Cross. (Hall)

finished third, and Collins also made it through to the final.

On the international front, Penhall and Gundersen starred for their respective countries as the USA and Denmark both qualified for the Inter-Continental Final of the World Team Cup in Vojens at the expense of England, despite a Kenny Carter maximum.

Cradley made the transition from June to July maintaining their unbeaten League run with victories at Reading and Birmingham, and against Belle Vue at Dudley Wood, but it was the Aces who ended their run on 3 July at the Manchester circuit. Without Gundersen, only Penhall and Grahame showed any resistance as Belle Vue romped to an 18-point win, putting them 2 points clear of Cradley at the top of the League, although the Heathens did have three matches in hand.

The next day was one that Penhall will never forget. On 4 July at White City in the Overseas Final, he drove a nail deep into the coffin of his popularity. Bruce had dropped only 1 point, to Dave Jessup, in his first four outings and looked red-hot favourite to take the £1,000 winner's cheque. He lined up for heat 19 alongside three other Americans – Dennis Sigalos, Shawn Moran and Kelly Moran. As the tapes went up, Penhall stayed back and let the other three go, content for them to battle it out whilst he remained half a lap behind pulling wheelies. As it happens, Sigalos and Kelly Moran qualified for the Inter-Continental Final, but the boos and jeers that greeted the end of the race were unprecedented. Penhall could not believe it as he rode back to the pits, where the television commentator Gary Newbon immediately interviewed him. Bruce was visibly shaken, as he tried to explain that it was in his country's best interests to have as many Americans as possible in the World Final, and he was just lending a helping hand. The television cameras were there to capture the event, and, once again, speedway was washing its dirty laundry in public.

The victory parade was an event itself. The top three – winner Dave Jessup, runner-up Kenny Carter and third-placed Penhall – were brought around the track on an open trailer and, as soon as it emerged from the pits, the stadium erupted. It became a cauldron of hatred, as the American was subjected to a measure of jeers, abuse and fist-waving the like of which had possibly not been seen before at a speedway track.

It was too much for Penhall, and he turned his back on his aggressors, well before the lap had ended. On the other hand, Jessup accepted the win with all the grace that one had come to expect of him, but standing on the other side of Dave, Carter had a grin on his face that expressed sheer delight. Could it have been that he had just received the winner's cheque from Littlewoods, or could it be that he was revelling in Penhall's downfall in public popularity?

Bruce read the situation completely wrong. It was not what he did; it was the way that he did it. The result would have been the same had he slipped off or if his bike had stopped. In either case he would have escaped the public animosity, but instead he was blatant in his actions, choosing to 'play to the gallery', and if he thought that his popularity would excuse him, then he was wrong. The Falklands War had rekindled British patriotism, and his actions had possibly cost English riders a place in the next round.

In fairness, he was put in an impossible position. If he had won the race and put Americans out of the next round, how would he be received when he returned to the States? It was America's first ever World Championship Final, and as World Champion, he was their ambassador, and he was expected to build up the meeting and sell it to the American people – and his actions had also cost him £1,000, remember.

The real fault lay well and truly in the hands of the organisers, for at this stage of the competition, to put four Americans in the last qualifying race of the round was ludicrous. However, the organisers were not on the trailer to take the torrent of abuse that Penhall was subjected to. The love affair was over. Penhall had indeed lost face with the British public in one of the sport's most controversial incidents. Bruce Penhall was no longer the blue-eyed boy. In the same meeting, Alan Grahame and Phil Collins failed to qualify.

Penhall immediately left England, either to visit his sick aunt or to audition for *CHiPs*, depending upon which newspaper you read, but the fact is that Cradley had to ride without him at Hackney and dropped another 2 League points. The Heathens were denied a guest rider, as the Control Board pointed out that Penhall's absence was due to domestic rather than professional reasons, so Adams put in an appeal that was eventually upheld. Bruce returned to ride at the Ballymena track in Ireland, where some 4,000 spectators saw Cradley beat an Ivan Mauger Select team by 2 points.

The middle of the month saw the American shake off the effects of any bad public relations by retaining the Yorkshire Television Trophy at Sheffield, and the next night at Birmingham, Grahame had his share of success, as he was runner-up to Hans Nielsen in the Olympique.

Bruce made his return to Dudley Wood on 17 July, and publicly apologised for his actions in the Overseas Final, claiming that he wanted Dennis Sigalos to qualify because Dennis' mother had been killed in the same plane crash as his own parents. He also apologised for missing the Hackney match and gave the fans the 'aunt' story. Anyway, Cradley beat their opponents Poole, and five days later, beat them on their own track to move to the top of the British League.

Erik Gundersen had top-scored for the Heathens in their last three matches. He lived in Bruce's shadow and quietly went about his business in the amicable way with which he was synonymous, but lo and behold, July found him on top of the British League averages, with Penhall in fourth place. Top rider and top team: the Cradley fans had a lot to celebrate until the Inter-Continental Final in Vetlanda. Penhall made it through with 9 points, but inexplicably, Gundersen failed. He changed parts, changed bikes, he even borrowed Penhall's bike, but it was not Erik's night and out he went.

Les Collins shocked many people by becoming the 1982 Inter-Continental Champion, but Carter's second place surprised no one, and he was looking to be a distinct threat to Penhall's world crown. As if to make that very point, he won the Golden Hammer at Cradley with a brilliant 15-point maximum, and replaced Erik at the top of the League Riders averages.

Meanwhile, King returned in the last week of July, as Cradley beat Birmingham and won at Swindon, and almost without anyone noticing, Alan Grahame sneaked his average up over the 10-point mark. Alan was having a great season, representing England in the Test matches against the USA and Denmark and finally getting the recognition that he deserved. But, if Gundersen lived in the shadow of Penhall, Grahame lived in the shadow of Penhall *and* Gundersen – such was the price of riding for the likes of Cradley.

The Heathens visited Ipswich for the first leg of the KO Cup quarter-final and amazingly came away with a 1-point advantage. It was amazing because apart from Penhall, Gundersen and Grahame, no other Heathen managed to beat an opponent.

August began well enough with Gundersen winning the Midland Riders Championship. In a meeting at Ipswich, Kenny Carter was put through the fence by Preben Eriksen and damaged his left lung. Doctors advised him to miss the rest of the season, but Carter vowed to ride in the World Final.

Cradley's assault on the League continued with a home win against Sheffield and a win at King's Lynn. Penhall had scored two successive maximums, and his run-up to the World Final seemed perfectly timed.

A 4-point win over Ipswich at Dudley Wood ensured the Heathens a place in the KO Cup semi-finals, but Cradley were unable to take the League points from contenders Coventry at Brandon, losing by 2 points, as Penhall scored only 6. Two days later, Bruce Penhall announced his retirement from British League racing. There had been rumours that he would retire at the end of the season, but his retirement would now become effective after the Halifax match at Dudley Wood on 16 August – 24 hours later! The rumours concerning Hollywood had all been true. He was to join the cast of *CHiPs*, a motorcycle cop television series, and his first episode would be based around the World Final in Los Angeles (it could only happen in America).

Adams was stunned and the Cradley supporters went into deep shock. As Cradley beat a Carter-less Halifax, Penhall said goodbye with a vintage maximum and told his once-adoring public that the opportunities that he had been offered were just too good to pass up. The studios had instructed him that he would not be allowed to ride again until the World Final, and Bruce walked out of the Cradley team forever.

Public opinion was split regarding Penhall's actions. He had his die-hard supporters who would have forgiven him anything, but the majority seemed to think that he should have put back into the sport what he had taken out and stayed until the end of the season. (Cradley supporters were not used to losing their riders to Hollywood. They were under the impression that every man out there was a 'bloody poofter'.) The speedway authorities took a very dim view of the affair, and Peter Adams sought legal advice with a view to suing the prodigal Heathen.

The rest of the Heathens put on a brave face and Alan Grahame took over as skipper, vowing that they would not falter in their quest to retain the League title. Their next home win against Eastbourne saw them poised to make history, as Cradley equalled the all-time record of 75 consecutive home League wins.

America's first-ever World Championship Final was staged on 18 August. It was reckoned to be between Penhall and Carter. The pressure on the American must have been almost unbearable, with film crews all over the place, plus the fact that he was defending the title in front of his own people, and, if he didn't win it, he would feel rather foolish with regard to the *CHiPs* people.

But, on the other hand, Carter was hardly fighting fit. After any strenuous movement, Kenny was forced to sit down as his breathing became laboured, but Penhall knew better than to take any notice of that. Carter was a one-off, whose determination knew no bounds, and he would be almost prepared to die to get his hands on the world crown. A more dangerous opponent did not exist.

The pre-final presentation was just about what you would expect it to be in America, with fireworks, stagecoaches, cowboys and the like. When the action finally got underway, Penhall received an early shock, when Les Collins headed him home in his first outing. It was a bad start for Bruce, but Les proved to be the surprise package of the final, finishing in second spot on the night.

It is testimony to Penhall that he stuck to the job in hand and won his next two races, but as he came out to face Carter in the now infamous heat 14, Bruce had already dropped 1 point – but Kenny had dropped none.

The race itself is one of the most controversial in the history of speedway. Uncharacteristically, Peter Collins made the gate, and after they had both passed Phil Crump, Penhall and Carter engaged in a personal dogfight, apparently oblivious to the fact that Collins was in front. They bumped and jostled one

1982 programme.

another until the first bend of the third lap, when Penhall made his move, and, in an attempt to try and stop him, Carter found himself under the fence, unconscious.

The race was stopped and Carter was excluded. When he regained consciousness, he pleaded with the referee, but it was to no avail. Pandemonium broke out as Kenny refused to leave the track, and eventually he was escorted away by security. An American television presenter took it upon himself to interview Carter on his return to the pits, and the cameras showed us the fiery Englishman, his chest heaving up and down, as he struggled to breathe. It was at this point that he uttered those immortal words: 'It were Browse – 'e stuffed me rart in t' fence.' The feud was over – for ever.

Penhall made no mistakes in the re-run and took another 3 points, and retained his title with a win in his final race. Carter, badly winded, scored only 1 point from his last ride, and finished in fifth place behind Americans Dennis Sigalos and Kelly Moran (two of the riders that Penhall had helped in the Overseas Final). Carter, as always, had to have the last word, and he left the Coliseum advising Penhall to never set foot in England again.

Bruce retired on the rostrum to pursue an unsuccessful acting career in Hollywood. *CHiPs* was shelved after about half-a-dozen further episodes, and he tried various other projects before returning to his family business. He had left the world of speedway in turmoil, a sport without a champion – never mind the problems that he had left the Heathens with.

Cradley ended August by beating Swindon on aggregate to earn a place in the Midland Cup final but, despite a brilliant display by Simon Wigg who scored 13 points, they failed to come away from Sheffield with any League points at the start of September. A home win against Coventry that put them in the record books was followed by a defeat at Leicester, and the Heathens began to look a little shaky.

Gundersen had effortlessly slipped into the number one slot, but his back-up man, Grahame, was having the odd bad match. King was beginning to show good form, but Collins had again become inconsistent. Verner was having the odd good match, as was Reid, but not knowing who, if anyone, was filling the empty space was having an unsettling effect on the Heathens, and they slipped under Belle Vue in the League table. Wayne Brown, Kenny McKinna and Steve Lawson all did well to help Cradley beat Eastbourne on aggregate and reach the KO Cup final in mid-September.

Gundersen hit top form as the Heathens destroyed Swindon at Dudley Wood, but he was unable to prevent a defeat at Halifax. Cradley entered October almost losing their unbeaten home record to Ipswich, when they trailed until the last two heats. Grahame and Collins put the Heathens ahead in heat 12, and Gundersen won the last race to ensure victory.

Two nights later, Cradley played host to Coventry in the first leg of the Midland Cup final. It turned out to be a night of personal feuds between King and Tommy Knudsen, and Grahame and Gary Guglielmi, and although Simon Wigg suffered an engine failure and King was excluded, the Heathens gained an 8-point advantage to take to Brandon for the second leg. All went well in the return at Coventry until the last two races. The Bees scored two 5-1s and Cradley lost their first trophy of the season by just 2 points.

A home win against Leicester was followed by a mere 2-point defeat at Ipswich, and that match put the Heathens out of contention for the League title. Ironically it was the new Champions Belle Vue who were Cradley's scheduled opponents in the KO Cup final.

Erik Gundersen was the Heathens' representative in the British League Riders final and finished in fourth place, Kenny Carter deservedly winning the meeting. Alan Grahame tuned up for the KO Cup final by winning the Newton Oils Marathon at Swindon, but followed this by falling in the sixteen-lapper at Ipswich, damaging his tendons and cracking a vertebra.

Meanwhile, back at Dudley Wood, Adams was reported to have received a five-figure sum from Penhall in an out-of-court settlement. How much a League Championship is worth is a matter of conjecture, for Penhall had surely cost Cradley that much.

Alan Grahame was obviously in a great deal of pain during the first leg of the KO Cup final at Dudley Wood and managed to score only 3 points. Lance King, however, hit top form and, along with Erik, scored 13 points. It gave the Heathens a precious 14-point lead to take to Belle Vue. The Dane surely laid Penhall's ghost to rest when he scored an immaculate 15-point maximum in the return leg at Manchester to hold the Aces to an 8-point win. Adams fought a tactical battle, putting rider replacement at number 1 and placing Erik at number 2. The ploy worked and Cradley were the new KO Cup holders.

The Heathens lost their last two League matches at Eastbourne and Hackney by just 1 and 2 points respectively but it was all academic. They had finished in second place in the League, 6 points behind the Aces and 6 points ahead of Ipswich. Since Penhall's departure, although they got close a few times, Cradley had failed to win an away match in the League, a fact that undoubtedly cost them the League Championship. There can be no doubt that at one time the Grand Slam had indeed been a possibility but, as it was, they were still the most successful team in the League, winning the Premiership, the League Cup and the KO Cup.

In Gundersen, they had a world-beater. He finished second in the British League Riders averages, behind Carter with 10.72 points, and was followed by Birmingham's Hans Nielsen and Penhall. At Cradley he now carried the mantle of People's Champion, and carried it with a pride and dignity that had not been shown by others before him.

Battling 'Big Al', Alan Grahame, had never given up fighting, as his average of 9.22 points showed and, but for a slump in form, he may well have maintained his 10-point figure. Phil Collins kept his average at 7.3 points, but should have improved it, and no doubt would have done but for mechanical problems and inconsistency. Lance King had been a success. He began like a locomotive, had a spell in the doldrums, got laid off with injury and came back to show his best form to date at the end of the season; his 6.3 point average did not reflect his real skill. Jan Verner had failed at reserve, as had a handful of others, but the seven matches that Simon Wigg had ridden had established him as a star of the future.

It had been a traumatic year for the Heathens – successful, but traumatic. Adams was left with some shoes to fill, but that's what you get when you flirt with showbiz stars. Dudley Wood would never be quite the same place again.

7

THE GREATEST TEAM EVER
1983

Peter Adams faced the forthcoming 1983 season having lost the services of arguably the best rider in the world. The loss would, however, allow him to form a much better balanced squad, not so top heavy as the 1982 team, and the winter saw him go about the task with solid determination. Jan Verner had not been allowed a permit for the oncoming season, so it looked as though Gundersen, Grahame, Collins and King would form the nucleus of the side. Joining them would be the highly recommended 20-year-old Dane Jan O. Pedersen. He had pledged his allegiance to Cradley as early as September 1982, and although he had been much sought after in the close season, he honoured his word to make his British League debut with the Heathens.

The 22-year-old Simon Wigg from National League Weymouth established himself as one of the top boys in the NL in '82, and his guest appearances for Cradley had been highly impressive. Adams had chased him from the off, and at first said that the asking price of £20,000 was too much. A deal was made, for an undisclosed sum of money, that involved Simon Cross going to Weymouth on loan for a season, and Wigg joined the Cradley camp.

Adams made up the team with an untried Australian, Dave Cheshire. The lad was only 16, but had quite a reputation in his homeland, and was considered by Ivan Mauger to be the best Aussie prospect since Billy Sanders. It was to be a nightmare season for Dave, starting as early as practice day, when he fell, broke his collarbone, chipped a bone in his shoulder and broke his ribs.

As if this wasn't bad enough, Adams received a phone call from Phil Collins, a matter of hours before the first match, saying that he wasn't feeling too well, and a short time later, Phil was rushed off to hospital with appendicitis. It was hardly the best start possible, but great things were in store for the Heathens.

New skipper Erik Gundersen's season began at Birmingham on 18 March, when he chalked up his first success of the season by winning the Second City Trophy. The very next night, he led the Heathens in the first leg of the Premiership against Belle Vue at Dudley Wood. Andy Reid had been called in to replace Cheshire, and Cradley used rider replacement for Collins, but only Gundersen and Wigg clicked, as the Aces took a 6-point lead on the night. It was quite a home debut for Wiggy, scoring 11 points and immediately making a smooth transition to the BL.

The next day the Heathens lost the Premiership, but not without a fight. They beat the Aces at Belle Vue by 4 points, but it meant a 2-point defeat on aggregate. The competition had been a fine advertisement for speedway, with some thrilling racing, and even though Cradley had to remove the trophy from their cabinet, they had performed well under duress.

The Heathens easily beat their old foes Ipswich at Dudley Wood in a challenge match, before beginning their League Cup campaign at Birmingham at the start of April. They maintained the same six-man line-up and came away with a 6-point win, thanks to a brilliant 14 points from Erik. His only defeat was at the hands of Brummie Hans Nielsen, and the duels between these two Danes were becoming a feature of League and world speedway. Wigg again scored double figures and as the fans watched intently, waiting for him to blow up, he just carried on gathering many, many points.

The Heathens were due to meet Coventry at Dudley Wood on Bank Holiday Monday morning, which meant that Gundersen, King, Ole Olsen, along with a number of other riders, would have to return from a meeting in Germany in a small aircraft. When they were over the Channel, the plane developed a fault, and at one stage, their lives appeared to be in danger, but fortunately a disaster was avoided, and they made a safe emergency landing. Gundersen was understandably shaken and it was reflected in the match as he scored only 7 points, but Olsen, who had kept everyone calm during the crisis, scored a vintage paid maximum, and led the Bees to an 8-point win.

After beating Leicester at Dudley Wood, the return at Blackbird Road proved to be a controversial affair. Lions manager Martin Rogers had agreed with Peter Adams that, as he had not got Phil Herne and Cradley had not got Collins, then the two cancelled one another out, and no replacements should be brought in. Before the match began, Adams was disgusted to discover that Rogers had called in Leicester's number eight, Joe Owen, and, after some debate, agreed to ride the fixture, only under protest. The result was a 43-35 win in the Lions favour, with Owen scoring 8 points. Adams immediately lodged an appeal, and resigned from the BL Management Committee.

In the next fixture at Cradley, Wigg, who had top-scored in the last four matches, again led the troops with 12 points. The Heathens beat Halifax 43-35, even though they lost King and Gundersen in a heat 3 pile-up. Lance damaged his foot, and Erik was stretchered from the track unconscious. The Dane suffered concussion and was found to have a chipped bone in his neck. After losing two riders, the referee allowed

Lance King. (Hall)

League and Cup Champions, 1983. From left to right, back row: Phil Collins, Peter Adams (manager), Erik Gundersen, Lance King, Simon Wigg. Front row: Peter Raun, Jan O. Pedersen, Alan Grahame.

Cradley to use their number eight, and young Simon Cross came in to score an incredible 9 points. When the going gets tough, the tough get going, and little Jan Pedersen got going and gave his best display to date, scoring 8 points and helping the Heathens to their 8-point win, despite a 15-point maximum from the Dukes' Kenny Carter.

Meanwhile, Simon Wigg's exploits had not gone unnoticed, and he was selected for the England team to face the Americans in the oncoming Test series. He in fact rode in three Tests, scoring 12, 10 and 9 points respectively, helping the Lions to a 3-2 series win. In a matter of just a few weeks, Wiggy had not only become the Heathens' number two, but had established himself on the international scene as well!

One week after his accident, Erik was still not fit to ride, and at Belle Vue, ironically, it was his great rival, Hans Nielsen, who stood in for him and top-scored with 11 points as the Heathens narrowly lost by 4 points. King had returned and so had Collins, but Phil was not match-fit and could only manage 4 points in his first match of the season for the Heathens.

The next match at Sheffield found Cradley at full strength for the first time in the season – and they lost! Cheshire, on his debut, understandably found the going tough and gleaned only a single point, Gundersen was still in pain and, although he was the Heathens' top scorer, he managed only 8 points. Collins was still unfit and Wigg suffered a mechanical nightmare, as the Heathens were beaten by 8 points.

Cradley's League Cup defence was not going well, and the reason was Alan Grahame. He was the lynchpin of the side, so often the match-winner, ever-trying and ever-present, but 1983 so far had seen him go through a patch of inconsistency that had him scoring about half the points that he usually did in a match.

Revenge is sweet and two nights later, when the Heathens played host to Sheffield, the Tigers were given a right mauling in a match in which Lance King scored his first BL maximum. A draw at Coventry followed, but a 4-point defeat at Halifax meant that Cradley's League Cup aspirations were over. It was only the beginning of May, and already the Heathens had lost two of the trophies that they'd picked up in 1982. In the match at the Shay, Alan Grahame scored 12 points and partner Collins came storming back to form but, on the down side, Cheshire crashed and found himself on the injured list again.

Adams immediately swooped and picked up Peter Ravn from Belle Vue. The 21-year-old Dane had been unhappy with the Aces, and after a couple of unsuccessful seasons in which he had averaged around the 4-point mark, he was given a free transfer. This move completed a trio of Danes at Dudley Wood, and it was to prove so important in Cradley's '83 season.

Ravn made his debut at Dudley Wood 24 hours after Cheshire's crash, Birmingham being the recipients of a good old Cradley thrashing. Collins scored a paid maximum, but the star of the show was none other than Peter Ravn, who gave one of the best performances of his career so far, scoring 9 points. The super-team was now complete.

With the League Cup now out of the way, the Heathens began their quest for the ultimate goal – the British League Championship. They began at Wimbledon on 19 March and won by 8 points, and followed that with a trip to Poole, where they notched up an incredible 51 points.

The first round of the KO Cup found the Heathens at Hackney, and saw them chalk up yet another victory and another maximum for King. A win at Dudley Wood against Reading completed Cradley's fixtures for May.

In the World Championship, Gundersen had finished second to Nielsen in the Danish Final, while Wigg had finished as runner-up to Peter Collins in the British Semi-final at Leicester. Phil Collins also made it through to the next round, but Grahame qualified only as reserve. In the British Final, Wigg was beset by mechanical problems and his two race wins were not enough to see him through to the next round, but Phil Collins was flying and became Cradley's only Englishman to progress. The Scandinavian Final saw Nielsen once again get the better of Gundersen, but Ravn, along with Ole Olsen, had also sneaked into the qualifiers. The quest for the League continued into June, but was interrupted by the re-run League Cup match at Leicester that Adams had successfully appealed for. It was a meaningless affair, but, even without Gundersen and King, the Heathens, led by 11 points from the rapidly improving Pedersen, proved masters on the night to win by 4 points, to prove a point, if nothing else. The only other interruption to the League programme that month was the return leg of the KO Cup match against Hackney at Dudley Wood, which proved to be a mere formality.

The Heathens' three League matches in June were all home fixtures, and out of Coventry, Eastbourne and Halifax, only the Bees managed to stop Cradley scoring 50 points (they scored 49). The maximums were coming thick and fast – Gundersen, Wigg, Grahame and Collins all got in on the act before the month was out. That is not to say that the other three were not pulling their weight; on the contrary, King was riding very well, and Ravn and Pedersen were well established as the best pair of reserves in the British League.

Janno grabbed a bit of the glory, as he and Alan Grahame won the Bonanza Pairs meeting at Hackney. Sensing that he was not going to get a ride, Andy Reid returned to Glasgow but Dave Cheshire, on the other hand, was given another outing in June, when Lance King was away in the States, but he failed to score. The Australian youngster had decided to stick it out in the second halves, or perhaps get a place in a National League team, but just as he had made his comeback, the luckless lad was involved in a workshop fire and was very badly burnt. He was rushed to hospital and given skin grafts, keeping him away from the track for many weeks. Rarely had a debut been so ill-fated as Dave Cheshire's had.

Simon Wigg meanwhile filled in the reserve berth for England in the Inter-Continental round of the World Team Cup, and was, along with Grahame and Collins, selected to represent the Lions in the Test series against Denmark. In the three-match series, which England won 2-1, Grahame was the only one of the trio who did himself justice, scoring 13 points in the one and only match that he rode in. The star of the series was Denmark's Erik Gundersen, who scored 39 points in the three matches.

In the first match in July, Halifax, despite a battling 13 points from Carter, were only able to muster 22 points at Dudley Wood, as the rampaging Heathens notched up seven consecutive League wins and moved to the top of the League table. A visit to Sheffield saw them lose only one race to further extend their winning run, and in the second leg of the KO Cup quarter-final at Poole, they overcame stubborn resistance by Michael Lee to win the match and move into the semis.

All of the team from number one to number seven were riding well, and the squad had that Championship look about them. Alan Grahame had recovered his form, Phil Collins was riding better than ever, and King was putting in some very classy performances that showed maturity far beyond his tender years. Gundersen continued to excel, both at home and away, and was well regarded as one of the world's top speedway riders. Some argued that he was merely a gater, who was unable to come from the back, and others countered that it was impossible to say, as he was hardly ever at the back! Indeed he was a lightning starter, but that was only one of his many attributes that he worked tirelessly, week after week, to perfect.

Simon Wigg had proved to be the jewel in the crown. He was probably the most improved speedway rider in the world at that time. Only a matter of months before, he had been riding in the lower division, and in the few short weeks since moving up to the BL, he was collecting the scalps of all the top boys.

Jan O. Pedersen had quickly settled in to look like one of the hottest prospects in the game, although his abysmal gating was making him work hard for his points. Janno wasn't afraid of hard work, however, and his dogged determination to come from behind became his trademark. His fellow reserve Peter Ravn already had a couple of seasons' start on Jan, and his superior gating usually gave him a higher return than his fellow countryman, but both Danes were excellent at the lower end of the team.

Dave Cheshire. (Hall)

But any rider can have an off night, and when King and Wigg both had one, in a classic top-of-the-table tussle at Coventry at the end of July, Cradley lost their first League match of the season by 2 points. Since the demise of Wolverhampton in the BL, Coventry had taken their place as the Heathens' arch-rivals, and the match was run in a cup final atmosphere, with the teams going into the last heat level. Although Grahame managed to split Tommy Knudsen and Gary Guglielmi, Wigg was unable to move up from last place, and a 4-2 to the Bees saw them win the match 40-38 and replace Cradley at the top of the League.

On the individual front in July, there were two big surprise successes for the Heathens. First, Phil Collins defied all odds to become the new Overseas Champion, with Carter and Mitch Shirra joining him on the rostrum. It was Phil's biggest honour to date and the icing was put on the cake when Lance King also qualified from the meeting. It was in fact Lance King who provided the second surprise, being a shock winner of the Golden Hammer, ahead of Gundersen and Dennis Sigalos. Ipswich's Sigalos was lively all night, and in his first outing, he lowered the track record to 62.3 seconds.

There was a break in the fixtures at the middle of July, and Peter Adams and all the boys made the most of it, taking a sponsored holiday together in Italy. Alan Grahame was the only one missing, as he stayed in Birmingham when his wife presented him with their first daughter, Karen.

August saw Hans Nielsen win the Inter-Continental Final from Mike Lee and Gundersen, and with King and Collins scraping through, Cradley could celebrate four riders in the World Final – five really, counting Ravn who had reached the final as reserve. Birmingham's Nielsen had won every round of the competition in '83 and looked favourite to become the new World Champion.

Gundersen had his revenge in early August when he again became Midland Riders Champion at Brandon, followed by Nielsen and Andy Grahame. It was a good performance from the Cradley boys, Ravn finishing fourth, Collins seventh and Pedersen eighth.

Two League matches at Dudley Wood at the beginning of August saw Poole score only 19 points, and then King's Lynn 21 points, when King celebrated his 20th birthday with a maximum. The Stars fared little better on their own track, as the Heathens came away from Saddlebow Road with a 16-point win and 2 more League points, but after a win in his first race, Pedersen fell and broke his wrist.

It was a blow, but Adams was quick to bring in young Simon Cross to fill the gap, Weymouth permitting. He came in at Dudley Wood on 20 August to face Leicester and in his first race he followed Ravn home for a 5-1 heat win in the second race. Although he failed to add to his score, the Heathens came out comfortable winners, 56-22.

In the Blue Riband at Poole, the Heathens again stole the thunder, Gundersen winning the event from Wigg and King, with Grahame finishing in fifth place! Peter Ravn continued to resurrect his career, having a fine World Team Cup final meeting at reserve for winners Denmark in Vojens. Gundersen scored a terrific maximum in front of his home crowd as England finished as runners-up to the Danes.

The confrontations between Cradley and Ipswich over the past couple of years had turned out to be torrid affairs, and a keen rivalry existed between the two teams. When the Heathens visited Foxhall Heath towards the end of August, they had regained their place at the top of the League while the Witches occupied second place. Cradley were pushed all over the track in a ferocious battle that saw Ipswich win the match and take over the top spot in the League. At the end of the meeting, all of the Heathens shook the Witches by the hand, but Adams refused in protest to Ipswich's tactics.

It was to be the last League match that Cradley would lose in 1983, as first Birmingham and then Swindon were crushed at Dudley Wood, before Cradley ended the month scoring almost 50 points at Blunsdon, taking 2 more League points from the Robins.

The World Final on 4 September at Norden, West Germany, was won on a very suspect track by Germany's own Egon Muller, from Billy Sanders and Michael Lee. Erik had just one bad race, in which he came last, but he still managed to finish in joint fourth place with Kenny Carter. King and Collins, who may have been overawed by the occasion, scored only 4 points each, and Ravn failed to get a ride.

In Cradley's next match at Reading the following night, Gundersen, King, Ravn and Adams had not made it back from Germany by the time the match began, and Cradley started with only four riders. By heat 4, the absentees had arrived, and the Heathens stormed to an 8-point win and were reinstated at the top of the League.

Simon Wigg grabbed a piece of glory at the beginning of September by winning the Favre Lubin Memorial

1983 programme.

Shield from Wimbledon's Kelvin Tatum. Tatum was having a season almost as successful as Wiggy's. The 19-year-old wonder boy was enjoying his first ever season in the sport, without serving any sort of apprenticeship in the NL, and he looked to be a sure-fire winner for England in the future. As the month continued, the Heathens scored a tremendous 20-point win at Belle Vue and thrashed Hackney at Dudley Wood, but amidst all the euphoria, a very disillusioned Dave Cheshire returned to Australia.

As the Heathens were preparing to face Reading in the KO Cup semi-final, news filtered through to Dudley Wood that Lance King had once again broken his collarbone racing in America and would be sidelined for most of the rest of the season. However, the momentum was now in full flow and, with Pedersen back in the team, Cradley beat the Racers both home and away to book a place in the final. Cradley were allowed a guest facility for King (as if they needed it) and scored an incredible 56 points at Eastbourne and also at Leicester, before managing only a mere 55 points at Dudley Wood against Belle Vue.

Poor old Swindon could only manage to score 18 points at Cradley against the mighty Heathens in the semi-final of the Midland Cup, and a 2-point win at Blunsdon in the second leg put Cradley into their second cup final. At this time, the media were referring to the Heathens as the best speedway team ever put together!

A sad reminder of the dangers of the sport was thrust home in late September when ex-Heathen Craig Featherby was killed at Peterborough while riding for Milton Keynes.

Ironically, it was a match against Ipswich at Dudley Wood at the beginning of October that saw Cradley clinch the League Championship. This time there were no mistakes as the Witches were subjected to the terrifying power of the Heathens. Only Sigalos resisted as Cradley trampled over Ipswich 49-29 on their way to their second League Championship. Even with the title in the bag, the Heathens were unrelenting and destroyed Hackney at Waterden Road before doing the same to Birmingham in a challenge match – their last match at Perry Barr.

The KO Cup and Midland Cup finals were prospective classic confrontations, as Coventry were Cradley's opponents in both. The KO Cup was the first to be contested and the Heathens did all the work in the first leg by drawing at Brandon. Ole Olsen, who had announced his retirement at the end of the season, battled gamely in both legs, but he was no longer the perpetual scoring machine that he once had been, and the outcome was inevitable. Cradley won the second leg by 16 points, and became the first team to 'do the double' since Ipswich had done so in 1976. The night had its down side, however, as Erik failed to win a race in his challenge for Mike Lee's Golden Helmet, and the King's Lynn star took a 2-0 advantage from the first leg.

The Midland Cup final was a very similar affair, Cradley winning at Brandon by 2 points. With Lance King back in the side, they won by the proverbial mile at Dudley Wood to take their second cup by 36 aggregate points.

The Heathens' last League match at Dudley Wood was against Wimbledon, and the score was 59-19, but the match is worth a mention because it was the Heathens' 93rd successive home League win. They had not lost a League match at home for five seasons!

Gundersen continued his success, winning the Tommy Jansson Memorial Trophy at Wimbledon, and also winning the big one – the British League Riders Championship at

Belle Vue. In the Brandonapolis at Coventry he finished second behind Carter, as third-placed Ole Olsen said goodbye to British speedway after seventeen seasons. It was the end of the Mauger/Olsen era. Both had retired to hand over to younger men such as Nielsen, Carter, Lee and Gundersen.

Cradley finished off the season with a series of challenge matches. They won them all, but the one at Poole was an unhappy night. Gundersen lost the second leg of the Golden Helmet Challenge and Pedersen broke his collarbone.

The Heathens finished 5 points ahead of their nearest rivals Ipswich in the British League, Coventry taking third place. After a shaky start, they had won the KO Cup and the Midland Cup, and had become probably the best club side ever. Even in challenge matches, opponents were shown the same degree of mercy as League rivals – none! They had finished the season with a team average of just below 60 points!

Gundersen topped the averages with nearly 10½ points, finishing third overall in the BL behind Sigalos and Nielsen, Wigg and King followed with over 9 points apiece and Grahame, Collins and Ravn all finished with over 8 points. Pedersen brought up the rear and he averaged well over 7 points a match. Incredibly, Cross in his four outings had averaged 5.39. It was the year in which every single member of the team clicked. Only Alan Grahame failed to better his average of the previous year, and who could complain at his performance?

The new boys had all been a success – a massive success, and now Adams faced the task of destroying the team to get within the dreaded points limit. It was a task that he never undertook, for although the speedway was over at Cradley for 1983, the action wasn't.

Wolverhampton had closed its doors at the end of 1982, but there were rumours that they would re-open in 1984 and rejoin the British League. Peter Adams had seemed unhappy at Dudley Wood during the last few weeks of the season, maybe because Derek Pugh was still the 'main man' and this didn't allow Peter the freedom that he would have liked. In mid-November, Adams dropped his bombshell by announcing that he would be leaving Cradley Heath to resurrect the old enemy Wolverhampton, where he would be in complete control.

His post was advertised, and Pugh set about choosing from some forty applicants the man who was going to have to break up the League Champions. In fact, Derek did more than that, as he made the job a little easier for the new manager by selling Simon Wigg for £25,000 to Oxford who were joining the BL in 1984. Just before Christmas it was announced that Colin Pratt was returning to Dudley Wood as team manager to face the most unenviable task in speedway.

8

BREAKING UP IS HARD TO DO
1984

Colin Pratt returned to Cradley having done it all. He had enjoyed an illustrious career as a rider, winning many honours and representing his country on numerous occasions, and he had ridden in most of the countries of the world that had speedway. He rode for Cradley in 1970, taking over the skipper's role from Roy Trigg, but just as Colin struck his top form, a road accident had finished his speedway career. Since then, he had taken on the role of trainer at Hackney, he had promoted at Rye House and had managed British League King's Lynn in 1983. Pratt had been actively engaged in track preparation and was knowledgeable in all aspects of the sport.

He arrived at Dudley Wood as promoter and team manager and must have realised that the 1983 Heathens were an impossible act to follow. Colin was not one to 'court' the media, as Adams and McCormick had before him, and was just content to go about the business of constructing the squad for the forthcoming season. He was a 'no nonsense' Southerner, who was swift to praise his riders' successes, but was just as quick to criticise their shortcomings if he felt it was warranted.

As Pratt took up the office, director Derek Pugh began to count the cost of the previous year's success. Crowds had indeed been up by 8 per cent but, although Adams had always maintained that his spending had been nominal, the fact of the matter was that the club had overspent, and Pugh reckoned to have lost a considerable amount of money on the season.

So, the new manager took over the helm with the club in debt, having to get rid of riders, having to find replacements and having to try to keep attendances up with an inferior team compared to '83. It was a thankless task, but it was one from which he never flinched. As the weeks flew by, Pratt began to make his moves. He would build the team around Gundersen, King, Grahame and Collins, which meant no room for Ravn or Pedersen.

Ravn was released to Wolverhampton, as was Dave Cheshire, but Colin realised the immense potential of little Pedersen and 'put him on ice' by loaning him to Birmingham. As it happened, the Brummies withdrew from the League at the last minute and Janno finished up at Sheffield, content to bide his time until he could be accommodated at Dudley Wood.

Steve Collins. (Hall)

Pratt's first signing was 23-year-old Mancunian Mike Wilding, who had ridden a few matches for Birmingham the previous year. His next signing was the one that he hoped would 'solidify' the team – 27-year-old Finn Jensen. The enigmatic Dane came to Cradley from Leicester with an average of just 3.8 points. Colin knew, in fact everybody in speedway knew, that on his day Finn could beat anyone in the world. His bikes were super-fast, but motivating the man had always been a problem; however, Colin was willing to persevere.

To complete his squad, Pratt searched in vain for a 3-point rider to use in the team until he could fit in the recalled Simon Cross. Close season interest in young Crossy had been lively, but all offers had been resisted and all prospective buyers were told 'hands off'.

On the eve of the season, Colin found his man – in fact he had been right under his nose all the while in the guise of Phil's younger brother, 17-year-old Steve Collins. Steve was the British Junior Grasstrack Champion and had been part of the Leicester team that won the Central Junior League and, although he had had limited experience, he certainly had the right pedigree, being the youngest member of speedway's most famous family. That was how the Heathens lined up to defend their League title – a little top heavy, but Pratt knew that if he could work Cross in and get the best out of Jensen, he had a good outfit.

The Premiership was, once again, the first fixture for Cradley and it looked as though Colin's hopes were to be fulfilled as the Heathens took a 2-point lead at Belle Vue, led by 10 points from Finn Jensen. He scored 6 points in the return at Dudley Wood, when great performances by Gundersen, Collins and Grahame won the match and put the first piece of silverware back into the boardroom.

The next three matches were all home fixtures in the League Cup, the first one seeing the return of Peter Adams with his new-look Wolves. A maximum from Collins put paid to their hopes and they were sent back to Wolverhampton with their tails between their legs.

When Sheffield were the visitors, they turned up without Alan Mason, so Pratt agreed to loan them Simon Cross for the night. Crossy nearly put the cat amongst the pigeons when he top-scored for the Tigers with 10 points, but Sheffield's other Heathen was not so lucky, Pedersen falling in his first race and retiring from the meeting.

A new rule had come into force that if a rider touched the tapes, he would be excluded. In the past, a certain amount of leniency had been exercised, but in 1984 there was to be none. In the Heathens' third LC match against Newcastle, no fewer than four riders fell foul of this rule and were duly excluded. Even though Cradley provided three of these, they still won the match by 6 points. Gundersen was one of the offenders – the new rule would cost him dearly during the season.

Defeats at the hands of Halifax and Sheffield made the Heathens' challenge look slimmer, but a massive victory over the Dukes at Dudley Wood lifted morale and Gundersen, King, Phil Collins and Grahame were all undefeated by the opposition. The win was made easier, and the match marred, when Kenny Carter fell in the first heat and broke his leg. A 2-point defeat at Coventry was immediately avenged at Cradley, and the Heathens saw out April scoring only 27 points at Belle Vue and failing by 12 points at Newcastle.

Mike Wilding became the first injury victim when he fell and fractured his foot, and Billy Burton was brought in to replace him. Gundersen, King, Grahame and Phil Collins were all riding well and Jensen was doing the job he had been brought in to do, but the reserves were, in the main, disappointing. Steve Collins was on a run of seven meetings without scoring a point, and he had not beaten an opponent since the beginning of the season. Pratt had said that he would not expect anything of the youngster and kept his word, but he was less charitable with Wilding, who was told to 'get his act together' or get out.

In the Gala Night at Poole, King finished second to Simon Wigg and, in a challenge match at Dudley Wood, he scored a brilliant maximum against Wimbledon. Lance also had a couple of good matches for the USA in the Test series against England. The series was a disaster for the Lions, as they won only one of the five Tests, Phil Collins being picked for three and Alan Grahame for two.

Cradley failed by a single point to win their League Cup match at Wolverhampton, despite bringing Simon Cross in. Cross was not in for Steve Collins, as originally planned, but was standing in for Jensen, who had been injured in Denmark.

Mid-May saw the Heathens travel to Wimbledon for their first League match of the season and, with Gundersen scoring only 4 points, they lost 35-43. The League Cup was run slightly differently in 1984, this time having semi-finals and, when Cradley beat Belle Vue at Dudley Wood, they booked their place in one of them. Gundersen was absent, but guest Bobby Schwartz did a good job, scoring 10 points.

Erik still had not returned when Cradley made their home League debut at the start of June. Wilding was back and so was Jensen, but they both failed miserably as the impossible happened and Wimbledon ended the Heathens' unbeaten run of 93 league victories at Dudley Wood when they ran out winners by 6 points. Simon Cross was not in the team that night as he had an engagement in the Junior Championship of Great Britain at Canterbury. It was a fine night for Simon, and he might have pulled it off had he not fallen in the run-off for first place with Marvyn Cox. As Gundersen returned, King went back to ride in the States, missing the first leg of a KO Cup match against Reading, but maximums by Erik, Alan and Phil ensured a comfortable home win.

In an effort to strengthen the bottom end, Pratt secured the services of Kerry Gray, when his National League club, Rye House, would allow it. Kerry made his debut at

Cradley, scoring 6 points as the Heathens beat Eastbourne and, although they failed by 5 points at Reading, Cradley progressed to the next round of the KO Cup on aggregate. A full-strength team that included Wilding and Cross at reserve visited Brandon and the result was a win for Cradley, thanks to maximums by Gundersen and King.

In the World Final hunt, the Heathens were doing well. Gundersen once again had to play second fiddle to Nielsen in the Nordic Final and, on the domestic front, Grahame and Phil Collins both qualified for the British Final. It was to be a British Final packed with controversy, with Kenny Carter right in the middle of it. He had decided to ride despite a broken leg, but on the night, the Brandon track was in a terrible state, due to the rain which was still falling. After the first few races, most of the riders wanted to call it off, but Carter, who had apparently disagreed with all and sundry in the changing rooms, was adamant that the meeting should continue. He argued that if he was prepared to carry on with a broken leg, then why shouldn't the others? The meeting did indeed continue – and Carter, showing immense bravery, became the new British Champion. Alan Grahame qualified from the meeting, but the conditions got the better of Phil Collins and he failed. But with King also qualifying from the American rounds, there were still three Heathens left in the competition.

June also saw the Test matches between England and Denmark, and the Danes, without Tommy Knudsen, lost the series 2½-1½, despite immaculate performances for the Danes from Nielsen and Gundersen. Phil Collins was beaten in England's point-scorers by only Chris Morton and, in the last Test at Halifax, Phil and Alan Grahame were the stars for the Lions.

July began for Cradley with two home matches against Sheffield and Poole. In the Sheffield match, they were without flu victim Gundersen, and for the Poole match, they were without Erik and Phil Collins as they were both representing their countries in a World Team Cup qualifying round. A couple of good guests and fine performances from Simon Cross ensured a Cradley victory in both encounters. The night after the Poole match, the Heathens, still without Phil and Erik, travelled to Eastbourne and lost by 7 points despite a blistering 12 points from Crossy. Jensen and Wilding were point-less, however, and after the match Pratt read them the riot act.

Cross had hit a rich vein of form, and scored 9 points at Dudley Wood as Cradley beat Belle Vue, 13 points as they entertained Wolves, and 10 points as the Heathens came away from Swindon with a win. He continued in the KO Cup quarter-final against Ipswich, top-scoring in both legs with 10 points, but with Jensen and Wilding failing to score at all in the round, Cradley lost on aggregate. Pratt carried out his threat. Mike Wilding was finished at Dudley Wood and was transferred to NL Scunthorpe.

July was a fabulous month for Lance King. He won the Overseas Final at Belle Vue and followed up that success by winning the Golden Hammer from Phil Collins and Billy Sanders at Cradley. In the next round of the World Championship, the Inter-Continental Final in Vojens, Lance once again found himself on the rostrum, this time in third place behind Shawn Moran and Simon Wigg, but Grahame managed to qualify for the World Final only as a reserve. Gundersen and Nielsen both booked their place in the final, but were way down the list of qualifiers; Erik, however, had a 'secret weapon'.

Ole Olsen had offered his services to his young countryman as an adviser in the run-up to the final. Ole had been Erik's hero as a lad and the Heathen jumped at the chance. Olsen took the job to heart, writing a special diet and exercise plan for his protégé and even persuaded him to stop smoking. Under the guidance of his mentor, Gundersen appeared in three open meetings in Sweden and won them all. Besides the prestige, the wins may have given Erik a psychological advantage because the runner-up in each meeting was Hans Nielsen. (Phil Collins was third in all three.)

King began August as he had ended July, when he won the Midland Riders Championship at Coventry after a run-off with the in-form Phil Collins. Gundersen had lost heart in the meeting when he was once again excluded for tape-touching. He was obviously more at home with the FIM ruling, which allowed tape-touching and, in the World Team Cup final in Poland, he led Denmark to another victory with a superb maximum. Phil Collins was rewarded for his current efforts with a place in the England team and scored 7 hard-fought points for the runners-up, while Lance King scored 6 points for third-placed America.

All three of the World Team Cup boys were unbeaten in Cradley's first match of August, as the Heathens pounded Reading in the first leg of the League Cup semi-final at Dudley Wood and, when they visited Newcastle, Collins scored his second successive maximum and Cradley came away with the League points.

Cradley Heath, 1984. From left to right: Derek Pugh (promoter), Alan Grahame, Mike Wilding, Phil Collins, Finn Jensen, Erik Gundersen, Simon Cross, Lance King, Steve Collins, Colin Pratt (manager). (Hall)

Swindon and Exeter proved to be poor opposition at Dudley Wood and were thrashed unmercifully as Cradley moved up to third place in the League table and, although they lost by 6 points at Reading despite a blistering 15-point maximum from Gundersen, the Heathens moved into the final of the League Cup on aggregate. They continued August by winning at Poole and losing at title-chasing Belle Vue, but Steve Collins had still not beaten an opponent since his reinstatement. Four days before the World Final, Wolves were the opponents, both home and away on the same day, and Gundersen completed his impressive run-up with two maximums in 24 hours.

On 1 September 1984 at Gothenburg, Sweden, 24-year-old Erik Gundersen became the second Heathen to take the World Crown. He lost his first race to Mitch Shirra and was taken aside by Olsen who told him that he could win the Championship on 13 points. After three outings, Erik had 8 points to his credit, but arch-rival Nielsen was unbeaten on 9 points and the two were due for a showdown in their next race. Heat 15 was a battle of nerves and it was the ice-cool Nielsen who lost his. As he made the gate, Gundersen swept around him on the outside and Kelly Moran followed through, leaving Hans to finish the race in third place.

Meanwhile, amidst all the excitement, young Lance King had been piling up the points and, after four outings, had scored 11 points, his only problem being that he faced Erik in his last outing. If he won, then he would be the new World Champion but Gundersen, inspired and fired up by his Svengali, fled from the gate and never looked back. Lance had to settle for second place, which put him in a run-off for the silver medal with Nielsen but, once again, the American missed out at the gate and took third place.

Gundersen had always been one of the most emotional riders in the sport and his ecstasy was there for all to see as he crossed the line to take the title and punched the air, clenched his fists and threw himself over his bike. As the television crew followed him into the pits to interview him, he wept openly and publicly thanked Olsen, without whom he reckoned it would never have been possible.

At this point, let us spare a thought for Alan Grahame. As reserve he was

Golden Hammer winner Alan Grahame. (Hall)

called upon twice and won his first outing and came second in his other. One couldn't help but wonder what his return would have been from five rides.

Erik returned to Dudley Wood to a rapturous reception as Cradley slaughtered Newcastle and the only thing that beat him all night was an engine failure. Young Crossy recorded a paid maximum and was again unbeaten in the Heathens' next match when they dispatched Halifax. Simon was riding with tremendous confidence and was beaten only by Mitch Shirra in the Poole Trades Gala, but it was Gundersen who was making all the headlines. He followed his World Championship win by winning the World Longtrack Championship in Germany, bringing his tally to three World Final gold medals in just four weeks.

Erik had been nominated as September's challenger for Hans Nielsen's Golden Helmet and, when Oxford visited Dudley Wood on the 22nd, another classic confrontation took place. In the first race Gundersen got his umpteenth exclusion for touching the tapes, but he made no mistakes in the other two and took the first leg 2-0. He scored a flawless maximum in the match as the Heathens beat the Cheetahs 46-32 and, if Nielsen had appeared to have the edge over Erik in the early part of the season, surely the reverse was true now.

Coventry and King's Lynn were unsuccessful challengers at Cradley and the Black Country boys were pushing hard behind Belle Vue and Ipswich in the League table. In the Coventry match, Gundersen got his by now almost obligatory exclusion at the tapes and Cross was stretchered from the track suffering from concussion and a cut leg, but the tough young Englishman was back against Lynn to score three heat wins. It seemed that the only thing left for Gundersen to do in '84 was to prove his superiority over Nielsen and he travelled to Cowley for the second leg of the Golden Helmet, beat his rival 2-0 and broke the Oxford track record into the bargain – mission accomplished!

The Heathens staged a late run at the beginning of October to try to hold on to the League Championship. They won at King's Lynn and Exeter, but their 6-point win at the Devon track was at the expense of Cross and Paul Fry. Cross crashed in the first race and retired with an injured arm and Fry, who had been brought up from the juniors to replace Steve Collins, fell in heat 11 and sustained collarbone and head injuries. It is worth a mention that the Falcons' part-time skipper, Ivan Mauger, scored his last ever maximum against the Heathens as the living legend completely retired from League racing at the end of the season.

Cradley then faced nine matches in ten days! They struggled without Cross against neighbours Wolverhampton in the first leg of the Midland Cup semi-final, but their home advantage was sufficient to earn them a 2-point lead. Simon's presence was sorely missed at Oxford as well, as the Heathens went down 33-45, but he returned for the next match at Dudley Wood – the first leg of the League Cup final against table-topping Belle Vue. An added spice to the brew was Erik's first defence of the Golden Helmet against October's challenger, Peter Collins. The Dane made no mistakes, taking the leg 2-0. In fact, he made no mistakes in the match either, along with Phil Collins, both scoring maximums as Cradley took a 10-point lead in the leg.

The next night found them in cup action again, this time at Monmore Green in the second leg of the Midland Cup semi-final, taking with them a mere 2-point lead. A solid

83

Finn Jensen. (Hipkiss)

team performance saw them hold the Wolves to a draw and win the semi by the 2-point advantage that had been attained at Cradley Heath.

Fine performances by Gundersen, King and Phil Collins helped flatten Reading at Cradley, but the next night the Heathens visited Foxhall Heath to take on a very strong Ipswich side. After the Witches had started off the match with two 5-1s, the writing was on the wall and they went on to win by 14 points and consolidated their second place in the League. However, Gundersen was unbeaten by an Ipswich rider, but was once more beaten by the tapes in one race. Two nights later Cradley played host to the Witches and, this time, Erik's exclusion at the tapes caused howls of frustration as Ipswich forced a draw in a thrilling match and put paid to Cradley's League title hopes.

He was at it again the next night at Belle Vue in the second leg of the League Cup Final, but still managed to score 11 points, as did Lance King and, although the Heathens lost the match by 6 points, they were League Cup Champions on aggregate. It was a night for celebration in the Cradley camp and Erik put the icing on the cake by defeating Peter Collins by 2-0 in the Golden Helmet, thus ending the season as the Match Race Champion. The following night, Gundersen managed to put four starts together and was beaten only by Mitch Shirra, but the rest of the Heathens lacked fire and were beaten at Reading by 2 points.

A break in the middle of the month allowed King to pop over to Czechoslovakia and finish as runner-up to John Davis in the prestigious Czech Golden Helmet. It was the position he also finished in the Brandonapolis at Coventry, with Tommy Knudsen taking the title and Phil Collins snatching third place.

On 25 October at Swindon, despite engine failures for Gundersen, Cradley still managed to take a 3-point lead in the first leg of the Midland Cup final. A couple of nights later at Dudley Wood, they finished the job and added the Midland Cup to the League Cup and the Premiership. It was the last fixture of the season at Dudley Wood and Cradley finished their programme by beating Sheffield at Owlerton in the last League match of the season, Alan Grahame ending a spell in the doldrums with a full maximum and Gundersen dropping another 3 points to the tapes.

In the British League Riders Championship at Belle Vue, Erik finished on the same points as Chris Morton and Hans Nielsen, thus necessitating a run-off for the

Championship. It proved to be the Dane's most expensive tape exclusion of the season and was reckoned to be his fortieth, leaving Morton to take the title from Nielsen. Apart from Erik's brushes with the starting tapes, it had been a wonderful season for him. He had written himself into the speedway record books and had gone through a purple patch that had seen him win just about everything except the Miss World contest. His average had dropped nearly a point from 1983 and his nine maximums were five short of the previous year, but it had still been the year to end all years for Erik Gundersen.

And how about young Lance King? He certainly had his share of glory in 1984 and had established himself as one of the top stars in the world in only his third season in the BL.

Alan Graham went through a sticky patch toward the end of the season that kept his average down to 7.87, but his counterpart Phil Collins, although having had the odd bad match, had put in some stirring performances, recording ten maximums and upping his match average to 8.4 points. Once again, the two Englishmen proved to be the backbone of the side, seemingly content to let Gundersen and King take the spotlight while they went about their business, forming one of the most respected pairings in British speedway.

Simon Cross had been forced to bide his time at the beginning of the season, but when he was finally unleashed, he justified all the faith that Colin Pratt had placed in him. Crossy proved himself to be one of the most exciting young prospects in the game, finishing with an average of 7.27.

Finn Jensen continued to be an enigma. Pratt had still not worked out how the Dane could beat Peter Collins in one race and then finish behind Steve Collins in his next! He was the recipient of many harsh words from the Cradley manager during the course of the season but, even so, he averaged over 5 points a match, which was considerably better than his previous season with Leicester.

Steve Collins had been thrown in at the deep end. Pratt had expected nothing of him and got exactly that, but it was early days for Steve and he was looked upon as an investment for the future.

The Heathens had lost the League Championship and the KO Cup, but

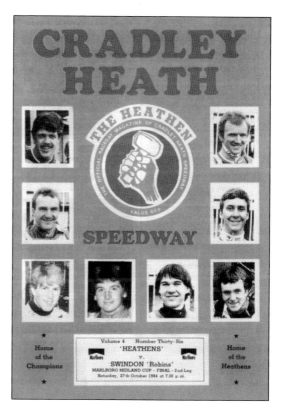

1984 programme.

any team that had retained the Midland Cup, won the League Cup and the Premiership, finished third in the League and boasted the new World Champion could not possibly be deemed unsuccessful. Pratt had been given an impossible act to follow and had done remarkably well in his first season as team manager at Dudley Wood. Even so, co-promoter and director Derek Pugh ended the season on a cautionary note, complaining that riders' wages and a 15 per cent drop in attendances had resulted in a loss of some £20,000 to £30,000 and announced that this would not be tolerated the following season. In trying to negotiate a drop in wages with the World Champion, the Overseas Champion, two England internationals and one of the hottest prospects in speedway, something had to give.

9

ANOTHER DOUBLE WORLD CHAMPION
1985

The 1985 season saw a very depleted British League with the departure of Wimbledon, Eastbourne, Newcastle, Poole and Exeter, who all left for the National League, leaving just eleven teams to contest the world's premier league. It was reckoned to make the remaining teams stronger and therefore more competitive, but even so, the points limit remained the same. The Heathens had finished the 1984 season over the limit and that meant that someone had to go. Remembering Derek Pugh's winter statement concerning the finances of the club, the chances were that it would be one of the big names. For one awful moment in the close season, Gundersen appeared to be favourite. He arrived back in Britain as Denmark's Sportsman of the Year to have talks with Pratt and Pugh, and asked for the same terms as the previous year, which didn't seem unreasonable for the reigning World Champion. Talks broke down and he stormed back home, threatening to quit Britain forever.

Meanwhile, King was approached, but he had acquired a business manager in the winter who was talking Monopoly money and, once again, talks broke down, with club and rider 'miles apart'. Phil Collins gave Pratt a ray of hope, being first to sign, and Alan Grahame quickly followed him. Grahame had not held out until the last minute this year, presumably assuming that if the management were looking to cut costs, then he was one of the costs that they would consider cutting!

One by one, they were all pulled into line. Jensen signed, and so did Simon Cross and Steve Collins, but Gundersen was still in Denmark, and King remained uncompromising with his demands. As the days ticked by, swift action was called for. King was out, and Jan O. Pedersen was recalled from Sheffield as his replacement. This left the door open for Erik, who flew in for last-minute talks, signed his contract and completed the squad for the 1985 season. Poole's Kevin Smith was named as Cradley's number eight.

If the Heathens' lead-up to the new season had been traumatic, then Denmark's had been even more so. A row had broken out between new Danish team manager Ole Olsen and Hans Nielsen, concerning Ole's involvement with Gundersen. Nielsen argued that Ole could not possibly have the team's best interest at heart when he was adviser to primarily one man – Gundersen. Tempers ran high in the winter, and Nielsen vowed never to ride for Denmark again as long as Olsen was team manager.

Cradley Heath, 1985. From left to right: Alan Grahame, Simon Cross, Erik Gundersen, Jan O. Pedersen, Steve Collins. Kneeling: Finn Jensen, Phil Collins.

Every dog has its day. In the mid-to-late 1960s, Sweden, with the likes of Fundin, Knutsson, Nordin, Persson and many more, was the top nation in speedway, and they were followed in the seventies by the English – Peter Collins, Malcolm Simmons, John Lois and the like. The early eighties saw the emergence of America as arguably the best national squad. In Penhall, Sigalos, Schwartz, Autrey and the Moran brothers, they indeed had a team to challenge any nation in the sport. But now the top dogs were the Danes and they were having their day. Ironically as Olsen (the greatest Dane to date) deteriorated, so the younger Danes began to bloom, and now they boasted Gundersen, Nielsen, Tommy Knudsen and Bo Petersen. Add to those four emerging riders such as Pedersen and Peter Ravn, and they looked more than a match for any other national team. But that, of course, was with Nielsen in the side.

The season began promisingly enough for Cradley with a win at Swindon in the League Cup. They followed this by beating Ipswich at Foxhall Heath and at Dudley Wood to take the Premiership. The Heathens then continued their League Cup campaign for the next three months.

They began April by losing at Coventry, despite a brilliant 15-point maximum from skipper Gundersen, but Erik was not so happy the next night at Cradley when machine problems dogged him all night, and he scored only 5 points, although the Heathens beat Wolverhampton by 4 points.

Due to a new ruling, Gundersen had been obliged to defend his Golden Helmet at every match. He had already been successful against Malcolm Simmons, Richard Knight, Billy Sanders and Kelvin Tatum, but at the end of the Wolves match, he trailed in behind new signing Bobby Schwartz in the match race, his bike coughing and spluttering, and the American became the new holder.

Erik did, however, manage to get the better of Hans Nielsen when Cradley visited Oxford, and a good all-round performance by the Heathens earned them a draw and another League Cup point.

Wins at home and away against Halifax and a victory at Dudley Wood over Coventry put Cradley on top of the League Cup table in mid-April, with arch-rivals Wolverhampton breathing down their necks in second place. The Heathens finished the month by losing at Reading and winning at Dudley Wood against Ipswich and King's Lynn. The Ipswich match was marred by the absence of Billy Sanders. A few days earlier, the speedway world was sent into shock when the news broke that Billy had committed suicide by shooting himself. The mighty Australian Ace was top of the British League averages at the time.

Bike problems aside, Gundersen seemed to be riding as well as ever, having already scored four maximums at that early stage of the season. Collins had also scored two maximums and Pedersen one, and with Jensen and Grahame both scoring well, the team seemed to be in fine fettle. In the last match of the month, Cross crashed, sustained concussion and missed the first match in May, but even so, Cradley still managed a 10-point win at Sheffield.

Two nights later, Pedersen was the one in trouble when he was involved in a frightening crash on a rain-soaked Belle Vue track. After a referee's inspection following the incident, the match was called off after only 4 heats with the score at 12-12.

The England *v.* Denmark Test matches featured some fun and games, due to the Olsen/Nielsen feud. Ole had picked Hans for the squad, and Nielsen was ordered by the Danish Motor Union to be present at the matches. Hans was then told by Olsen that he would not be given a ride and would have to sit in the pits, thus preventing him from earning money from other meetings that he may have been able to ride in.

All this goes to show that, although the Danes were the top nation in speedway and their professionalism was to be applauded, they could in fact be just as pig-headed and silly as any other national team. Olsen had often been accused of being ruthless on the track in the past, and it was a trait that he displayed in his management of the Denmark side, although it should be said that perhaps Nielsen had brought it upon himself.

In the first Test at Coventry, Ole carried out his threat and Hans was left in the pits. When skipper Gundersen had an awful night, scoring only 5 points, it should have been all over for the Danes, but remarkably, led by 15 points from Peter Ravn, they raced to a 14-point win. Cross was given an outing at reserve, but failed to score, while Phil Collins scored only 6 points in a disappointing England display.

The next Test was at Nielsen's home track – Oxford, and Olsen found himself in a dilemma. Hans had been doing his 'sitting in the pits thing' up until heat 14. The Danish first reserve Jens Rasmussen was already in the race and his partner, Bo Petersen, got himself excluded. It left no alternative but to bring in Nielsen, but Hans refused to ride unless he was personally asked to by Olsen. Olsen refused, and an angry, heated Danish exchange followed. After much persuasion by the Danish riders and the Oxford promoter, Hans, on a cold engine, was coaxed out on to the track and managed a third place. His late inclusion was not enough to save the Danes, and England won the match, as Collins helped himself to 13 points.

Phil also battled gamely in the final Test at Dudley Wood, scoring 12 points, but the Lions lost by 2 points and the series belonged to Denmark. Gundersen was the top-scoring Dane in the match with 15 points, but he had had a poor series, whereas Phil Collins had topped the English scoring in all three matches.

May continued for the Heathens with wins at Dudley Wood against Belle Vue and Reading, and, in the first match, Gundersen regained the Golden Helmet from Champion Chris Morton and successfully defended it against Reading's Per Jonsson. Erik was given a leave of absence for a week to compete in the World Longtrack Championship rounds, and he was missed at King's Lynn when Cradley lost by 10 points, but Jeremy Doncaster guested admirably as Sheffield were beaten at Dudley Wood.

The skipper returned at the beginning of June to face Oxford at Cradley. A hard-fought match saw Phil Collins become the fastest man ever around Dudley Wood in the first race, when he led Hans Nielsen home. He was the only Heathen to beat Hans in the match, and the Cheetahs came out on top by 2 points, but in the Golden Helmet Match Race, Gundersen got the better of his arch-rival to retain the title.

It was to be Erik's last successful defence, however, for in the next match at Ipswich Jeremy Doncaster became the new holder as Gundersen fell in the Match Race. The Dane had been unbeaten in the match, but subdued displays by Pedersen, Cross and Jensen allowed the Witches a 2-point win.

Erik was off on his travels again and missed the next three matches. A poor guest performance by Simon Wigg did little to help as Cradley lost by 10 points at Wolverhampton, but on the other hand, Neil Collins showed what a difference a good guest could make, as he helped Cradley to victory at Belle Vue.

The Heathens got off to a poor start in their League debut, losing to Sheffield at Dudley Wood. Erik was still away, winning the World Pairs Championship with Tommy Knudsen, but he returned at the end of June to lead Cradley to a win in their last League Cup match against Swindon and to score an untroubled maximum as the Heathens defeated Belle Vue at Dudley Wood.

Meanwhile, in the World Championship rounds, Gundersen was once again runner-up to Nielsen in the Danish Final, but Jensen and Pedersen also qualified for the next round. In the Nordic Final, Erik got the better of Hans, but even so, he had to settle for third place behind Knudsen and Jan Andersson. Jensen was a non-qualifier, but tiny Pedersen moved on to the next round.

On the domestic front, Cradley had Phil Collins, Alan Grahame and Simon Cross through to the British Final. Phil did himself proud, finishing in fourth place, but Crossy only managed the reserves spot for the Overseas Final. A couple of controversial exclusions at the hands of the much-loved referee Frank Ebdon spelt the end of the road for Grahame.

July began with the Midland Riders Championship at Brandon, and it proved to be another battle of the 'Great Danes' as this time Nielsen scuppered Gundersen for the title. Hans was at the top of the British League Riders averages and was showing an incredible consistency that was netting him maximum upon maximum. He rarely missed the gate, and he was looking an ominous challenger for Erik's World Crown. The Championship would surely be between these two, with British Champion Kenny Carter being a possible spoiler.

The Heathens began the month with KO Cup matches, which they drew at King's Lynn and won by a mile at Cradley, to move into the second round. They unsuccessfully challenged Coventry at Brandon in the League, despite four heat wins from Gundersen, but King's Lynn offered little resistance at Dudley Wood and the Heathens showed them no mercy.

The Golden Hammer turned out to be a benefit to the arch-rivals. Gundersen started off well enough, beating Nielsen and setting a new track record of 61.8 seconds in the first race, but he faded as the meeting progressed. Public enemy number one, Kenny Carter, won the title with a workmanlike performance, signalling to the Danes that they might not have it all their own way in the World Final at Bradford. Nielsen had his revenge over Erik, beating him and Phil Collins in a run-off for second place, and the impressive Jan O. Pedersen finished in fifth position.

Janno was riding with a new-found confidence, due to his successful run in the World Championship rounds, and it was reflected in his scores for Cradley. The fact that his

Phil Collins, Finn Jensen, Jan O. Pedersen. (Hall)

gating was awful made his performances more impressive, but Jan's problem was his stature. He was one of the smallest riders in the League, and was referred to somewhat unkindly by a famous speedway commentator as the 'stick insect'. He was so slight that, as the tapes went up, so did the front wheel of his bike because he did not have sufficient weight in his upper body to hold it down. So the tiny Dane had to 'do it from the back', and it forced him to serve an apprenticeship that was to make him one of the best riders in the world.

The Overseas Final at Bradford saw American Shawn Moran stake his claim as a World Championship contender when he won a run-off for the title with Carter. Lance King, who had been absent from Britain all season, caused a few raised eyebrows when he finished in third place, and Phil Collins' 6 points saw him take the last qualifying place.

The final qualifying round, the Inter-Continental Final, took place at the beginning of August in Vetlanda, Sweden, and incredibly once again Carter was the victim of a broken leg after a crash in his second outing, and England's best world title chance was down the tubes. Gundersen had crashed the week before in West Germany and had suffered spinal and shoulder injuries but, although he was obviously in pain, he was not about to give up his crown without a fight. Even so, he scored only 7 points, but it was enough to book his place in the final. Pedersen was right behind him on 6 points, but it was sufficient, and he would be taking his place alongside Erik at Bradford for the final. Phil Collins was right behind Janno on 5 points, but that was not enough, and Phil

John Bostin. (Hall)

would be in the final only as reserve. Shawn Moran, King and Nielsen took the honours, and all three were now casting a shadow over Erik's title aspirations.

Only three League matches were scheduled for the Heathens in August, but by then Gundersen had recovered and was in majestic form. Although Cradley were swamped at Halifax, no one got near him in five starts. In the return at Dudley Wood, he was again unbeaten and just a few days before the final, he raced to a 15-point maximum at Swindon and took over 1 second off the track record, but once again he failed to save the Heathens.

Just for good measure, as he had the year before, Erik did a short tour of Sweden, accompanied by Ole Olsen, and won the Norrköping Open and the Buster Open in Stockholm, before finishing third behind fellow-countrymen Knudsen and Nielsen in an open meeting in Malmö. He also led Denmark to a famous success in the World Team Cup final in Long Beach, California, to complete his best month of the season so far.

The 1985 World Championship final took place at Bradford Stadium on 31 August and was expected to be decided in heat 4, when Gundersen and Nielsen clashed. The inside gate had been the home of the first three race-winners and seemed to be a distinct advantage – and Nielsen had it in heat 4. He made the most of his good fortune and streaked from the tapes like a bat out of hell. Not only was Erik not able to catch him, but he was kept in third place by World Final debutant American Sam Ermolenko. One race – 1 point.

As the meeting progressed and the track dried out, overtaking became possible, and Gundersen made no mistakes. He won his next two races and finished the first half of the meeting with 7 points. His problem was that Nielsen was unbeaten on 9 points, and Ermolenko, who was proving to be the surprise package of the final, was revelling in the conditions and had scored 8 points. A battle of nerves was developing as the second half began; Gundersen set a new track record, winning heat 13, and Ermolenko dropped a point to Kai Niemi in the next race.

Two heats later, Nielsen made his mistake. He attempted a swoop around the other three riders and ended up on his backside. First-bend bunching was the referee's decision and, although Hans had been given another chance, his bike was damaged and he was forced to use another machine. He finished third in the re-run behind John Cook and Tommy Knudsen, putting him on 10 points, along with Gundersen and Ermolenko.

Nielsen and Ermolenko both won their final races, ensuring them of a run-off for the Championship, and if Gundersen was to join them, he had to win a difficult heat 20. His opponents were Shawn Moran and Lance King, who, if they got out of the gate, would surely team-ride to give fellow countryman Ermolenko a better chance. The Americans did indeed fly from the tapes, with Erik sandwiched between them, but as they attempted to pair up, the Dane found a massive surge of power and rounded both of them to book his place in the run-off for the 1985 World Championship.

The run-off was a tense affair, and as the tapes rose, Nielsen made a flyer from gate 2, but Gundersen, off gate 4, hung on around the first bend to come out of it slightly ahead. It was a lead that he gradually increased and, with Ermolenko unable to do anything from the back, that was how they finished, and the World Crown stayed at Dudley Wood.

World Champion Erik Gundersen makes a triumphant return to Dudley Wood. (Hall)

Pedersen, after winning his first race, found that failure to make the gate at this level was severely punished, but even so, he managed to score in all of his subsequent rides, and his 7 points placed him in ninth position overall and established him on the international circuit.

September opened for Cradley with a win against Swindon at Dudley Wood and an encouraging 6-point win at Monmore Green, Gundersen not dropping a point in either match. He was again unbeaten in five outings at Cradley when the Heathens entertained Ipswich in the first leg of the KO Cup semi-final, but the rest of the team were beginning to look jaded, and the Witches went away with a 6-point lead.

Reading were the next visitors to Dudley Wood, and they were subjected to Erik's eighth successive maximum. Although support for him was thin on the ground, the Heathens still managed a 4-point win. Young Andrew Silver, the National League whiz kid stood in for the absent Finn Jensen and provided some fireworks when he head-butted Mitch Shirra after a torrid heat 8.

Alan Grahame had a guest booking to ride for Wolverhampton at Reading a couple of nights later, and it proved to be an expensive outing for Alan as he fell, broke his collarbone and found himself sidelined for almost a month.

Steve Collins had failed to live up to expectations after almost two years at Cradley, and Colin Pratt decided to loan him to NL Birmingham, in the hope that the lesser competition would boost his confidence, and in his place he brought in local junior Nigel Leaver. The 20-year-old Nigel hailed from Walsall and had spent some time as Alan Grahame's mechanic. He was given his chance in the second leg of the KO Cup semi-final at Ipswich, and although he fell in his first outing and came last in his second, he finished in second place behind John Cook in the last heat, beating Richard Knight in the process. Predictably, however, the Heathens lost the tie and made their exit from the competition.

Two nights later, Cradley played host to Oxford in a League match, and Gundersen scored an immaculate maximum, beating Nielsen in his last two outings. The Heathens were forced to use Kevin Smith, but lively performances from him and Leaver helped the Heathens to gain a 41-37 win.

Cradley had managed to qualify for the League Cup semi-finals, but were only able to hold Coventry by 2 points at Dudley Wood in the first leg, and a heavy defeat at Brandon in the return saw them crash out of another cup competition.

September was concluded with defeat at Belle Vue and a win at Cradley against Ipswich, but Gundersen apart, the team were an uninspired bunch. They were not in with a chance of the League Championship and were out of the major cup competitions so, with nothing to go for, inconsistency was running rampant in the side.

Collins and Grahame, before his injury, were the prime sufferers, and Cross didn't look half the rider that he had at the start of the season. Jensen was as enigmatic as ever, and was often the subject of a verbal battering by Pratt, but Pedersen was winning more fans every week with his never-say-die style of riding. Indeed, only he and Gundersen showed any resistance at all when the Heathens were mauled at Oxford at the start of October.

The two Danes were again the only Cradley contestants worthy of any note in their next match, when Coventry won by 10 points at Dudley Wood. Pratt was furious at Kevin Smith, who had been booked to ride and not only failed to turn up, but didn't even telephone the track to say that he would not be appearing, the result being that Cradley were forced to contest three races with only one rider.

Another dire performance followed as the Heathens were beaten by 20 points at Sheffield, despite the return of Alan Grahame. Colin Pratt announced that 'heads would roll' if their present form did not improve, and this inspired an away win at King's Lynn and a win at Cradley against a weak Wolverhampton team. The Heathens even managed to make a fight of it at Ipswich. They lost by just 6 points, before beating Reading on aggregate to book themselves a place in the Midland Cup final against Hans Nielsen and Oxford.

Erik meanwhile picked up the last major trophy of the season by winning the British League Riders Championship at Belle Vue, from 'home boys' Peter Collins and Chris Morton. He was not so lucky in the first leg of the Midland Cup final at Cowley when he fell in heat 8, and was forced to withdraw from the meeting, and Cradley found themselves 12 points adrift by the end of the match.

Jan O. Pedersen. (Hall)

95

1985 programme.

Before the return leg, the Heathens found time to squeeze in the Dudley/Wolves Trophy, and after winning 45-33 at Dudley Wood, they completed a demolition job on their old rivals by winning the Monmore leg by an astounding 30 points.

On the very last day of October, Cradley set about trying to whittle down Oxford's 12-point advantage in the second leg of the Midland Cup final at Dudley Wood. Not only did they fail to pull back the points, but they were unable to hold the Cheetahs on the night and lost the match by 2 points. It completed a fabulous year for Oxford, in which they won the British League Championship, the KO Cup and now the Midland Cup. But not so for Cradley, who had a quiet season by their own standards. They had begun well enough by winning the Premiership, but were only able to add the Dudley/Wolves Trophy to it and finished in seventh place in a League of eleven teams.

Gundersen was, again, the jewel in the crown. He had a wonderful season, retaining the World Championship, winning the British League Riders Championship, leading Denmark to victory in the World Team Cup, winning the World Pairs Championship and finishing third in the BL averages, behind Nielsen and Shawn Moran, with 10.37 points. Erik was in fact the only Heathen to finish with over an 8-point average. Phil Collins followed him with 7.93 points, a step in the wrong direction for Phil, and he ended the season threatening retirement, unless more dirt was put on British tracks.

Little Jan O. Pedersen finished on the same average as Phil and looked a sound bet for the future. His army of fans was growing every week, and he finished the season second only to Gundersen in the popularity stakes.

Alan Grahame's average had fallen slightly from 1984, and the matches that he missed when he broke his collarbone were the first since 1978. Simon Cross was down on '84 too. Jensen managed to up his average slightly, despite causing Pratt to tear his hair out on many occasions.

Although speedway officially ends on the last day of October, special dispensation was given to Ivan Mauger to hold his farewell meeting at Belle Vue on Sunday 2 November. The highlight of the meeting was to be the appearance of Bruce Penhall; in fact, Mauger had centred his publicity for the event around the American. Hundreds of Cradley fans made the pilgrimage to Manchester to see Bruce ride – maybe for the last time – but they, along with thousands of others were to be disappointed, as he failed to show. Ivan was stunned and explained that Bruce's absence was a complete mystery to him, as Penhall had confirmed the booking only days before. Bruce lost a lot more of his diminishing fan club that day. As usual, it was Gundersen who saved the day, winning the meeting and giving the Cradley fans something to cheer about.

Just before Christmas, Colin Pratt had something to cheer about too. He and Eric Boocock were named as the new joint managers of the England team.

10
A LATE REVIVAL
1986

With the Heathens finishing on a team average of 47.28 points in 1985, Colin Pratt could have been excused for sitting back in the winter, happy in the knowledge that he could have retained his seven riders for the oncoming season, if he so wished. It was not a choice that he was given, however, as the dreaded points limit was dropped to 45 during the winter, and once again he faced the prospect of letting another rider go. There was also a new ruling that stated that every team had to include a rider from their junior ranks, so young Nigel Leaver's place seemed assured. Phil Collins had decided to give it another go and became the first to sign as early as January. Erik Gundersen, newly married to childhood sweetheart Helle, was also expected to be a definite starter, as was Jan Pedersen, so Alan Grahame's future at Dudley Wood was looking uncertain. Finn Jensen was offered terms, refused them, and was promptly transfer-listed, without further ado. Even so, Pratt needed a bit more breathing space points-wise to allow him room to negotiate, so Grahame was put out on loan to Swindon. Alan protested at his treatment after eight seasons with Cradley, but his pleas fell on deaf ears, and he did indeed line up with the Robins for the 1986 season.

Pratt made enquiries for National League hotshot Andrew Silver, but decided that the asking price was beyond Cradley's financial resources, so he plumped for an old Cradley favourite – Stevie Bastable. Steve was set to make his comeback at Dudley Wood at the age of 29, over a decade after his debut for the Heathens. Since his departure, following the ruck with McCormick, he had ridden for Birmingham and Swindon, and had spent the last two years with Coventry, but the ex-British Champion had had a lean time lately, and Pratt was gambling that Steve would be better than his current 5.92 average suggested. Lance King, still under contract to Cradley, had made his intentions clear that he wanted BL racing in 1986, but once again he found that he didn't fit into the Heathens' plans and the new season saw him on loan to Bradford.

Colin Pratt still had to find that elusive number seven rider and had only 3.6 points in which to accommodate him, and after an unsuccessful attempt to loan Jan Steachman from Wolverhampton, with time running out, he took on another Cradley junior – 19-year-old Paul Taylor from Worcester.

Although Pratt and 'trackman' Mick Flanaghan (son of Ted) had worked hard on the track in March, a bad frost had caused the official practice day to be cancelled, but they had at least managed to finish the installation of a new, higher safety fence. The season began with the management announcing that a junior circuit would be built inside the track, and Gundersen himself pledged to help the British youngsters who would train on it, but although the idea was well-received, it never got off the ground.

The first match at Dudley Wood was to have been against Sheffield Tigers, but the Moran brothers had been delayed in America and old rivals Ipswich agreed to step in at the last minute for a challenge match. Led by Gundersen and Pedersen, the Heathens won the match by 2 points, but the star of the night was the young Englishman Jeremy Doncaster, who was unbeaten.

One week later, the Heathens began their League Cup campaign at Cradley with a match against Belle Vue, but the Aces lost Peter Collins after one ride with an ankle injury, and the Black Country outfit came out comfortable winners.

Another victory followed when Ipswich made a quick return to Dudley Wood, before the Heathens made their first away visit of the season. Belle Vue were their hosts, and with only Gundersen performing, the Aces easily won the match 46-32. Erik dropped his only point in five starts to Carl Blackbird, but it was the Dane who had the last laugh as he relieved Carl of his Golden Helmet after the match.

It was to be a short reign as Match Race Champion for Erik, however, for one week later, at Dudley Wood, Kenny Carter deposed him, after the Heathens had gained a 4-point win over Bradford. The evening hit a sour note in the second half when the Gold Sash race was to be contested. This was a new race introduced by the League that featured the top scorers from both teams (although, in reality, it rarely did), and the Dukes' representatives on this particular night were Carter and Dudley-based Neil Evitts. Carter cried off after discovering a crack in his frame, but Evitts, never the most accommodating of riders, flatly refused to take part in the race and it turned into a two-man affair with Cross beating Gundersen.

The first Gundersen/Nielsen clash came at the end of April when Oxford visited Dudley Wood, and Hans proved to be the master, beating Erik in the match and also in the Gold Sash race. No one got near him all night, and with Simon Wigg and Andy Grahame supporting well, the Cheetahs snatched a 2-point win. Once again, the World Championship was reckoned to be between the two flying Danes, and everyone in the sport closely monitored their encounters throughout the season.

Erik shrugged off the temporary setback to record four successive maximums. He scored 15 points at Reading, as Cradley lost by 6 points, and he did the same again at Belle Vue, when they lost again in the first leg of the KO Cup. He was unbeaten in the next two matches at Dudley Wood when the Heathens beat Reading and then Belle Vue on aggregate to progress to the second round of the KO Cup.

The match against the Aces saw Bastable at his best, dropping only 1 point to Chris Morton. Steve had been a disappointment up until then, 5 points being his top score, and on only two occasions at that. Pedersen and Collins, although having some good matches, were inconsistent, as was Cross who either rode like a World Champion or like a reserve. At the bottom end, Leaver and Taylor flourished briefly, but both struggled on the away tracks. Towards the end of May, the Heathens almost had the match in the bag at Ipswich, going into the last heat 2 points up, but when Richard Knight and Phil Crump finished ahead of Pedersen and Collins, the Witches won the match by 2 points. Cradley finished the month by beating Sheffield at Dudley Wood and losing by just 4 points at Swindon, Gundersen notching up another maximum. Alan Grahame was injured and was unable to take his place against his former club, but two weeks earlier he had won the British semi-final at Blunsdon from Phil Collins.

May also saw the staging of the England *v*. Denmark Test series, and Dudley Wood played host to the opening match. It proved to be a thriller, with Denmark winning by 2 points. Olsen had stood down as team manager in the winter, and the Danish spearhead of Gundersen, Nielsen and Pedersen was too powerful for the English. Phil Collins put himself about a bit, but had only 9 points to show for his efforts, and Simon Cross had only one outing and fell. It was a series that the Danes completely dominated, losing only one match out of five, and Gundersen led by example, topping their scoring and averaging an incredible 15 points a match.

While all this was going on, speedway was rocked by some terrible news. Kenny Carter had killed his wife by shooting her and had then turned the gun on himself and committed suicide. Although he was always looked upon as a villain at Dudley Wood, the Cradley fans mourned him as much as anyone.

The beginning of June saw Carter's team-mate Neil Evitts become British Champion. Phil Collins pulled out a vintage performance to take the silver medal, but Simon Cross never got to grips with the Brandon circuit and scored only 2 points. Coventry became a 'bogey' track for Crossy, and it was to be some time before he came to terms with that particular raceway.

June opened at Cradley with a match against arch-rivals Wolverhampton. Wolves were boasting a new number one, the flamboyant American 'Sudden' Sam Ermolenko, and, forever the showman, he was to become just as provocative to the Heathens fans as Warren in the sixties and Olsen in the seventies. Although he beat Gundersen in the last race of the match, which Cradley won 44-34, when it came to defending his Golden Helmet, Sam had to take second place to Cradley's favourite son.

Gundersen and Pedersen were both unbeaten as the Heathens forced a draw at King's Lynn, and Erik successfully defended the Golden Helmet against Steve Regeling, before he nipped off to win the World Pairs final with Nielsen, at Pocking, West Germany.

Even without him, the Heathens were still too good for Swindon at Cradley; 22-year-old Paul Fry battled hard for his 2 points from the number seven spot. Fry had been showing up well in the junior league matches, and Pratt had decided to give him a run in the team at the expense of Paul Taylor.

Erik returned, as only Erik could, with a 15-point maximum at Oxford. Twice in the match he had the better of his great rival Nielsen, and as if to prove a point, he beat him in the Golden Helmet Match Race as well. If Hans appeared to be having things all his own way earlier on in the season, then he had surely been warned that the World Championship would be far from a formality for him. Cross and Bastable mustered only 1 point each at Cowley, and it cost Cradley the match, as they lost by only 3 points.

When lowly King's Lynn visited Dudley Wood, they drew one of the lowest crowds ever, and the people that had stayed away to watch World Cup football on the television had made a wise decision, as the Heathens romped home 57-20. Gundersen, Collins and Pedersen were all unbeaten, and Bastable dropped only 1 point. Such was the

Cradley Heath, 1986. From left to right: Steve Bastable, Phil Collins, Simon Cross, Erik Gundersen, Paul Taylor, Colin Pratt (manager), Jan O. Pedersen, Nigel Leaver. (Hipkiss)

mediocrity of the opposition that it was the Stars' young reserve Ray Morton who unsuccessfully challenged Gundersen for the Golden Helmet. One week later, Gundersen and Pedersen were again unbeaten at Dudley Wood, as Cradley had a convincing win over Ipswich, but the night ended on an unhappy note for Erik, when he surrendered the helmet to Jeremy Doncaster.

The last match in June was a sweet victory at Monmore Green, Gundersen scoring his fifth successive maximum and leading the Heathens to a 10-point win. Janno dropped his only point to Ermolenko in the last race of the night, and the 14lb in weight that he had put on in the winter was beginning to pay dividends. Erik scored another psychological victory over Hans Nielsen at the end of the month by winning the Oxford Supporters Trophy at Hans' own track, followed by Nielsen himself, with Jan O. Pedersen taking third place.

The three Danes went into battle once again at the beginning of July in the Nordic Final at Kumla, Sweden. This time it was Nielsen who took the honours from Swede Jimmy Nilsen, Pedersen and, in fourth place, Gundersen.

The Heathens began their League campaign at the start of the month at Dudley Wood against title favourites Oxford, and they failed miserably. Gundersen won two races, came second behind Nielsen, and suffered an engine failure in his last race. Nielsen, on the other hand, roared to a 15-point maximum and pulled back any of the psychological advantage that Erik may have built up in the previous few weeks. Incredibly, it was a match that the Heathens were winning up until heat 10, but the

Cheetahs sneaked slightly ahead, and then two 5-1s in the last two races saw Cradley plummet to a 33-45 defeat, their biggest home defeat in ten years. Pedersen's and Gundersen's bikes were still in transit from the Nordic Final, and both experienced problems with their second machines and had to finish the meeting on borrowed bikes. Following the match, Cradley's misery was complete as Simon Cross failed to take the Golden Helmet from the new holder, Marvyn Cox. The Heathens had crumbled under pressure from a very determined Oxford team, and Pratt was furious, describing his team's performance as 'pathetic'. They fared little better at Reading, losing 32-46, but back in League Cup action, and led by maximums from Gundersen and Pedersen, the Heathens forced a draw at Bradford.

The Cradley skipper continued his unbeatable form at Dudley Wood back in the League when the Heathens took 2 more points off Sheffield, and he romped home five times as Cradley returned to Bradford and forced another draw. Cradley completed their League Cup qualifying matches towards the end of July by playing host to Coventry, and Tommy Knudsen became the first rider to beat Gundersen in four matches. His efforts, however, were not enough to stop the Heathens recording a 4-point win, but three nights later, it was the turn of the Bees, and they came out 8 points in front at Brandon, despite a 15-point maximum from Erik. Cross once again failed on the Coventry circuit, and his 2 points did little to help Cradley's cause. Despite the result, the Heathens had still qualified for the semi-finals.

The final League Cup match at Sheffield was a formality, but Cradley almost pulled it off, losing by just 2 points. Gundersen had netted yet another 15-point maximum and

Simon Cross leads Andy Smith. (Hall)

headed the League Cup averages with a tremendous 11.29 points, just 0.03 points in front of Nielsen, which was some indication of how much the two Danes were dominating British speedway.

The last match of July saw the Heathens visit Oxford in the League to renew the battle of the Danish titans. They met twice in the match, Erik winning the first and Hans taking the second, but Gundersen also finished behind Simon Wigg in one race, and his 13 points and Janno's 11 were not sufficient to prevent Oxford from winning the match 43-35. Support for the two top Heathens was thin on the ground, with Collins scoring 6, Cross 3, Fry 2, and Bastable and Leaver failing to score. After the match, Marvyn Cox, who had managed to hold on to the Golden Helmet, surprisingly beat off Gundersen's challenge to retain the Match Race Championship.

It had been a wonderful month for Erik, perhaps his best ever, for besides his terrific consistency for Cradley, July saw him become the Inter-Continental Champion, beating Nielsen into second place at Bradford. Pedersen had a quiet meeting, scoring only 7 points, but it was enough and the Heathens had two riders through to the World Final.

Three nights later, Erik won the Golden Hammer at Dudley Wood for the first time ever, finishing in front of Simon Cross, who had put on his best performance of the season so far. Erik continued into August in much the same vein, leading the Danes to victory in the World Team Cup final and top-scoring for them in the process. In the middle of the month, England beat the USA 3-0 in their annual Test series, but the form of Collins and Cross did not warrant either a place in the national squad.

Cradley's first match in August was an away fixture at Belle Vue, a task made all the more difficult by the absence of Pedersen, injured in a clash with Bobby Schwartz in the World Team Cup final. But as the Heathens took a 2-point lead in the opening heat, they never looked back. A great all-round team performance saw them eventually increase their lead and win the match by 8 points, Gundersen and Cross performing heroics on the way.

The next two matches at Dudley Wood saw the Heathens defeat Bradford and then resist a spirited effort by Wolverhampton in the first leg of the Dudley/Wolves Trophy to take a 4-point advantage. The second leg at Monmore was run without Erik Gundersen who was suffering from food poisoning, but guest Jeremy Doncaster was superb, scoring a maximum and leading Cradley to a famous 8-point win to retain the trophy.

The 1986 World Final was a bitter-sweet occasion for Cradley fans. On 30 August at Katowice, Poland, Erik Gundersen was deposed as World Champion. Many thought that heat 2 would decide the destiny of the Championship, for that was when the two 'big guns' Gundersen and Nielsen were due to meet, and with Sam Ermolenko thrown in for good measure, it was surely one of the most important heats in the meeting. As it transpired, Erik led from the tapes and won from Hans and Sam – job done? – not quite.

His next outing was easy by comparison, his opponents being three Englishmen – Kelvin Tatum, Chris Morton and Neil Evitts. Erik missed the gate and failed to make up ground, as his clutch slipped cruelly from start to finish. He won another race before the interval, but Nielsen had made no further mistakes and looked unlikely to. Jan Pedersen had also only dropped 1 point, to Jimmy Nilsen, and Erik knew that even if he won his last two races, a minor rostrum place was the best that he could expect. As it happened, even that was beyond him, as the nightmare continued in his worst ever World Final appearance. He finished third in his next outing and retired in his last, giving him a total of 7 points and tenth place overall.

The sweet side of the final was Pedersen's performance. He clocked up another win after the interval and headed the leader board with Nielsen, whom he had to meet in his last race. Hans found himself behind fellow-countryman Tommy Knudsen in his fourth race and as Tommy moved a little wide on the pits bend, Nielsen barged through and Tommy hit the fence. With the race stopped, the fans, many of whom felt that Nielsen should have been excluded, waited anxiously for the referee's decision. When it came, Knudsen was excluded and Nielsen's luck was in.

Knudsen remonstrated with the referee to no avail, and ended up riding through the tapes, while Nielsen, despite some strong words from Gundersen, regained his composure, comfortably won the re-run and made sure that the very last heat was a showdown between Pedersen and himself for the title.

In heat 20, Hans shot from the tapes in front and stayed there; Janno was unable to make up any ground on him, and that was how it stayed. Nielsen was the new World Champion, Pedersen was second and young Kelvin Tatum was a very creditable third. No handshake for the victor was forthcoming from Gundersen. His bitter disappointment had made him ungracious in defeat, but Erik always wore his heart on his sleeve and in Katowice he was devastated.

It had been a tremendous effort by Pedersen – a totally mature and professional performance that had endeared him to so many of the impartials and increased his popularity even more. As for Hans Nielsen, he hadn't won many fans with his tactics at Katowice, but he had won the title, and that's what mattered to him. Nobody had deserved it more. For a couple of years at least he had been relentlessly consistent – the ultimate team-man who could team-ride a raw reserve to cross the line ahead of top-class opposition. Before Katowice, he was probably the best rider ever not to have won the World Championship.

September began on a sad note for Cradley. Alan Grahame, who had been out of the Swindon side for some time with injury, was diagnosed as having Hodgkin's disease and was ordered by his doctor to stop riding immediately until his condition could be treated, and hopefully improved.

On the home front, Gundersen put his disappointment behind him to top-score for the Heathens, dropping his only point to unbeaten Kelvin Tatum, as Cradley forced a draw at Coventry in the first leg of the League Cup semi-final. Although he beat the Bees' John Jorgensen in the match, Erik failed when he challenged him for the Golden Helmet Match Race.

Back in League action, Cradley drew at Sheffield and won at Dudley Wood against a fighting Wolverhampton, Gundersen dropping a total of only 1 point in both matches. Bastable was showing some better form, which was just as well because since the World Final, Pedersen had slumped to his lowest patch of scoring all season. He continued to struggle as the Heathens beat Coventry by 4 points at Dudley Wood to book a place in

Nigel Leaver. (Hall)

the League Cup final, thanks to Gundersen and Cross.

The middle of the month brought some consolation for Erik as he won the World Longtrack Championship in West Germany, and followed this with a win in the prestigious Golden Helmet in Czechoslovakia. He continued his run of success by relieving Phil Crump of the Golden Helmet at Cradley when the Heathens beat Swindon by 6 points, and successfully defended it against the Australian when Cradley drew at Blunsdon. The Heathens had gone six League matches without defeat and were moving rapidly up the League table.

Their League campaign was inter-rupted by a visit from Reading in the first leg of the KO Cup quarter-final, when the Heathens won by a massive 22 points and Gundersen successfully defended the Golden Helmet against Jan Andersson. The next night found them at Ipswich, taking the points with an impressive all-round performance. Jeremy Doncaster had fought a virtual one-man battle for the Witches, but although he was unable to stop Cradley's 14-point win, he did take the Golden Helmet from Gundersen for the second time that season. Young Paul Fry, who had put in some gritty performances since his arrival, was a victim of the match when he crashed in his first outing and fractured his collarbone, keeping him out of the next three matches.

His replacement in the next fixture was another Cradley junior, Wayne Garratt, a 17-year-old youngster from Halesowen. Even though Wayne debuted with only 1 'gift' point and Pedersen was still in the doldrums, the Heathens proved to be too strong for opponents Belle Vue and won the match convincingly. The win lifted them to second place in the League behind the mighty Oxford, but whereas Cradley had lost four League matches and drawn four, the formidable Cheetahs had yet to be beaten and already looked to have the League Championship in their pockets.

Even though they lost at Reading in the second leg of the KO Cup quarter-final, the Heathens won the round on aggregate and progressed to the semis. Pedersen at last found his form at the end of September, and was unbeaten in the qualifying races for the Coalite Classic at Bradford but, come the final, he was forced into second place by World Champion Nielsen. Janno continued the good work as October began, and top-scored for the Heathens with 11 points, as they narrowly missed out on the League points at Coventry, losing by just 2 points. Three nights later, he scored a brilliant maximum as Cradley exacted their revenge on the Bees at Dudley Wood, taking the match by 43-35.

The Heathens had found themselves with their usual fixture pile-up in October, and the matches were coming thick and fast. The night after the Coventry match, they visited King's Lynn, and the Stars were even poorer on their own track than they had been at Dudley Wood and could only muster 23 points against a rampant Cradley. Gundersen, Pedersen and Collins were all unbeaten, and Cross dropped only 1 point to the opposition. Coventry were a different proposition, however, and when the Bees lost by just 4 points at Dudley Wood in the Midland Cup semi-final, their progress seemed assured.

Another 2 League points were gained at the expense of Reading at Cradley, and when Bradford visited a couple of nights later, in the first leg of the KO Cup semi-final, the 22-point lead that the Heathens established put them in a comfortable position for the return leg. Collins and Cross had hit their best form of the season, and with Gundersen and Pedersen scoring freely, and Bastable scoring steadily, although the League Championship seemed to be out of their grasp, Cradley seemed to have peaked at the

right time to do some damage in the cup competitions. Their first pitfall came, as expected, at Brandon, when the Bees overcame the 4-point deficit and added another 4 points to put the Heathens out of the Midland Cup final.

The second pitfall came swiftly, just two nights later, when Cradley played host to Oxford in the first leg of the League Cup final in front of the biggest crowd of the season. Nielsen began ominously, beating Gundersen in the first heat and lowering the track record to 61.5 seconds. Although Pedersen later claimed his scalp, it was the only point that the World Champion dropped in the match, as he led the Cheetahs to a 2-point win. It was a match, however, that was won on a 'professional foul', for in heat 9, when Pedersen and Cross were in a comfortable 5-1 position over Wigg

Steve Bastable. (Hipkiss)

1986 programme.

and Oxford reserve John Surman, Surman 'slid' into the fence and stayed down, forcing a re-run, which Wigg won from the gate. The Cradley fans were incensed, and many cancelled their coach tickets for the return at Cowley. The return, however, never took place as the cruel weather that speedway experienced in October aborted any attempts to stage the fixture.

Two nights later, Cradley took the League points at Wolverhampton, Cross and Gundersen remaining unbeaten and Collins dropping only 1 point to Ermolenko. Phil was riding well, but seemed to be unsettled. Already the rumours were rife that he would not be returning in '87, and young Crossy had indicated that the shortage of meetings in the British League might mean that grasstrack would be his priority the following year. He wasn't riding as though he'd lost interest, however, and scored a marvellous 15-point maximum as Cradley beat King's Lynn at Dudley Wood in their last League match of the season to confirm their runners-up spot in the League Championship.

There was, of course, the matter of the KO Cup final to be resolved – another titanic battle between Cradley and Oxford. The first leg was to be held at Cowley on 30 October and, like the League Cup final, was rained off, much to the disgust of the travelling Heathens supporters. Thus the Cradley leg held on 1 November became the first leg, with the Cowley leg rearranged for the 3rd.

The first leg was another classic battle, which ended in a 39-39 draw. Oxford had the adrenaline flowing and the Heathens looked jaded by comparison. Nielsen led his team impeccably and was unbeaten by any of the Cradley team in five outings. He paired up with Marvyn Cox in the last heat to score a 5-1 and force the draw. The return leg at Oxford was now decided to be for the KO Cup final and the League Cup final, and after being assured at 4.30 p.m. that the match was still on, hundreds of Cradley supporters set out for Cowley, only to be told on their arrival that the ill-fated fixture had again been thwarted by rain, and the track was unsuitable for racing. Their angry reaction was understandable, but pointless. They had seen their last speedway match of 1986 – there were to be no more and there were to be no cup winners, which was a highly unsatisfactory state of affairs but that is what the weather gods had decreed.

The year 1986 had belonged to Hans Nielsen. Just as Erik had seemed to have the edge on his great rival, Hans had turned the tables on him, relieving him of his world title and beating him into second place in the British League Riders Championship at the end of the season.

Incredibly, Nielsen topped the BL Riders' averages for the third consecutive year with a stunning 11.52 points, but Gundersen was right behind him on 11.09 points, his highest average ever. The season had all been about the two Danes, and their many clashes had produced some thrilling racing – Gundersen, by his own high standards, had enjoyed a fabulous year. He had recorded an amazing 22 maximums in LC and BL matches and had hardly put a foot wrong, apart from Katowice.

Jan O. Pedersen had flourished into a genuine world-class performer, and looked set to scale even greater heights of success, finishing the year on an 8.58 average.

Phil Collins had ended the season on an almost identical average to the previous year, but he had ridden his last match in British speedway. He announced in November that he would be moving to the USA to live and would resume his racing career over there. Ironically, his brother Peter also retired at the end of 1986.

Simon Cross had upped his average by a full point during the season, and had shown flashes of brilliance which indicated that he could be one of the top riders in the sport, but he left the fans on tenterhooks, as he ended the season undecided about his future and set off to winter in Australia.

Steve Bastable had done little better for Cradley than he had for Coventry the year before, averaging 6.08, and although he had often borne the brunt of Colin Pratt's criticism, he had been the match-winner on the odd occasion. Pratt had reason to be pleased with the showing of both Leaver and Fry, both shoved in at the deep end and both averaging well over 3 points a match. They had proved to be a pair of bonny battlers and an undoubted asset to the club.

It had been a strange year for the Heathens as a team. They had started off poorly and looked unlikely to win anything, and had not even been in the Premiership for the first time since its conception. But an impressive burst of form saw them climb the League table and put themselves in with a chance of three cups and an outside chance of the League title, and then – nothing. Oxford never lost a match in the League, making it impossible for the Heathens to overtake them, Coventry knocked Cradley out of the Midland Cup, and the other two cup finals were never completed! True, the good old Dudley/Wolves Trophy was still on the mantelpiece, but it had been there since 1978 and was almost regarded as a piece of the furniture (sorry Wolves).

But Colin Pratt must have been reasonably satisfied. As always, he didn't know what horrors the winter might hold for him, but what he did know was that he already had his first problem – what was he to do about poor old Alan Grahame?

11

BIG AL'S FIGHT FOR SURVIVAL
1987

Colin Pratt had become a master at playing 'the numbers game'. It was a talent that had been born out of necessity, for since he had arrived at Dudley Wood, Colin had been forced to weaken the team every year to get within the assigned points limit, which had remained at 45 for the 1987 season. He decided to persevere with the 'old guard', and tried to persuade Phil Collins to reconsider his plans, but it was to no avail. Before settling in the USA, Phil had embarked on a winter tour of Australia, but crashed in his first meeting and spent the winter in an Australian hospital recovering from a broken leg.

Simon Cross was Colin's next target. Crossy had a super winter in Australia, winning the Western Australian Championship, and returned to England with a much more professional approach to the sport. His enthusiasm for speedway had been rekindled, so Pratt did not have to be as persuasive as he thought he might.

Gundersen and Pedersen had both expressed an early desire to stay at Cradley, but during the winter, the League Council had introduced new pay rates and they impressed neither of the Danes. Pratt, determined that his top three would be Gundersen, Pedersen and Cross, set about finding sponsors to subsidise his riders' earnings. Lance King, still a Cradley asset, engaged in talks with the Cradley management, but once again found himself out in the cold and on his way back to Bradford for a second loan agreement.

Meanwhile, as the weeks ticked by, Pratt engaged in a bit of 'loaning' himself, taking on board David Walsh from Sheffield. The 23-year-old Yorkshireman had found success with National League Ellesmere Port, before trying his luck with the Tigers, and his average of 4.76 points gave Pratt some room to manoeuvre. Steve Bastable seemed to be out of the picture. He returned to Brandon, only to be loaned out to Bradford just before the season began.

Alan Grahame was a problem. After six months of treatment that included taking twenty tablets a day and having two injections a month, he announced himself totally cured of Hodgkin's disease. Pratt must have realised that he was taking a risk with the 33-year-old veteran, but it was Big Al's testimonial year, and maybe taking this into consideration, Grahame was offered terms – and promptly turned them down! Pratt meanwhile had once again shown interest in young Andrew Silver, but his National League club Arena Essex had

Dean Barker. (Hall)

put a £28,000 price tag on his head, answering a lot of critics who wished to know why managers had so many foreign riders in their teams. After Grahame had unsuccessfully approached Swindon, Bradford and Sheffield, he became resigned to the fact that it was Cradley or nothing and signed for a considerable drop in wages.

Nigel Leaver had expressed a desire to ride in the National League to gain experience, and he was allowed to move to Arena Essex, and even though Paul Fry was retained, it still left the number seven spot to fill. Colin's last move, on the eve of the season, could have been an inspired one, had it worked out. He looked to National League Eastbourne to solve his problem and signed 16-year-old Dean Barker on a trial period to make up the team. Part of the deal was that he would also take on one of the hottest prospects in speedway, Martin Dugard, as the Heathens' number eight. Leaver was named as the Cradley number nine.

The season began, as it usually did for the Heathens, with the Premiership. Due to the unfinished business of 1986, Cradley's opponents were Oxford. The Cheetahs were not quite so formidable as the previous year, having fallen foul of the points limit, and when Hackney had decided to move up into the BL, Oxford had loaned them Simon Wigg.

The first leg was Cradley's curtain-raiser on 21 March, and in the very first race of the season, Gundersen beat Nielsen. In fact, Erik beat everyone and recorded a superb 12-point maximum. Simon Cross, riding at number five, had to face the Oxford skipper twice, and twice he had to take second place, but they were the only 2 points that Crossy dropped all night. Pedersen struggled with his bike all through the match and scored only 7 points, and with the other Heathens scoring only 8 points between them, the result was a 4-point win for the Cheetahs, who even without Wigg remained Cradley's bogey team.

One week later at Dudley Wood, the Heathens contested the brand-new British Trophy, and their opponents in the first leg of the competition were Wolverhampton. Pedersen got his bikes sorted out and roared to a 12-point maximum, and with Gundersen dropping just 1 point to Ermolenko and everyone else chipping in, Cradley won the leg by 14 points.

A nice 'bonus' to the evening was a visit by Bruce Penhall, who had flown into the country to take part in a series of match races against Peter Collins in Peter's farewell meeting at Belle Vue the following day. After the Mauger farewell meeting some eighteen months earlier, the fans speculated as to whether or not he would put in an appearance, but here he was, back at Dudley Wood, taking a lap of honour with his great pal, another ex-Heathen, Bobby Schwartz.

Bruce was interviewed and, as usual, said all the right things, and won back an army of fans in the space of just a few hours. He seemed more relaxed and appeared to be philosophical about the fact that he was obviously not destined to be a big Hollywood star. Indeed, he seemed to be resigned to take his place in his family's multi-million dollar demolition business, content to do a little television commentating at American speedway events to keep the wolf from the door of his wife and two children.

Apart from the Belle Vue meeting, Bruce was a man on a mission – a mission to tell British speedway about his new protégé, Greg Hancock. Hancock was hailed by Penhall as a future World Champion, but at just 17 years old, he was still at high school in Costa Mesa. Nevertheless, before Penhall left Dudley Wood that night, Greg was already a part of the Heathens' future plans.

An hour after the match was over, Bruce was still there, signing autographs, talking with the fans, making himself totally approachable and generally putting a shine back on his tarnished image. He did indeed appear at Belle Vue, and amazed everyone present by beating Peter Collins 3-0 and looking almost as classy as ever in the process. He talked on the microphone and publicly apologised for his absence from the Mauger meeting, claiming that filming in Italy had fallen behind schedule, and as the crew were in a remote part of the country, means of communications could not be found in time for him to let Ivan know the situation. It was all good stuff, and the sceptics were won over. It was Penhall at his best, but you just had to admit it – he seemed such a bloody nice bloke. As a public relations exercise it was brilliant, and Bruce left the country with hundreds more fans than when he arrived.

It was Erik Gundersen who top-scored in the farewell meeting, but it was one of those affairs that featured a run-off for the top six scorers, and poor old Erik finished fifth!

April began on a sad note with the news that Johnnie Hoskins, the 'Father of Speedway', had passed away at the grand old age of 95. The Heathens began the month with the return leg of the Premiership, at Oxford, and they lost the trophy. The meeting of the 'Great Danes' never took place, as they were programmed to meet in heat 1 only, and Nielsen was excluded from that. Erik cruised through the match unbeaten, and although Pedersen gave excellent support, scoring 12 points from 5 rides, and Cross did well, scoring 8 points, the other four mustered only 4 points between them and Cradley lost the match 36-41.

A disturbing trend was developing in the Heathens' team. Cross was emerging as a genuine top-class rider and his change in attitude and approach was paying dividends. Along with Gundersen and Pedersen, Cradley could boast, perhaps, the most powerful heat-leader trio in the country, but the rest of the team were not performing at all, and Pratt was swift to pounce. He excluded Dean Barker from his criticism – after all, the lad was only 16, riding in the best speedway league in the world, and he was a long way from home, and besides he was showing up well in the junior league matches. Colin also had a little bit of sympathy for David Walsh, realising that he might need a little time to settle in, but warning that he would be looking for an improvement in the very near future. It was Grahame and Fry who were the Cradley manager's main targets. At Cowley, neither rider scored a point. It was a situation, they were told, that would not be tolerated.

As the Heathens began their League Cup campaign at Dudley Wood on 11 April, Walsh and Grahame responded with 5 points each, and with Gundersen scoring another maximum, and Cross and Pedersen scoring double figures, Sheffield were beaten by 8 points. A few nights later, at King's Lynn, Cradley scored their second LC victory, even though they lost Alan Grahame in his first outing with neck and knee injuries. His place was taken the following night at Dudley Wood by Martin Dugard, and the youngster impressed, scoring 9 points, as the Heathens thrashed Hackney 52-26, Gundersen and Pedersen both scoring maximums.

King's Lynn supplied unusually spirited opposition at Dudley Wood on Easter Monday morning, but the three Cradley heat-leaders were all unbeaten, and Janno relieved Steve Regeling of the Golden Helmet to become the holder for the first time, as the Stars were beaten 44-34. It was to be a short reign for Pedersen, however, for on that very night at Coventry, he looped at the gate in his first outing, injured his back, withdrew from the meeting and lost the Helmet by default. Without him, the Heathens crashed to defeat 26-52, Cross scoring only 5 points on his bogey track.

Janno made his comeback five nights later at Dudley Wood, dropping only 1 point to Lance King, who inspired Bradford to put up a fine show, pushing Cradley all the way and losing by only 8 points. Gundersen scored his third maximum in four matches and Cross scored 10 points, but Exeter's Alan Rivett, who had been signed as Cradley's number ten, scored only 1 point and didn't seem to be the answer to Alan Grahame's absence.

Rivett failed to score at all as the Heathens went down by 4 points at Belle Vue at the beginning of May, despite the top three battling hard. The Aces' Paul Thorp got the biggest cheer of the night, beating both Cross and Gundersen in the same race. Belle Vue had seen fit to pay National League Stoke a staggering £25,000 for Thorpy, and still riding from the reserve berth, he was regularly top-scoring for the Aces and was collecting many big scalps in the British League. However, two nights later, he was mastered at Dudley Wood, as maximums from Cross and Gundersen helped the Heathens to beat the Aces. Alan Grahame had made a premature comeback, and after struggling to score just 2 points, he was ordered by the doctor to take a further week's rest.

Martin Dugard was again brought in to cover for Big Al in the return leg of the British Trophy at Monmore Green, but he found the tricky Wolverhampton circuit not to his liking and scored only 3 points. Only double-figure scores by Gundersen and Pedersen saved the day, as Cradley lost the match by 10 points but moved into the next round of the competition on aggregate.

May also saw the staging of the England *v.* Denmark Test series, the Danes already having won two matches in Denmark. It was again a five-match series in England, and the Danes were at their most powerful, boasting Gundersen, Nielsen, Pedersen and Tommy Knudsen. Even so, they were beaten at King's Lynn, but got their revenge in the next match at Oxford, where they lost the services of Pedersen for the rest of the series after a clash with Cradley team-mate Cross in heat 14. The third Test at Dudley Wood was a classic, but it had a very unsavoury ending. Even without Pedersen, the Danes started off in devastating fashion, and after a few heats seemed to have the match in the bag, but as the second half of the meeting began, England, led by Kelvin Tatum and late substitute Andy Grahame, staged a wonderful revival that included 5-1 wins over Gundersen and Nielsen. Erik displayed the more aggressive side of his nature after finishing last in the first race after the interval. The track had dried out and Colin Pratt had ordered it to be watered in the interval. Upon his return to the pits, the Danish captain was furious and argued angrily with Pratt.

By the last heat, the match had reached boiling point and the atmosphere was electric, as Tatum and Cox for England lined up at the tapes with Knudsen and John Jorgensen, with both sides level on 51 points. The two Englishmen made the gate and seemed to have the match wrapped up, as Knudsen could not make up any ground and Jorgensen was looking unlikely to move out of last place. The stadium was in uproar as Jorgensen, with no one near him at the time, slid into the fence. He was clearly unhurt and the track staff were quickly there to assist rider and machine off the track, but he clung onto his bike and resisted any attempts to help him until the race had been stopped.

His 'professional foul' caused a re-run of the race, which was won from the gate by Knudsen, and the Danes had forced a draw. The patriots came out in force during the lap of honour and the Danes were soundly booed, but the rulebook had tied the referee's hands. Joint England manager Eric Boocock promised to install a bed for Jorgensen in the next Test if he wanted to lie down, and branded the Danes as cheats. The series ended in a draw, 2½-2½, and Simon Cross justified his inclusion in the England side by top-scoring in the final Test at Wolverhampton.

With Pedersen still recovering from his injuries, the Heathens chose to use rider replacement at Bradford and brought in young Wayne Garratt for Grahame. A sizzling 15-point maximum

Goodbye to Phil Collins. (Hall)

from Gundersen and 13 magnificent points from Cross saw Cradley score a famous 4-point victory. Walsh and Fry scored well into the bargain.

Alan Grahame returned in the middle of May, but Pratt elected to use guest riders in place of Janno. At Dudley Wood, Kelly Moran did a fine job, scoring 11 points as Cradley thrashed Ipswich, and Marvyn Cox did almost as well, scoring 9 points as the Heathens lost by just 2 points at Swindon. At Hackney, however, 'fall guy' John Jorgensen scored only 2 points and cost Cradley the match as the Hawks won by 8 points, despite double-figure scores from Cross and Gundersen who broke the track record in the first heat.

Pedersen was prepared to defy doctors' orders to ride in the Danish qualifier of the World Championship but, at the end of the day, the DMU seeded him through, Nielsen winning the meeting from Gundersen. Cross meanwhile qualified for the British Final by finishing fourth in the Swindon semi-final. He finally laid his Coventry bogey to rest on his 22nd birthday by finishing runner-up to Kelvin Tatum in the British Final. It was a measure of how much Simon had improved over the last few months.

Gundersen returned to England to find himself top of the League Cup averages with a fantastic 11.35 points. He had joined the Swedish club Vagarna, but it was a Tuesday night engagement, which he said would not interfere with his Cradley commitments, and in fact, it did not.

Cradley Heath, 1987. From left to right: Dave Walsh, Alan Grahame, Paul Fry, Erik Gundersen, Jan Jakobsen, Colin Pratt (manager), Simon Cross, Jan O. Pedersen. (Hall)

A fine win at Sheffield was followed by a visit to Dudley Wood by high-flying Coventry. The Bees had managed to put together the best outfit in the BL in 1987, and were to become Cradley's main rivals in the forthcoming months. With Pedersen back in the squad, the Heathens were at full strength; however, Coventry, using rider replacement for the injured Rick Miller, led from heat 1 and finished off a thrilling match winning by 2 points.

Pratt had reason to be concerned. The team was unbalanced. Gundersen, Pedersen and Cross were all capable of scoring double figures against any team in the country, and more often than not, they did. That added up to approximately 30 points, and if the other four Heathens could score 10 points between them, that would mean a Cradley victory every time out, but that was not happening.

After a 4-point defeat at Reading, the Heathens entertained local rivals, Wolverhampton, but the match was abandoned after nine heats with the score at 37-17 in Cradley's favour. Pratt was incensed when he was told that the match would have to be re-run because, at the abandoned stage, the Heathens were in an unbeatable position.

It was Erik's turn to win the next round of the World Championship, and in Sweden he became Nordic Champion, for the first time ever, ahead of Jimmy Nilsen and Hans Nielsen, but Pedersen did enough to qualify as well, scoring 11 points.

The League Cup programme continued with a slender defeat at Oxford (Nielsen unbeaten) and a 4-point win at Wolverhampton. Monmore Green was a sorry stage for Alan Grahame when, more out of frustration than anger, the more thoughtless of the Heathens supporters booed him. Alan had been struggling, hardly able to keep his bike up going into the bends. His illness had not been completely cured and he was advised to take an intensive course of radiotherapy. Pratt had no option but to rest him for one month and Alan's career at Cradley seemed to be in jeopardy.

Wayne Garratt was brought in as the Heathens played host to Oxford, and when the Cheetahs won by 4 points and put a severe dent in Cradley's League Cup aspirations, Pratt knew that he had to make a swift move to plug the gap.

He looked toward Denmark once more and came up with an old friend of Pedersen's – 22-year-old Jan Jakobsen, and he made his debut as Cradley beat Reading at Dudley Wood in the last match of the month. Jakobsen scored 3 points before he fell in his last outing. He was not the most graceful of riders, being very tall for a speedway rider, and at times he looked ill at ease on a bike, but he got stuck in and displayed the type of spirit that Pratt had begged Fry and Walsh to display. Gundersen was absent from the match, winning the World Pairs Championship with partner Nielsen.

The Heathens began July by playing host to Swindon, and with Cross having an off night, scoring only 7 points, and Gundersen dropping 3 points when he fell, Cradley found themselves level going into the last race and only a 4-2 heat win saved the day. Gundersen beat Jimmy Nilsen for the bonus point and kept the Heathens' League Cup hopes alive. Jakobsen scored 6 points, and Pratt had reason to be pleased with his new acquisition. Young Dean Barker had scored 4 points and was beginning to look useful, but Walsh was once more at the tail-end of the scorers with just 2 points. He fared little better as the Heathens beat Ipswich in their first British League match at Dudley Wood

Jan Jakobsen. (Hipkiss)

and, menacingly, Pratt was threatening that the axe would fall.

The Heathens completed their League Cup matches with a big win over Wolves in the re-staged match and a super win at Ipswich that clinched them a place in the semi-finals. In the Wolves match, Pedersen was excluded twice and scored only 5 points, and at Foxhall Heath, Cross scored only 7 points, but 'Jakko' had settled down quickly and, along with Barker, who was improving every match, they compensated sufficiently.

In the Overseas Final at Belle Vue, Mitch Shirra became the new Champion, while favourite Kelvin Tatum was a shock non-qualifier, but Cross was comfortably through to the next round, scoring 9 points, and he was rewarded with a place in the English World Team Cup squad.

Lance King showed that he had not forgotten his way around Dudley Wood, as he beat Gundersen and Pedersen when Bradford visited in the League and forced a shock draw, but he was not so lucky four nights later when he returned for the Golden Hammer. Gundersen put on a majestic performance to take the title with 15 points. It was a good night for the Heathens, with Cross taking third place after losing a run-off with Nielsen, and Pedersen finishing fourth. Phil Collins was also in the field, being over in England on holiday, but he looked sadly out of touch and scored only 6 points. It was a poor night for Dave Walsh too; he cracked his collarbone and was out for two weeks.

It gave Alan Grahame an opportunity to make his comeback and he seized the opportunity with both hands. Although he scored only 2 points in his return at Monmore Green, outstanding performances by Gundersen and Pedersen allowed the Heathens to draw with Wolves in the first leg of the Midland Cup. But Big Al had better things in store, and scored 10 marvellous points when the Heathens beat League visitors Sheffield.

Wayne Garratt found himself recalled when Dean Barker dropped his bombshell and returned home. Still too young to drive, Dean had found home visits difficult to make and was feeling homesick, so Pratt had no option but to let the lad go just as he was showing so much promise.

Alan Grahame's testimonial meeting was held on 26 July and took the form of a four-team tournament. Alan was on top form and was unbeaten in the match; in fact, the only race he lost all afternoon was to Tommy Knudsen in the Champion of Champions final race. A lot of big stars were missing because of the Inter-Continental Final, but Crossy put some of his colleagues to shame by paying his own air fare back in order to take part in the meeting. Simon had cause to be generous – he had just qualified for his first World Final with 8 points. Erik Gundersen had become the new Inter-Continental Champion in Vojens with an unbeaten performance, Jimmy Nilsen being runner-up and Hans Nielsen taking third place. Janno's fourth place meant that Cradley would have three representatives in the World Championship Final.

The Heathens made short work of Wolverhampton in the second leg of the Midland Cup, and did the same to Bradford at Cradley in the first round of the KO Cup, but the match belonged to Alan Grahame. From the reserve berth, he recorded his first ever 18-point paid maximum as a Heathen. He had left the team with just over a 3-point average, allowing Pratt to use him at reserve upon his return, and it was a move that was paying huge dividends.

However, as Grahame enjoyed a rich vein of form, Jakobsen lost his, and with Fry struggling and Garratt finding the points hard to come by, the pressure was once again put on the heat-leader trio (and Big Al) to score consistently well. They all did their job at Swindon and came away with the League points, and would have done the same at Hackney but for some awful luck which saw Pedersen have two engine failures, Cross have one and Gundersen get excluded at the tapes.

Cradley's next match at Dudley Wood was a combination of the first leg of the British Trophy final, and the Midland Cup semi-final and their opponents were Oxford. Pedersen nursed a sick motor all night and managed only 5 points, but with Gundersen and Cross trying their hearts out, and some clever tactical use of Grahame from the

reserve berth that netted him 10 points, the Heathens beat the bogey and won the match by 8 points. Cross was the only Heathen to lower Nielsen's colours in a thrilling last race.

Alan Grahame scored only 4 points at Reading, and Cradley lost the match by 2 points, highlighting Pratt's dilemma. His three heat-leaders had all scored double figures, but with Walsh back and scoring only 1 point, and Fry and Jakobsen both doing the same, the lack of back-up cost the Heathens the League points. The 'big three' made no mistakes at Oxford in the second leg of the British Trophy and the Midland Cup

Paul Fry. (Hall)

semi-final, and with Grahame and Jakobsen chipping in, Cradley won by 2 points, took their first trophy of the season and booked a place in the Midland Cup final.

The Heathens stormed through August, thrashing King's Lynn at Saddlebow Road and beating Oxford by 8 points in the League at Dudley Wood. It was the third time that Cradley had beaten the Cheetahs in two weeks, and the Oxford hoodoo was finally laid to rest. The match produced one of the best races of the year, when Pedersen refused to allow Nielsen to shake him off in heat 13 and hung on to overtake the Oxford skipper on the last bend, inflicting upon him his only defeat of the night on the eve of the World Final.

The last day of August saw the Heathens take on Coventry at Dudley Wood on Bank Holiday Monday morning, with the return at Brandon the same evening in the League Cup semi-final. Top-of-the-table Bees were too good in both matches, winning by 6 points at Cradley and 12 points on their own track to deny the Heathens a place in the final.

The 1987 World Final was held at the Olympic Stadium in Holland on 5 and 6 September, the event being run over two days for the first time ever. Over the years, the one-night, twenty-heat final had been a tremendous success, so that left only one thing to do – change it! Heat 1 on the first day saw the favourite Nielsen finish third behind Jimmy Nilsen and Crossy, and Hans went on to record two heat wins. Gundersen meanwhile had clocked up three wins, and was looking the new favourite to finish in front on the first day, but the two Danes were programmed to meet in their next race. A lightning gate by the Cradley skipper and a bad first bend by Nielsen gave

Dave Walsh and Alan Grahame. (Hall)

Erik a good lead, and although Hans stuck to the task, he was beaten by half a wheel. The reigning World Champion won his last race to finish the meeting on 12 points, but Gundersen was subject to some rough treatment in his last outing and was pegged back to third place behind Sam Ermolenko and Per Jonsson. The win gave Sam 13 points, the same as Erik. There was no run-off, and they went into the second day as joint leaders, with Nielsen right up their exhaust pipes waiting for either to make just one mistake. Pedersen was still in the running with 10 points, but Crossy, with only 7 points to his credit, must have known that his chance had gone.

The story of the second day is simple. Erik made mistakes, so did Sam, but Nielsen didn't, and he finished the day with a further 15 points. Gundersen started abysmally with two third places, but then he rallied to finish the day with three wins and 11 points. Ermolenko dropped exactly the same amount and finished on the same total score of 24 points. Nielsen had 27 points and another world title. Erik beat Sam for the runner-up spot, and left all the Cradley fans wishing it had been the old one-night formula. Pedersen had a patchy second day, adding a further 9 points to his score and finishing in seventh place overall. Simon Cross finished in eleventh place overall, but he did have the distinction of being the only rider to have beaten both Nielsen and Gundersen over the two days.

Cradley's World Championship heroes returned to thrash the living daylights out of Swindon at Dudley Wood, and an 8-point win at Bradford saw the Heathens progress to the KO Cup semi-final. David Walsh had moved down into the reserve berth and, perhaps sensing that the axe was about to fall, scored 10 points at Odsal, but as he did, Alan Grahame, who had taken Dave's place in the team proper, found the pace too hot and scored only 1 point!

The very next night at Cradley, the Heathens took on their old rivals Oxford in the first leg of the KO Cup semi-final. The match was ridden under difficult conditions on a very wet track, and when rain began to fall towards the end of the match, there were casualties. Oxford's Nigel De'ath was taken to hospital following a spill in heat 10, and two races later, Cross, who had been determined to get the better of Nielsen, swooped under the World Champion on the bottom bend, picked up some unexpected drive and crashed into the fence. His bike rebounded across the track and hit last man Andy Grahame, and after Andy became the second hospital visitor of the night, it was decided to call a halt to matters, with the score standing at 39-33 in Cradley's favour.

England had beaten the USA 2-1 in the Test series a couple of weeks earlier, and Cross had confirmed his arrival on the international scene by top-scoring for the Lions and finishing the series with a 13.50 point average, the highest of any rider on either side. He also did well in the World Team Cup final, although England had to play second fiddle to the Danes, who, led by Gundersen, won the event for the sixth consecutive year.

Cross continued to show excellent form for the Heathens too, once again scoring double figures as Cradley won by 10 points at Wolverhampton. Pedersen, however, was in a class of his own, scoring an immaculate maximum and enhancing his reputation of being a Monmore specialist. Wolves were without Sam Ermolenko, who had been suspended for the rest of the season for failing to supply a urine sample for a drug test at a previous meeting.

Coventry were red-hot favourites to win the League Championship, and did their cause no harm at all by beating the Heathens by 10 points at Brandon and by 2 points at Cradley. The Bees were a formidable outfit with Tommy Knudsen and Kelvin Tatum forming the warhead, 'fall guy' Jorgensen, Rick Miller and David Bargh all providing solid backing, and Dave Clarke, who was gaining a reputation as one of the best reserves in the League. The Heathens, man for man, were just as good when they were all going well together – which they never did!

Walsh had retained his good form, but Jakobsen and Fry were inconsistent, and Alan Grahame was looking completely out of touch. He had scored only 4 points in the last five matches, and questions were being asked about poor Alan's health. He flourished briefly as the Heathens beat King's Lynn and Belle Vue at Dudley Wood to move up to fourth position in the League table, but he was soon back in the doldrums.

Pedersen made a mockery of his World Final position when he beat Nielsen twice at Oxford, as Cradley held the Cheetahs to a 4-point win in the KO Cup semi-final. It meant that the Heathens were 2-point winners on aggregate, and were in their second successive KO Cup final. Indeed, it seemed as though the tables had turned, and now Cradley was Oxford's bogey team!

Dave Walsh had injured his collarbone at Cowley and was absent as the Heathens began October, and Wayne Garratt was once again recalled to the squad as Cradley lost by 4 points at Sheffield. Pratt was furious as, besides the 'big three', who all scored double figures, Fry scored 1 point, and Jakobsen, Grahame and Garratt all failed to register. Hackney and Wolverhampton were both dispatched by Cradley with relative ease, as Cross coasted to maximums in both matches and moved up to tenth position in the BL Riders averages.

The best that the Heathens could hope for in the League was the runner-up spot, but Pratt knew that they were so finely balanced that a slip-up or an injury to one of his top three would spell disaster, unless he could get the rest of the team to respond. Grahame stood down and Nigel Leaver was brought in as Walsh returned, but at Bradford Gundersen had a bad match, scoring only 5 points, and Pratt's concerns were confirmed as Cradley lost by 6 points.

Once again, storms and heavy rains played havoc with the end-of-season fixtures, so it was decided to treat the KO Cup final and the Midland Cup final as one tournament, as the Heathens' opponents in both were the new runaway League Champions, Coventry. The first leg took place on a foggy night at Brandon on 20 October. Disaster struck the Bees as early as heat 4, when Kelvin Tatum picked up some unexpected drive, lost control and ploughed into the fence, taking Pedersen with him. It looked to be a heavy fall for both riders, but Janno got up and Kelvin didn't. Tatum was not only excluded from the re-run, but was forced to retire from the meeting injured, thus robbing the Bees of one of their top riders.

Cradley immediately seized the initiative, scoring a 5-1 in the re-run when Walsh followed Pedersen home to put the Heathens into a 2-point lead. Coventry rallied briefly, but Cradley would not be denied and forced a draw, despite a brilliant performance from Bees' captain Tommy Knudsen. Cradley's unlikely star of the night was Dave Walsh. He gave the best performance of his career so far, scoring paid 15

Erik Gundersen leads Hans Nielsen and Andy Grahame. (Hall)

points from six outings to put the Heathens in with a great chance in the second leg at Dudley Wood the following evening.

Tatum was still unfit for the return and Coventry drafted in Kelly Moran, but he scored only 7 points as Knudsen fought a virtual one-man battle against Cradley. Cross, Gundersen and Pedersen all scored well in the match, but the star of the night was once again Walsh, who topped the Heathens' scorechart with paid 12 points. As they won the leg by 8 points, Cradley became KO Cup Champions and Midland Cup Champions in one fell swoop. Pratt had constantly criticised Dave all through the season, and with good reason, but he had been a revelation in both Cup matches from reserve.

Leaver had failed to add any input, so a couple of nights later, Grahame was reinstated at Oxford for Cradley's next League match, in which he failed to score. Nielsen was at his majestic best, reeling off his umpteenth maximum of the season, but Erik, Jan, Simon and Dave gave the Cheetahs a fright, as the Heathens failed by only 2 points.

Cradley beat Reading in their last League match at Dudley Wood, and promptly went to Wolverhampton to establish a 12-point lead in the Dudley/Wolves Trophy. They followed this with a win at Belle Vue, which ensured their runners-up position in the League Championship.

The end-of-season matches turned out to be rather painful for the Heathens. Their final home match of the campaign, the return leg of the Dudley/Wolves Trophy, proved

1987 programme.

to be a formality, but Pedersen clashed with Preben Eriksen in his first outing and withdrew from the meeting with bruising and abrasions. Even without him, Cradley thrashed the Wolves to win the trophy by 30 points on aggregate.

Marvyn Cox stood in for Pedersen for the Heathens' last match of the season, a League visit to Ipswich. The Witches won by 4 points, but it was academic as the result would have no bearing on Cradley's League position. However, Gundersen had an unfortunate end to the season when he was stretchered off in his second outing with damaged ligaments and concussion.

The season had been a huge success for the Heathens, winning the KO Cup, the Midland Cup, the British Trophy and, of course, the Dudley/Wolves Trophy, besides finishing second in the British League. On an individual basis, it had once again been Hans Nielsen's year, but Erik had always been right behind him. Nielsen topped the BL averages with a stunning 11.53 points, and Erik was the next rider, over a full point behind him on 10.5 points and 11 maximums, but Hans knew that if he made just one slip, then it was Erik who would replace him as top dog. Gundersen seemed more relaxed in his speedway than at any other time, especially in the World Final when he had shown maturity and dignity of the highest degree.

Little Janno had finished eighth in the BL averages, with 9.6 points, and although he had a disappointing World Final, he did much during the year to confirm that he was indeed one of the best riders in the world and probably the most exciting bar none. Simon Cross had been voted 'Cradley Rider of the Year', and rightly so. His talent and ability had never been in doubt but, coupled with a new approach and attitude, Crossy really did 'arrive' in '87, finishing the season with a 9.33 average.

David Walsh finished with a 5.1 average, and if he had ridden the first part of the season as he had the last few matches, he would have added a fair few points to that. At one stage, his future with the Heathens looked to be in doubt, but Walshy came good when he was needed, and even his severest critic, Colin Pratt, must have been impressed with Dave's cup final performances.

Alan Grahame ended a very traumatic season with an average of under 5 points. He began poorly, but after an enforced rest, he seemed to be completely revived, but it was not to be, and poor Alan finished the season with a question mark over his health. After a promising start, Jan Jakobsen faded badly, and his 3.94 point average was well below what he seemed capable of when he arrived. Dean Barker looked to be a good prospect for the future, and left holding the Cradley junior track record, but his link with the Heathens was a tenuous one and Cradley would surely be only one of many who would seek young Barker's signature in the future.

Points were needed to achieve prizes and prizes (which Cradley had won many of in 1987) in turn, made points – 47 to be exact. The oncoming season looked ominous for Colin Pratt, as further cutbacks would have to be made.

12
WORLD CHAMPION AGAIN
1988

Colin Pratt and the Heathens were given a reprieve in the winter of 1987/88 with the announcement that the points limit was to be raised to 48, and Colin found himself, for the first time, not forced to break up his existing squad. The League Cup competition had been scrapped for more League matches and the thirteen-heat match formula was increased to fifteen heats – an extra reserves race and a nominated riders race. Also, programmed starting positions were introduced, ensuring that the top riders could not start from the inside grids in all of their races, and one relished the prospect of seeing Hans Nielsen starting from the outside grid against the likes of Gundersen who might be starting from the inside grid. The biggest transfer in the close season was the entire Belle Vue team, who were forced out of their Hyde Road Stadium after so many years and set up home in the greyhound stadium just down the road.

Pratt meanwhile set about the task of forming the '88 Heathens squad. The higher points limit meant that he could retain his heat-leader trio of Gundersen, Pedersen and Cross, and indeed he did. Lance King must have given up hope of ever returning to Dudley Wood as he was again put out on loan, this time to King's Lynn. Colin then made tentative inquiries about young Greg Hancock, only to be told that Greg had decided to stay in the States for another twelve months.

Dave Walsh's late burst of form in '87 had persuaded Pratt to take him on board again for the oncoming season, and when Sheffield refused another loan period, Cradley bought him outright. But Pratt didn't have so much faith in Jan Jakobsen, and he was replaced by another Dane, Gert Handberg. The 18-year-old Gert had been recommended by former Heathen Kristian Praestbro, and was way up in the Danish averages after just eighteen months in the Superleague. He had already won the Danish Junior Championship, and upon his arrival at these shores was found to be a shy introvert, who spoke no English at all. It was just as well that Cradley already had two of his countrymen in its camp.

Alan Grahame had once again declared himself fit, and Colin must have done some soul-searching before finally offering Alan another contract. Paul Fry had decided to try his hand in the National League with Stoke, and Wayne Garratt was brought up from the juniors to become a full-time Heathen and fill in the number seven spot.

Bad weather hit the season even before the start, and Cradley were forced to cancel their official practice – twice. There was no respite and their opening challenge match against Sheffield was also cancelled, so the Heathens were obliged to plunge straight into League action without the benefit of a practice. Their opening night at Dudley Wood saw them defeated by Ipswich. Gundersen was brilliant and was unbeaten in five rides, but apart from Pedersen and Cross, he received scant support, and Cradley lost their first match by 6 points.

Erik carried on where he left off at Reading, but his 18-point maximum was not enough to stop Cradley's second defeat, as they lost by just 2 points. Pratt pleaded with the supporters to be patient, but even so, he ordered Grahame and Walsh to a Wednesday night practice session, as the early pattern of the previous season seemed to be repeating itself.

A more determined Heathens side easily beat Bradford at Dudley Wood at the beginning of April. Gundersen enjoyed another 15-point maximum, but no one in the squad could be faulted in an impressive all-round team performance. Young Handberg gave his best showing so far, scoring 7 points.

The Heathens' next visitors were the much-fancied Coventry in the first leg of the Premiership, and the fans were reeling in horror as Cradley found themselves 14 points down after just five heats! An extraordinary match developed as, due to some clever tactical moves, the Heathens clawed back the deficit to go into heat 14 just 2 points in front of the Bees. When Walsh and Garratt failed to make any impression on Coventry's reserves, David Clarke and Andy Hackett, Cradley found themselves 2 points adrift with one race to go. In the last heat, Tommy Knudsen and Kelvin Tatum scored a 4-2 over Gundersen and Pedersen, and the Heathens were left with a 4-point deficit to take to Brandon for the return leg. It was an unfortunate night for Handberg, who blew his fourth motor of the season.

His engine troubles continued at Bradford as Cradley tumbled to another defeat, but at Monmore Green, even though Simon Cross had a quiet meeting, once again the Heathens proved to be masters of the old enemy, thrashing the Wolves at their own den by 12 points. Walsh responded to Pratt's threats of replacement by scoring 8 points, but the assault was led, as ever, by Gundersen and Pedersen.

Cross was having a much slower start to the season than the previous year, and it had reflected in Cradley's success rate. It was the old problem. The bottom four were so unreliable that if any of the heat-leaders failed to score double figures, then the Heathens were in trouble. As Crossy found his form in the middle of April, then so did Cradley, beating Sheffield at Dudley Wood and drawing at Owlerton.

They completed their first double of the season when Wolves were their visitors, but the Heathens finished the month with a completely lacklustre performance at Dudley Wood when they were trounced by Oxford. Nielsen was beaten only by Cross, and equalled the track record in the first heat, but Simon Wigg was the Cheetahs' trump card, celebrating his return to the Cowley outfit with a paid maximum. Pratt had not expected much of young Garratt, and he was sympathetic with Handberg's awful run of machine problems, but he was becoming exasperated by the efforts of Grahame and Walsh, and once again threatened to wield the axe.

May saw the top three Heathens make progress in the World Championship. Hans Nielsen won the Danish qualifier from Pedersen and Gundersen, and Crossy qualified from the British Final behind Wigg, Tatum and Chris Morton. Cradley's first match of

Cradley Heath, 1988. From left to right: Alan Grahame, Simon Cross, Dave Walsh, Derek Pugh (promoter), Erik Gundersen, Jan O. Pedersen, Wayne Garratt, Colin Pratt (manager), Gert Handberg. (Hall)

the month saw them make their first visit to the new home of Belle Vue, and Gundersen immediately showed a liking for the new circuit by equalling the track record in his first race. However, it was an unfortunate debut for unlucky Alan Grahame, who fell in his first outing and broke his collarbone. Even so, the Heathens put up a spirited display, and but for exclusions to Cross and Gundersen, might well have won the match, but at the end of the day, a 5-point win by the Aces gave the home side the League points.

Pratt elected to use a succession of National League guests to replace Grahame over the next few matches, but they were, in the main, ineffectual. However, Handberg and Garratt responded to the crisis as Cradley beat Belle Vue, Reading and King's Lynn at Dudley Wood, and beat Swindon at Blunsdon, before thrashing them at Cradley to notch up their fifth consecutive League win. Wayne Garratt had taken a knock at Swindon, so 17-year-old Justin Walker was called up from the juniors and thrown in at the deep end, where he displayed a lot of guts and determination.

The Heathens ended the month in defeat at Oxford and began June with another defeat at the hands of red-hot Coventry at Dudley Wood, before narrowly defeating visitors Reading. In the World Championship, Nielsen became Nordic Champion, ahead of Gundersen and Pedersen, and Cross moved on by virtue of his fifth place in the Commonwealth Final at King's Lynn.

Mid-June found the Heathens beginning their defence of the KO Cup, and they did so with the return of Garratt and Grahame. It was a successful start with a 12-point win over Sheffield at Dudley Wood but back in League action at King's Lynn it was the same old story with the 'big three' lacking support, as they all scored double figures, but couldn't prevent the Stars from winning by 8 points.

In the second leg of the KO Cup, Handberg joined the top scorers with 9 points, enabling Cradley to win by 4 points and move comfortably into the next round of the competition. Gert continued his good run, as the Heathens finished the month by easily beating visiting King's Lynn.

Erik Gundersen celebrated his testimonial year in 1988 (as did Tommy Knudsen and Reading's Jan Andersson) and Erik's meeting took place on 8 June in front of a healthy crowd. The weather had severely threatened proceedings but the meeting got under way, and the fans were treated to some thrilling racing, as Simon Cross won a brand-new GM bike when he won the six-lap final from Simon Wigg and top-scoring Jan O. Pedersen. Bruce Penhall returned to win a match race from Ole Olsen, Gundersen and one of Cradley's legends, Bernt Persson. Dan McCormick was there, and so was Bruce Cribb, taking a full second off the track record on his ice-bike. Altogether, it was an unforgettable night, and it was no more than Cradley's greatest servant deserved.

The Heathens began July by beating Oxford for the first time that year at Dudley Wood, despite an awesome 18-point maximum from Nielsen. Five nights later at Cowley, they topped that by beating the Cheetahs by 4 points to complete a swift double. Gundersen and Nielsen each had one victory over the other, but more importantly, the two wins moved Cradley to within a point of second-placed Oxford in the League table with one match in hand.

However, League leaders Coventry once again would not be denied when they visited Dudley Wood, and they claimed their fourth win of the season over Cradley. Gundersen, Pedersen and Cross all did their job, but the rest of the team scored only 9 points between them, and the dreaded heat 14 reserves race saw the Bees take another 5-1 heat win. Consequently, Coventry won the match by 6 points and dented the Heathens' League title hopes into the bargain.

On the individual front, Gundersen was a lucky winner of the Jubilee Trophy at Belle Vue, after Pedersen had gone through all the qualifying races unbeaten. In the grand final, it was Erik who crossed the line first to take the trophy. Janno made no mistakes at Oxford, however, when he beat the mighty Nielsen from behind to win the Supporters Club Trophy, and if Gundersen was sounding out warning shots to Nielsen, then surely Pedersen was too.

The three World Final favourites clashed again in the Golden Hammer at Dudley Wood towards the end of July. Cross began the meeting in devastating style when he equalled the track record in the first heat, but a couple of indifferent races saw him finish with only 10 points. When Gundersen won heat 3, with Nielsen trailing in last on a sick bike, it looked as though the World Champion's challenge was over before it had begun. But Hans continued his affair with Lady Luck, and as everyone else dropped further points, he did not, and found himself in a run-off for the Hammer with Pedersen and Chris Morton, which he won, with Gundersen relegated to fourth place overall.

The Heathens staged a revival in the middle of the month, winning at Ipswich and putting the fear of God into Coventry, losing by just 2 points at Brandon. The main reason for their better displays was the return to form of Alan Grahame. Walsh and Garratt were both lacking confidence and so, to a certain extent, was Handberg, but with Big Al supporting the heat-leaders, Cradley were transformed into a winning team.

He scored paid 11 points as Belle Vue were dispatched from Dudley Wood, and followed that with paid 10 points at Bradford as the Heathens won by 4 points. Alan improved even further in the next round of the KO Cup, dropping just 1 point in five outings as Cradley easily beat King's Lynn in the first leg at Dudley Wood. He then scored just as many at Saddlebow Road in the return leg, when Cradley won by 10 points.

Whilst all this was going on, Gundersen and Pedersen were rattling off the maximums, but Crossy had lost a little of his consistency, no doubt due to his shock elimination from the World Championship. Simon had looked as though he would go all the way especially when, in the next round of the competition, he completely buried his 'Brandon bogey' and won the Overseas Final from Tatum and Wigg. But in the last qualifying round, the Inter-Continental Final at Vetlanda, Sweden, he scored only 5 points, which had made him the World Final reserve.

There were no such slip-ups by the 'Great Danes' in the Inter-Continental Final as they indeed filled the first three places; Pedersen rode brilliantly to take the title, breaking the track record three times in the process. Nielsen and Gundersen, along with Sweden's Per Jonsson, were involved in a run-off for second and third places. The meeting finished in bizarre, almost farcical, circumstances and highlighted another unfortunate aspect of the sport that was becoming commonplace. The FIM had

decided to do the draw for the World Final before the Inter-Continental Final had taken place, and in those days of ultra-professionalism, it took the top riders no time at all to work out that third place in Vetlanda would give them the best draw in the World Final. In the run-off, Nielsen led from the tapes, followed by Gundersen, with Jonsson bringing up the rear. As he came out of the final bend, Nielsen slowed up dramatically, and whether his actions forced Gundersen to do the same or whether Erik was playing Hans at his own game is mere speculation, but both merely coasted across the finishing line, with Jonsson too far back to take any advantage. So, Cradley had two riders through to the World Final,

Gert Handberg. (Hall)

Simon Cross. (Hall)

with Cross in with an outside chance if any of the qualifiers were injured beforehand.

Crossy was devastated, brought down to earth with a bang after the heady heights of having recently been crowned Overseas Champion. Simon had also performed brilliantly in the World Pairs final, when he represented England with Kelvin Tatum at Bradford on the last day of July. Tatum had also ridden well, and the English riders finished in the runners-up spot just 4 points adrift of the eventual, almost inevitable, winners Denmark, represented by Nielsen and Gundersen.

Cradley were forced to ride at Reading without Pedersen, who had been detained in the Midlands on unforeseen legal business. As the Heathens were unprepared for this, they tracked only one rider in two races, and the result was an 8-point win for the Racers, who took the bonus point into the bargain. Grahame maintained his impressive form as Wolverhampton and Swindon failed to make any impact at Dudley Wood, and in the last match, Gundersen completed his World Final run-up with a faultless maximum.

The 1988 World Final took place at Vojens, Denmark, on 3 September, the venue being yet another reason to fancy a Danish winner. The last few World Finals were reckoned to have been about Gundersen and Nielsen, but in '88, Pedersen could not have possibly have been discounted. He had become quite simply the most exciting rider of his time. True, he did not have the aggression of Nielsen or the lightning starting of Gundersen – in fact, gating was the worst weapon in his artillery – but what he did have was masses of talent, just as much as the other two and probably more. He had developed a relaxed style of riding that made the job look easy; his balance was superb; and he oozed class – and there was nobody in the world that could overtake like Jan O. Pedersen. The World Final was expected to be, and indeed was, about these three Danes. Gundersen began well, winning his first race, but Pedersen faced Nielsen in his and dropped his first point to the defending champion. It was Hans' turn in his next outing, and he dropped his first point as Gundersen led him home from the gate. Janno came second to Ermolenko in his next race, and it was the last point that the tiny battler dropped in the meeting. Erik stormed through his next two races, as did Nielsen, but Gundersen had to face Pedersen in his last race, and Janno had Ermolenko breathing down his neck for third place on the leader-board. As they met, Gundersen made the gate, but on the back straight, Pedersen shot past him as though his skipper

The late Wayne Garratt. (Hall)

had stood still. Club and country comradeship was swept aside as Janno pulled away, denying Erik the 15-point maximum that would have secured him his third world title. Cradley fans were divided on the issue, but Pedersen knew that a win would pull him 1 point clear of Ermolenko, and assure him of at least third place in the Championship. As Nielsen won his last race, Gundersen knew that a run-off with his great rival was the only way in which he could regain his crown, and he approached it in an uncharacteristically cool manner. He won the toss for gate positions, but elected not to say which one he had chosen and left Nielsen looking perplexed as he rode off to the tapes. In the all-important race, Gundersen gated fractionally ahead of Nielsen, who appeared to lift slightly on the first turn. That was all Erik needed, and he increased his lead to join the immortals of speedway by winning the World Championship for the third time.

He returned to Dudley Wood on 14 September to be met by a marching band and a rapturous reception, and dropped only 1 point to Paul Thorp in an important match that saw the Heathens take an 8-point lead in the first leg of the KO Cup semi-final against Belle Vue. Three nights later he was unbeaten, as Cradley established a 12-point lead over Wolverhampton in their home leg of the Dudley/Wolves Trophy. Pedersen too was going like an express train, and with Handberg and Grahame riding well, a drop in form by Simon Cross was being covered, but it must be said that Simon had taken a few knocks of late and was not fully fit. When he fell in his first outing at Wolverhampton in Cradley's next League match, Simon was eventually forced to retire from the meeting, and only an inspired performance by Grahame kept the Heathens in the hunt, but eventually they conceded the match by 4 points.

Cradley's next match at Ipswich was steeped in controversy, thanks to that 'ever-popular' referee Frank Ebdon. With the score at 43-41 to the Witches after fourteen heats, Jeremy Doncaster and Armando Castagna lined up against Gundersen and Pedersen. Doncaster came to grief on the first bend as he tried an outside swoop. No other rider was involved and Ebdon excluded Pedersen. Even the Ipswich supporters were sympathetic, and Pratt was so furious that he refused to allow Gundersen out for the re-run, leaving the home riders to coast around for a 5-0 heat win. With just one rider in the last race, Cradley could not possibly have won the match anyway, but Ebdon's actions had robbed the fans of one of the best climaxes of the season.

The Witches crumbled under the Heathens' vengeance three nights later at Dudley Wood, as Cradley romped to their biggest win of the season, 57-33. A strange-looking Heathens scorechart read as follows: Handberg 9(3), Walsh 9(3), Grahame 9(2), Cross 8(2), Gundersen 8, Pedersen 7(2), Garratt 7(1). Their next home match saw the Heathens exceed that score, when a pitiful Sheffield side failed to win a single heat, losing the match 62-28. Cradley added insult to injury by tracking both reserves, Walsh and Garratt, in the nominated riders race. Gundersen celebrated his 29th birthday with a maximum.

Erik was called upon by the FIM to be present at a conference in Rio, but asked to be relieved of this duty to enable him to ride in the Belle Vue leg of the KO Cup semi-final. His request was denied and he was told that as World Champion his presence would be required – period. Cradley were at least allowed a guest rider, but Colin Pratt's choice surprised many Heathens fans. He chose Wolves' Sam Ermolenko. There was certainly no arguments about the man's ability, which was proved by his seventh position in the BL Riders averages with just over 9½ points, but some imagined that the American had a genuine dislike for Cradley, and that he would do them no favours at all. One can only assume that Colin took the view that Sam was a professional, who would do his best out of professional pride, if nothing else.

The Heathens booked themselves a place in the KO Cup final, courtesy of Pedersen and Grahame. Pedersen was incredible, scoring a paid 18-point maximum and sweeping inside both Thorp and Morton in the last race to join Grahame at the front, securing a 2-point win on aggregate. Grahame was the hero, scoring 12 points against an Aces team that had just moved into second place in the League table. Sam Ermolenko scored 3 points.

Erik was still absent when the Heathens beat Bradford at Cradley to keep their hopes alive for second place in the League, but upon his return, their hopes took a knock when, despite a spirited performance, they failed by 6 points at Belle Vue. Pedersen and Grahame, in almost a repeat performance of the previous week, were both tremendous, Pedersen dropping only 1 point to the opposition in six rides, and Alan remaining unbeaten by an Ace in five outings.

The next night, Cradley contested the first leg of the KO Cup final, and it was a story that could have been taken from the *Boy's Own* comic. Their opponents were the formidable Coventry, who already had the League Championship sewn up, being an unbelievable 20 points ahead of their nearest rivals, Belle Vue. Only Nielsen headed the Bees' top men, Knudsen and Tatum, in the BL Riders averages. Coventry had strength in depth from number one right through to number seven – no lemons in sight. The Heathens had so far failed to beat the Bees in '88 and, to make matters worse, the first leg was at Brandon. There were also a couple of unanswered questions. Could Grahame maintain his marvellous end-of-season form to join Pedersen and Gundersen as the Cradley warhead, and could Cross shake off his present bout of inconsistency that had seen him point-less in Cradley's last outing?

On 22 October Cradley beat Coventry 50-40 at Brandon, to set them right on course for another KO Cup Championship. The reason (not to take anything away from the rest of the lads) was the performance of a lifetime from Alan Grahame. He rode like a man possessed to score a paid 15-point maximum to lead Cradley to a famous victory against a seemingly invincible Coventry. He defied all the efforts of the Bees' big guns and teamed up with Cross three times and Pedersen once to give Cradley vital 5-1s that eventually broke the Bees' back. Alan was well supported by Pedersen and Cross, and with Gundersen and Walsh scoring well, the Heathens were home and dry in the first leg.

The return leg was the next night at Dudley Wood – Cradley's third match in as many days. Coventry started off as though they meant business and quickly established a 4-point lead, but the Heathens would not be denied and, led once again by the new, improved Alan Grahame and serviced by some late-match heroics by Dave Walsh, Cradley won the match 50-40 to take the KO Cup by 20 points on aggregate. It was ironic that Pratt's 'whipping boys' had come though for him at the very end of the season. Grahame top-scored with paid 12 points from five rides, and again the Heathens' scorechart had a strange look about it: Handberg 9(2), Gundersen 8(1), Cross 8(1), Pedersen 8, Walsh 5(2), Garratt 2.

It was the third successive year that Cradley had won the KO Cup, and thus it became their own property – and they promptly handed it over to Alan Grahame! It was a noble gesture, and a fitting one for a man who in the twilight of his career had fought back from a serious illness and injury to find the best form of his illustrious career.

He was at it again the following night at Monmore Green when he top-scored with paid 13 points, as Cradley won their second trophy in 48 hours in the second leg of the

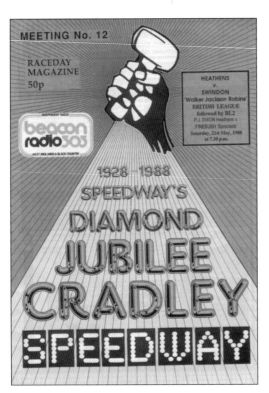

Dudley/Wolves Trophy. Although the Heathens lost the match by 2 points, the 12-point advantage that they held from the first leg was more that enough to see them through and retain the trophy for a decade.

Cradley found themselves with a night off – only one, mind you – before beating King's Lynn at Saddlebow Road, but they failed at Swindon in their last League match and finished in third place in the British League behind Coventry and Belle Vue.

The Heathens' last outing of the season was an entertaining challenge match against the old enemy Wolves, which they won by 6 points. But a nice end to the season was the announcement that they had been awarded the Premiership, as Coventry were unable

1988 programme.

Erik Gundersen's testimonial programme.

Wednesday June 8th 1988
at 7.45 p.m.

THE TOLBA/GM CLASSIC

at Cradley Heath Speedway
Souvenir Brochure £1.20

ERIK GUNDERSEN

10 YEARS IN
BRITISH SPEED-WAY

to stage their leg of the competition. Jan Pedersen had a nice end to the season too – he won the British League Riders Championship at Belle Vue, from Gundersen and Nielsen, emphasi-ing the stranglehold that the three Danes held on the sport.

It had been another successful season at Dudley Wood. The Heathens had won the KO Cup, the Premiership and the Dudley/Wolves Trophy. They boasted the World Champion, the third-placed man, the Overseas Champion, the Inter-Continental Champion and the British League Riders Champion and runner-up.

Erik had once again topped the averages for the Heathens and finished fourth in the BL Riders averages with 9.96 points. Janno was right behind him on 9.88 points, and seemed poised to take over the number one spot at Cradley. Even though he had had a wonderful season, it seemed ironic that Pedersen should have won the Supporters' Rider of the Year award in a season that had seen Gundersen regain the World Championship in his testimonial year at Cradley Heath. Janno had become the darling of the crowd, and even wowed them in Los Angeles when he was unbeaten as Erik led the Danes to victory in the World Team Cup final.

Simon Cross had a strange season, finishing with an 8.22-point average, but he had established himself as a serious contender at the very highest level. But for a slump in form following his World Championship elimination, he would no doubt have improved his final figure. He had become an England regular, and besides representing his country in the World Team Cup final, he also gave a very good account of himself when he was selected for the World Pairs final. Simon finished the season on a high note, however, when although England lost 2-1 to the Danes in the Test series in October, he top-scored for the Lions with 37 points from three matches.

Alan Grahame – well, what can you say? The year saw the best and the worst of Alan Grahame. His career at Cradley seemed to be in jeopardy after the first few weeks of the season and when he broke his collarbone, many thought that it spelt the end of the road for him. But he stunned the sceptics, and the fans that had booed him in the early part of the season were heard chanting his name at the end of it. Although Grahame had always maintained that he was over his illness, only he knew how he felt at the times when he had seemed too tired to carry on. But he was a professional sportsman – no play, no pay – and he stuck it out. There is a lesson for us all in the way that

Grahame's grit and determination took him from the depths to the heights in a fairy-tale year for him.

Gert Handberg had a start to the season that every rider has nightmares about. With only a handful of meetings under his belt, Gert found himself a long way from home and hundreds of pounds in debt, after blowing more motors than the average rider does in a career. His confidence suffered and it was reflected in his scoring, but Pratt was patient with him and persevered, rather than putting the lad under pressure. Colin was rewarded with some very classy performances from young Handberg, whose season average was 5.1 points.

Dave Walsh must have ended the season wondering if his late burst of form would be enough for Pratt to hold on to him. Colin had put a lot of faith in Dave, and when faced with the option of buying the rider or losing him, he elected to buy, but Walshy had let his average drop to 4.5 points.

Wayne Garratt flourished briefly and on occasions looked as though he could make the grade, but in the main, he struggled, as indeed he was expected to at this level. He nevertheless looked a good prospect for the future.

Just before the end of the season, the Cradley supporters were treated to a glimpse of the future. When he was out in Longbeach with the England team, Colin Pratt had spotted a young American rider and invited him, along with Greg Hancock, to come over to England and try out the Dudley Wood circuit. One cold night in October, after the match, Billy Hamill and Greg Hancock were to be seen roaring around the Cradley boards for the first time ever.

13

TRIUMPH OVER TRAGEDY
1989

After one season's grace, it was once again time for Pratt to play the numbers game, as in the winter a new points limit of 44 was announced, forcing the Heathens to shed 4 points. This was later amended to 46 points, but that still meant changes had to be made.

The New Year began on a grim note with the announcement that Sheffield was to close, depleting the British League even further. More bad news followed when Tommy Knudsen crashed in South Australia and broke his back, seemingly ending the career of one of the world's best riders.

Wayne Garratt heard as early as February that he did not feature in the Heathens' 1989 plans, and the shocked youngster looked to the National League to resume his career. Alan Grahame refused the terms that were offered to him, arguing that he had taken a pay-cut three times in the last four years and was not prepared to take another one for the oncoming season. A war of words broke out between Grahame and Pratt; the Cradley manager pointed out that the '89 wage scales were linked to points, so if Alan scored more points, then he would make more money, and anyway, did Cradley's loyalty to Grahame in his 'dark days' count for nothing? He further commented that he didn't want anyone at Cradley who didn't want to be there, and it looked as though Alan was out in the cold. Out in the cold also was Dave Walsh. He had refused the terms offered to him and moved into the National League with Berwick.

So who was left? Gundersen, Pedersen and Cross, of course, and Gert Handberg was returning, in the hope that luck would deal him a better hand than in '88.

Pratt had always made his intentions clear to include Greg Hancock in the team at the earliest opportunity, and saw Grahame's departure as the ideal time to bring in the young American. However, on the eve of the season, his plans were ruined when the Speedway Riders Association put the block on any further foreign riders, and Colin was obliged to telephone Greg and tell him that he was unable to get him into the Heathens squad. Alan Grahame was not yet fixed up, so a quick peace was established and the veteran signed on for another season.

Justin Walker was given his chance at the reserve berth, but with days ticking by, Pratt was still short of a 4.5-point man to complete the team. In desperation, he turned to Wayne Garratt, only to be told: 'Thanks, but no thanks, I'm on my way to Arena Essex.' He was just as unsuccessful in his attempts to woo back Jan Jakobsen, and as practice day came around, the Heathens were only six in number. Just before the opening

Cradley Heath, 1989. From left to right: Simon Cross, Erik Gundersen, John Bostin, Gert Handberg, Alan Grahame. Kneeling: Greg Hancock, Jan O. Pedersen. (Hall)

match, the identity of the mystery man was revealed – 27-year-old John Bostin. John was a former Cradley junior, who had left to try his hand in the National League, but his main interest was grasstrack racing, in which he was very successful. It seemed a strange move to some, but with the first match literally hours away, Pratt's options were limited, to say the least.

Cradley's opener was a Gold Cup match against Bradford and, tracking a fearfully weak tail-end and with Gundersen and Grahame suffering engine failures, the Heathens were relieved to take the match by 2 points. Just 48 hours later, they were in action at Dudley Wood again, this time in the first leg of the Premiership against Coventry on Bank Holiday Monday morning. The Bees were, of course, without Tommy Knudsen, and a rider of his stature is almost always impossible to replace. The result was that Coventry arrived a shadow of their former selves and were beaten 55-34, Cross scoring a five-ride maximum. He was also unbeaten in the return the same evening, as was Pedersen, and the Heathens romped home to a 57-33 victory and claimed their first trophy of the season. Gundersen dropped only 1 point, Grahame rode well, and Bostin rode with grit and determination.

Pratt had made no secret of his determination to win the League Championship. It had been the only title to elude him since his arrival at Dudley Wood, and both he and skipper Gundersen were saying that this year would be the one. However, the Heathens were brought down to earth with a bump at the end of March when they visited Belle Vue and lost a Gold Cup match by 20 points.

They started April a little better by beating local rivals Wolverhampton at Dudley Wood, but their win was limited to 8 points because of engine failures by Cross and Pedersen and the exclusion of Gundersen. Handberg got the biggest cheer of the night when he beat 'Super-wolf' Ermolenko in heat 8.

A lacklustre performance at Bradford cost Cradley another 3 Gold Cup points, but they just managed to contain Belle Vue at Dudley Wood, winning by 4 points, despite further engine failures for Gundersen and Grahame. The match marked the Dudley Wood debut of the most talked-about youngster in British speedway at that time, the Aces' young whiz-kid Joe Screen, who impressed with a paid win and a paid second place.

Pratt always maintained that the Gold Cup competition was of secondary interest to Cradley, and that their main goal was the League Championship, and they began their League campaign four nights later at Oxford, who were boasting on paper perhaps the most powerful side in the League. The Gundersen/Nielsen duels began with one victory each, and it was the only point that either rider dropped in the match, Erik scoring 17 points for the Heathens. Unfortunately, that was to be almost half the Cradley total, as they scored only 38 points at Cowley. Apart from Pedersen, who scored 10 points, and Cross, who scored 6 points, the rest failed miserably. It was hardly the start that Colin had hoped for.

The next night at Dudley Wood proved to be another expensive one for Gert Handberg, who blew an engine in his first heat, but it was his first one of the season and by this time last year he was already on his fifth! To his credit, he picked himself up to have a good match, as did all of the team, and the result was a 53-37 win over Reading.

Cradley's first visit to Monmore Green was for their final Gold Cup qualifying match, and the Heathens needed to win to be in with a chance of reaching the final. The Wolves were leading by 6 points after eight heats, when they were hit by a blitz of Cradley 5-1s – five on the trot, in fact. It was a sweet night for the Heathens fans as their team thrashed the Wolves 51-39 in an incident-packed match that saw Handberg end up under the safety fence after being hit by Graham Jones – after the race! The racing was tremendous, and the Cradley/Wolves clashes were becoming more thrilling than ever.

The Heathens played host to Oxford back in the League at the end of April but, once again, they were unable to get the better of the Cheetahs and were held to a 45-45 draw. Although Nielsen beat Pedersen and Cross in the last heat to save the match for Oxford, he had to take second place to both Gundersen and Pedersen in subsequent races, and in heat 13, Dudley Wood was in uproar as Grahame and Pedersen scored a 5-1 over the former World Champion. It was a dramatic match that Cradley should have won, and probably would have done, but for an engine failure by Erik and a snapped footrest for John Bostin.

Janno saw out April by winning individual meetings in Austria and West Germany, and was becoming just as popular on the Continent as he was in England. The end of April also brought out the green sheets, and Cradley's average had dropped sufficiently to allow Pratt to fit Greg Hancock into the side, which he immediately did. His actions met with a furious response from some of speedway's hierarchy, and Belle Vue manager John Perrin led the assault, accusing Cradley of manipulating the rules. He reckoned that the engine failures and the falls that the Heathens had been experiencing had been a ploy to get the team's average down in order to accommodate the American. Pratt's reply was that if that was the case, then how come Cradley were still in with a chance of reaching the Gold Cup final? Mr Perrin was unconvinced. In fact, he was so unconvinced that he went away and promptly signed American Gary Hicks!

Greg Hancock arrived in England battered and bruised, just in time to take his place in the Cradley team at Dudley Wood for the first match in May against King's Lynn. He had wrenched the ligaments in his shoulder in his last match in the States, and as he trailed in last in his first race, it was obvious to all that he was far from fit. In his next outing, he retired from the race and indeed the rest of the meeting, making it impossible to judge his potential on his debut. The 19-year-old was desperately disappointed with his performance, but he must have been grateful for all the sympathy and encouragement that he received from riders and supporters alike. Cradley had after all won the match by 8 points and could afford to be magnanimous.

Greg was unlike the other Americans. He was quiet, shy, well-mannered and keen to please, and seemed quite introverted compared to the other somewhat brash Yanks. He had been taken in by Lance King, who, ironically, was on the opposing side in Greg's debut match. Hancock had been paired with Gundersen, as were all the new boys – the master and the pupil – and to make room for him, after much deliberation, Pratt moved Justin Walker back down to the juniors.

A wave of concern went through the Cradley camp, as Simon Cross became a shock elimination from the British Semi-final at Wolverhampton, after Alan Grahame had won the meeting. His failure at the final fence in last year's World Championship competition had affected his form badly, and one shuddered to think what would happen to him, having failed to negotiate the first hurdle. He replied by scoring a brilliant maximum, as the Heathens unmercifully pounded the Wolves at Dudley Wood.

Over in Denmark, Gundersen became Danish Champion, with Pedersen right behind him and Brian Karger taking the last rostrum place. Hans Nielsen had to settle for fourth place, but it was enough to see him through to the next round of the World Championship. Before returning to England, Pedersen won the prestigious Gold Bar meeting at Vojens.

Back in Britain, 'born again' Alan Grahame was the third-placed man in the British Final, finishing behind Simon Wigg and Kelvin Tatum and booking himself a place in the Commonwealth Final at Belle Vue.

Hancock had his best match to date, scoring paid 4 points, as Cradley entertained Coventry and easily beat the Bees for the third time in the season. However, he struggled at Smallmead as the Heathens were unable to overhaul Reading and suffered an 8-point defeat in an outstanding match. Greg then had his first look at Brandon and did well, scoring paid 4 points, as Cradley, led by Gundersen and Cross, went on the rampage and beat the Bees 53-37. The previous season, this would have been nothing short of a sensation, but the absence of Knudsen had seen the Coventry team collapse and they were currently at the foot of the League table.

The Heathens' League campaign was going well. After nine matches, they had lost only two and headed the League table, but they were only 1 point ahead of Oxford, who would be pushing them all the way. The Cradley heat-leaders also featured prominently in the BL Riders averages. Nielsen occupied the top spot (it seemed as though he had been there since the outbreak of the Second World War), but Pedersen was well placed in second, Crossy had sneaked into fourth and, with Erik in fifth position, it made the Cradley boys the most successful heat-leader trio in the country. Further good news followed when it was learned that Bradford had beaten Belle Vue in the final Gold Cup match. It gave the Heathens a place in the Gold Cup final against rivals Oxford.

Cradley completed May by entertaining Swindon on Bank Holiday Monday morning and visiting the Robins in the evening. The morning match saw the Heathens completely swamp Swindon – so much so that they entered Hancock and Handberg in the nominated riders race, which Greg won from Jimmy Nilsen and Andrew Silver. Handberg had a fabulous match, scoring paid 13 points, and so did Hancock, scoring paid 9 points. The American was looking better in every match as his injuries slowly improved. His efforts helped Cradley to a 58-32 victory. The Heathens did almost as well at Blunsdon in the evening, shocking the Robins with a tremendous all-round performance to take the match 57-33 and consolidate their position at the top of the League.

The beginning of June meant further World Championship duties, and in the Commonwealth Final, Alan Grahame scored only 7 points, but it was just enough to see him through to the Overseas Final. On the very same day in Finland, Hans Nielsen

Erik Gundersen welcomes Greg Hancock to Cradley. (Hall)

Erik is visited by his Cradley team-mates at Pinderfields. (Mike Patrick)

became Nordic Champion after a run-off with Jan O. Pedersen, and Gundersen took third place to give Cradley at least two riders in the last qualifying round.

Cradley's first match of the month was a tough one – the first leg of the KO Cup quarter-final at Oxford. It began well enough, as Gundersen beat Nielsen in the first heat, and a red-hot match developed with neither side willing to give an inch. Cross beat Nielsen in heat 10, but the Heathens found themselves 2 points down going into the final heat. A thrilling finale saw Pedersen beat Nielsen and Gundersen beat Wigg, to take the heat 4-2 and draw the match.

In the return leg the following evening, the Cheetahs provided stiff opposition, taking an early lead, but the Heathens would not be denied. When they stepped up the pace and scored a 5-1 over Nielsen (courtesy of Pedersen and Grahame), they established a 10-point lead and maintained it to book a place in the semi-finals. There was talk of a Grand Slam – the League Championship, Gold Cup, KO Cup, Ryder Cup, FA Cup, Rugby League Cup, but hold on – let's not get carried away. Pratt, as ever, was cautious. He had been in the game a long time and was well aware of the pitfalls – or so he thought, for even Colin Pratt could have not imagined what cruel cards the hand of fate would deal him over the next eighteen months.

Anyway, let's not get depressed. The Heathens continued their fabulous run, beating King's Lynn at Saddlebow Road and dispatching Bradford and Swindon from Dudley Wood with consummate ease. Their only hiccup came at the beginning of July, when bottom-of-the-table Belle Vue turned the form-book upside down and forced a draw at

Cradley. It was a costly slip-up that allowed Oxford and Wolverhampton to join the Heathens on the same League points.

Pedersen was riding tremendously well, and was looking like his skipper's main challenger for his World Championship. In between matches, Janno had nipped back to Denmark and won the Danish Longtrack Championship, and June had also seen him win the Olympique at Monmore Green.

Alan Grahame was in the news too. He had finished fifth in the Overseas Final at Coventry, and had assured himself of a place in the Inter-Continental Final, alongside Erik and Jan. His current form had earned him a place back in the England team too. In the first Test match against the USA at Dudley Wood, he scored paid 12 points, as the Lions roared to a 20-point win. England won the series 2-1 against a depleted American team, so depleted in fact that they were obliged to use Greg Hancock, after just a handful of meetings in this country. Although Greg failed to make any impact in the series, he was settling in very well at Cradley, and his amiable disposition was winning him an ever-increasing army of fans.

Pedersen continued his threat to the World Championship by winning the Golden Hammer, in which the Danes reigned supreme, Gundersen beating Nielsen in a run-off for second place. Handberg gave his best performance in England to date when he scored 10 points to finish sixth in a world-class field.

The 1989 World Championship had reverted to a one-day event and was to be held at Munich, and a 'dress rehearsal' was arranged in July to allow the riders to try out the brand-new track. Nielsen won the meeting from Gundersen and Simon Wigg, but Pedersen crashed, cracked his shoulder blade and spine, and bruised his kidneys.

Even without him, Cradley took a further 2 League points at Bradford, thanks to Gert Handberg, who was a revelation, scoring paid 13 points. A further point was added at Monmore Green, when the Heathens forced a draw in a classic Cradley-Wolves confrontation. A thrill-packed match saw the Heathens requiring a 5-1 in the last heat if they were to draw, and guest Kelvin Tatum and Gundersen proved to be equal to the task. Wolves were suffering from their own injury problems – big ones in fact. Sam Ermolenko had crashed in West Germany and shattered his leg, and while Wolves and Cradley were battling it out, Sam lay in hospital with his future as a speedway rider hanging in the balance.

Simon Cross was having a fine season, and was thrilled when he learned that, once again, he had been chosen to partner Kelvin Tatum in the World Pairs Championship. He had also been selected to ride for the Rest of the World team against Denmark in Vojens, but he became Cradley's second casualty when he crashed in Vojens and tore his shoulder ligaments. The injury kept him out of the World Pairs final, which was won yet again by Gundersen and Nielsen, and also kept him out of the Cradley side for almost a month.

Pratt chose his guests well, and both Peter Ravn and Neil Evitts did a good job as the Heathens established a 10-point lead in the first leg of the KO Cup semi-final at Reading. Pedersen made his comeback at King's Lynn on 12 August and top-scored with paid 14 points, but his efforts were to no avail, as Martin Dugard proved a poor replacement for Cross. Gundersen had a subdued night, and the result was a 47-43 win for the Stars. Erik had a punishing itinerary with Continental engagements, and reckoned that in the previous season, he had covered over 45,000 miles, which had cost an estimated £3,000 a month in air fares!

The day after the Lynn match was the date for the last qualifying round of the World Championship, held at Bradford, and Kelvin Tatum became the new Inter-Continental Champion after beating Erik Gundersen in a run-off. Nielsen took the third spot with Janno finishing in fifth place, despite retiring from the meeting after his cousin John Jorgensen had put him in the fence in his last outing. Alan Grahame was not up to the task and his 3 points saw him eliminated at the final stage.

A dejected Grahame again scored only 3 points at Dudley Wood when visitors Reading shook Cradley in the second leg of the KO Cup semi-final. The Heathens went into the final race requiring a 5-1 to stay in the competition, and when Pedersen and Gundersen went out and did the job, although the Racers had won the match by 6 points, Cradley were through to the final on aggregate.

Cross returned on the 26th to face Oxford in the first leg of the Gold Cup final at Dudley Wood, and was promptly excluded from his first race for tape-touching. Gundersen suffered the same fate in his second outing, and when Pedersen was excluded in his second outing also, it proved too much of a handicap for Cradley, as they lost their home leg by 6 points. Cross was the only Heathen to lower Nielsen's colours.

Two days later saw Bank Holiday Monday cover both legs of the Dudley/Wolves Trophy. Cradley hosted the first leg in the morning, and the Heathens fans were left reeling as Cradley were held to a draw by a very determined Wolverhampton team. The visitors' key to success was their guest Kelvin Tatum. Twice he came from behind to beat Gundersen, and was unbeaten in five outings, and with Erik suffering an engine failure, and Handberg and Hancock failing to make an impression, Cradley were faced with a difficult task at Monmore Green. The return match in the evening was a torrid affair, packed with all the drama that was a trademark of the clashes between these local rivals. Wolves had retained their 'trump card' Tatum, but Pratt objected to their second guest, Kelly Moran, on a technicality, which was upheld. A nice friendly start to proceedings!

Both sides began the match as though their very lives depended upon it, and after heat 5, the Heathens led by 2 points, but Gundersen made an appeal from the pits for riders to 'cool it', as he thought that things were getting out of hand. In the following race, Pedersen suffered engine failure, allowing Wolves to take a 2-point advantage, but worse was to come for Janno. In his next race, he caught the back wheel of Neil Collins and crashed into the fence. The Cradley fans anxiously waited for him to get up – but he didn't. The ambulance collected him and took him to hospital, where X-rays revealed that he had broken his arm. With the World Final only five days away, Pedersen was well and truly out of it, but worse still, his '89 season was over. Meanwhile, back at Monmore, the spills were coming thick and fast, as Hancock hit the deck, Wolves' Grahame Jones broke a couple of ribs, Tatum withdrew after a spill that left him with concussion, and Handberg and Bostin both bit the dust. Gundersen was having none of it. As the tapes went up, away he went, oblivious to the carnage that was going on behind him, and winning his first five races

1989 spelt the end of Erik Gundersen's career. (Hall)

by a mile. An appeal by the referee failed to calm down proceedings, and as the last heat arrived, Wolverhampton were leading by 3 points. Gundersen and Cross lined up against Robert Pfetzing and Jan Staechmann, and although Erik made his customary gate and headed for an 18-point maximum, Cross was unable to pass Pfetzing, and Wolves won the match and the trophy by just 1 point.

The Wolverhampton foot parade from the pits to collect the trophy was like a scene from *Dad's Army*. Ermolenko, already on crutches, led the walking wounded, followed by Grahame Jones, who was physically assisted as he clutched his broken ribs. The rest of the team trudged across the track wearily with Tatum somewhere in the middle of them, looking dazed and confused. It had been one hell of a match – but what a price to pay, with speedway's most prestigious meeting less than a week away. Pedersen's physical pain was nothing compared to the mental anguish that he suffered, knowing that he had been in with an excellent chance of becoming World Champion before hitting the Monmore shale.

Gundersen was Cradley's only representative in the World Final in Munich on 2 September. Following the rehearsal meeting, the riders seemed to be of the opinion that the track was too narrow coming out of the bends, and that gating would be at a premium, as overtaking would be very difficult. Erik found this to be the case in his first race, when he faced Nielsen. Although both trapped together, Hans was slightly ahead coming out of the first bend and it was all over.

Gundersen kept his composure and won his next heat, but in his third outing disaster struck, when he was a comfortable leader from Tatum, Wigg, and Jeremy Doncaster, before his bike gave up the ghost and effectively dashed any hopes that he may have had. Even though he won his last two races, 11 points was only good enough to give the spirited Dane fourth place.

Nielsen meanwhile, never put a foot wrong. He revelled in the 'gater's paradise', and put together five picture-book starts to become World Champion for the third time. The English boys had a good final, Wigg and Doncaster taking the other two rostrum places, but even so, it had been a poor final with a distinct lack of overtaking.

Even though an engine failure had robbed Erik of second place, he seemed philosophical about it and accepted the circumstances with good grace, and proved it in Cradley's next match at Reading, when he scored a 15-point maximum and led the Heathens to a 56-34 win. Cross looked as though his injuries were behind him, dropping only 1 point, and with guest Shawn Moran performing admirably and Hancock riding brilliantly, the Cradley machine was still rolling on towards its goal.

Gundersen continued in super style, setting a new Dudley Wood track record of 61.2 seconds in the first heat of their next match against Coventry. Although the Heathens won the match easily, a last-heat incident saw Tatum put Cross into the fence and Simon was forced to go to hospital for precautionary X-rays.

Crossy began Cradley's next outing at Swindon as he had finished the last one – on his back – and, as he scored only 3 points, the Robins came out winners 54-36. It could have been closer, and indeed, it should have been closer, but Lance King, guesting for Pedersen, complained of bike troubles all night. Even so, a rider of his calibre should have been capable of more than 0 points.

Cradley arrived at Cowley in mid-September with a mountain to climb in the second leg of the Gold Cup final and even with Kelvin Tatum in the side they were easy prey for the Cheetahs who boasted the world's number one and two in their side. Even so, Hancock put on a stirring display, and he was beginning to claim some famous scalps, but Crossy looked as though his latest string of injuries were taking their toll on him. With Grahame having an indifferent match, the Heathens lost 54-36 and their dream of a Grand Slam was over.

Something else was over too – Erik Gundersen's career. Two days later, on a sunny Sunday afternoon at Bradford on 17 September, the 1989 World Team Cup final took place. Even without Pedersen, Cradley had a healthy representation, with Gundersen skippering Denmark, who included Handberg, Cross riding for England, and Hancock at reserve for the USA. Colin Pratt was also present, of course, as the England manager.

Heat 1 began with Gundersen on the outside gate, Cross on the inside and Lance King and Jimmy Nilsen in between them. As the tapes went up, Gundersen made the gate, but going into the first corner, he locked up slightly. It was the kind of thing that one sees dozens of times in a season, but the result, on this black Sunday, was one of the most horrific pile-ups in speedway history. Erik's back wheel was clipped and the other three riders ploughed into him. King and Nilsen appeared to lock together before they hit the Dane, and Cross, who had completely missed the gate, tried to avoid the accident by switching to the white line, but he too was caught up in the carnage, and his bike was bought to a sickening halt by the riders and machinery in his path.

Two ambulances were on the track in seconds, where Gundersen lay completely motionless. King was first to his feet, suffering from a chipped bone in his neck, Cross was taken to hospital with facial wounds, and Nilsen went to hospital with a damaged thigh. Gundersen, meanwhile, was receiving lengthy attention as he lay prone on the track. He had swallowed his tongue and had stopped breathing. Fortunately, the quick-thinking track medical staff had recognised his condition and had put him on a ventilator. He was eventually taken away by ambulance, but the spectators were unaware that Erik was fighting for his life.

After a lengthy delay, it was announced, inexplicably, that Erik was conscious and was talking to the doctors and the meeting was recommenced. The truth, in fact, was that he was being rushed to Pinderfields Hospital in Leeds, and that his life was in grave danger. Only the Danish team were aware of the gravity of the situation, and Nielsen – the usually ice-cool Hans Nielsen – told the story in his face. He was completely stunned and visibly shaken, and in his own words he 'went through the meeting on auto-pilot'.

As the hours of Black Sunday ticked by, speedway supporters and riders alike were shattered as the extent of Erik's injuries were revealed through the media. He had indeed not regained consciousness, and as further hours passed, the news got worse. He was now on a life-support machine, as he was unable to breathe for himself. He had broken his back and there was damage to his spinal column. By the next day, he had still not regained consciousness, and it was reported that he had broken his neck and that wife Helle was keeping a bedside vigil.

The shock waves rippled through the sport, and the next evening at Wolverhampton, when the Wolves were due to ride at Oxford, although they were all present the riders did not want to ride the match. It only went ahead when it was announced over the tannoy system that Erik had regained consciousness for the first time.

It is difficult for an outsider to know what the relationship between Gundersen and Nielsen really was. On the track, they were either deadly rivals, or, together, for Denmark, they were the greatest World Pairs Champions ever. At one time, earlier on in their careers, they had reportedly been great friends, but a rift had developed when Ole Olsen became Danish team manager, and, since then, they had often been critical of each other. Off the track, they were like chalk and cheese. Gundersen was bubbly and ebullient, whilst Nielsen was somewhat sombre and withdrawn, but one thing that they did have in common was their immense respect for each other. Nobody was more upset by what had happened to Erik than Hans was.

There was a general gloom about the sport. Riders such as King, Hancock and Handberg contemplated retirement, and some supporters considered taking up other pastimes. Such was the profound effect that Gundersen's accident had on everyone, but Pratt and his men vowed to carry on. With almost a week's grace before the next match, Pratt was faced with the prospect of not only finding suitable guests for Gundersen and Pedersen, but for Handberg too, who was away in Italy contesting the World Under-21 Championship.

The week passed and Dudley Wood welcomed none other than the team who were 1 point ahead of Cradley in the League – Oxford. The Heathens faced them with Kelvin Tatum, Shawn Moran and Sean Wilson as their guest riders. On paper, Cradley didn't seem to have a chance, and Pratt must have speculated as to how many people he would have through the turnstiles, all things considered. Many fans who had just a few days earlier said that they had finished with speedway for good turned out in force, because 'they felt that they just had to', and so did hundreds more, making it one of the best gates of the season. The crowd was somewhat subdued before the meeting got underway, some openly weeping at the plight of Cradley's favourite son.

The match itself was one that warrants a book of its own. Heat 1 saw Oxford's Andy Grahame leap from the tapes and stay there, but behind him, Sean Wilson held out Nielsen to take second place! When Hancock won the next race to level the scores, the crowd began to warm to the match. On the first bend of heat 3, Cheetahs' Martin Dugard made a mistake, causing Cross and Grahame to crash heavily into the fence. Neither moved, to the horror of the spectators, and the all-too-familiar ambulance made its way onto the track. Fans sank to the floor in despair, and some left the stadium, unable to take any more. Eventually, Grahame got to his feet, looking badly shaken, but not so Cross – he was on yet another trip to hospital for more X-rays. The consequences did not bear thinking about. Cradley may possibly have been without their three heat-leaders for the rest of the season. Heat 4 saw Tatum equal the track record, and a see-saw match developed that saw Oxford in an 8-point lead by heat 7, only for the Heathens to come back and take a 6-point lead by heat 12. Alan Grahame, who had decided to continue, got a standing ovation when he beat Nielsen in heat 13, and in a last-heat decider, Cradley, who had been without Cross all night, incredibly won the match by 2 points.

Young Sean Wilson had one of the best nights of his career, dropping only 2 points to Oxford, and Kelvin Tatum was as always a splendid guest, whilst from the Heathens, Hancock and the very brave Alan Grahame were heroes. Cradley had won, against all odds – and the fight continued. Erik's fight continued also, and although he was still in a critical condition, it seemed that his life would be spared.

Gert Handberg returned as World Under-21 Champion, somewhat surprisingly, as Erik's accident had affected him more than most, but the fans hoped that the win would boost his confidence and help him to put the Bradford nightmare behind him.

Pratt began to look for a replacement for Gundersen, and it was reported that he had even approached Bruce Penhall, only to be politely turned down. In fact, it was the young Swede Mikael Blixt who became the favourite. Colin had been impressed with his efforts in the fated World Team Cup final, and things even got so far as Blixt turning up at Dudley Wood and having a spin after one of the meetings, but it was the last that Pratt saw of him.

Some guests are good and some are bad. There is absolutely no way of knowing how a guest will perform on the night, and Pratt was now faced with the dilemma of finding at least two for each one of Cradley's remaining matches. Theoretically, with the average that both Gundersen and Pedersen had attained, he could have had the pick of the British League, bar a couple, but there were many setbacks – many, many setbacks. Cradley Heath was a Saturday track, as were Coventry, Swindon, King's Lynn and Bradford. Add to that the fact that riders may not be available for other reasons, and the rules involving guest riders, such as not being allowed to ride on the same track in a certain amount of days etc., and it amounted to one giant headache for Colin Pratt. But for all that, the Heathens could not have wished for a better man at the helm. Colin was no quitter and he would stick to the task in hand regardless. He also had another problem regarding guests. The Heathens were still challenging for the League and the KO Cup and it would be to the advantage of most teams if Cradley were to lose matches – so how would guests from these teams perform? Some did and some didn't.

Only a late rally at Belle Vue saw the Aces beat the Heathens, Simon Cross electing to rejoin the team and take over as skipper, despite being battered and bruised. He probably wished he hadn't the next night at Dudley Wood, when in his last outing,

Jan O. Pedersen leads Carl Blackbird. (Hall)

Wolves' Grahame Jones knocked him into the fence and poor old Crossy found himself back at Russells Hall Hospital for the third home match in succession! The fans feared for his health, not from all the bangs that he was taking but from radiation poisoning!

It was a disappointing night for Cradley as neighbours Wolverhampton beat them at Dudley Wood to replace the Heathens in second place in the League table behind Oxford. The match highlighted the perils of the guest system, as Mitch Shirra top-scored for Cradley with 11 points, an adequate replacement for Gundersen or Pedersen, but the Heathens' other guest, American Kelly Moran, mustered only 2 points.

Simon Cross was ruled out with concussion a couple of nights later at Monmore Green, and Cradley were obliged to use three guests – Shawn Moran, Jimmy Nilsen and Brian Karger – but it was poor performances by Grahame and Handberg that cost the Heathens the match, as they lost to their local rivals for the second time in 48 hours, this time by 48-42. Hancock was superb, scoring 14 points, and his determination to keep the Heathens in the hunt for Erik's sake was making him the most popular rider in the Heathens' outfit.

Cross returned to lead his team at Coventry at the beginning of October and led by example, scoring 15 points from six starts, but Lance King again failed as a guest, scoring only 3 points – but even that was 1 point more than Cradley's other guest, Peter Ravn! The result was a win for the Bees by 53-37, and the Heathens' fourth successive League defeat. Although they were still clinging on to their third spot in the League table, Cradley seemed to be precariously balanced.

The Heathens did pick up the League points at Bradford against all odds. It was, of course, the scene of the World Cup carnage, and that must have been uppermost in the riders' minds. To make matters worse, the weather was abysmal, and Cradley asked for two track inspections during the match. The Heathens were only able to field six riders in the meeting, electing to use rider replacement, and able guest Chris Morton. With conditions getting worse, Cross, who despite his injuries had dropped only 1 point in three outings, asked the referee if he could withdraw from the meeting, and was given permission to do so, leaving Cradley with just five riders. Things became desperate when Handberg got 'spooked' and walked out of the meeting, promptly being fined £50 for his actions. So how the hell did Cradley manage to win by 3 points? The answer in a nutshell was John Bostin. He rattled off three heat wins in his last three outings to top-score for the Heathens with paid 13 points from six rides. The diabolical conditions had persuaded John to use his grasstrack engine, and while all the other riders were struggling to get some grip with their highly-tuned engines, Bostin on his 'flat' engine was leaving them for dead!

The next day at Dudley Wood, Cross, who was revelling in the captain's role, led the Heathens to a huge win over King's Lynn, scoring a paid maximum. As the match took place on a Sunday, Pratt was able to book two good guests in Kelvin Tatum and Simon Wigg and both scored well, along with Cradley's latest hero, Greg Hancock.

Just after the season had begun, Tatum publicly announced that he was fed up with the reception that he was receiving at the various tracks around the country. He had become a regular 'boo-boy', and Kelvin had not taken kindly to that sort of treatment. At Cradley, whether he was a guest or opponent, he became a great favourite, and the Heathens fans gave him a rousing ovation every time he appeared, in appreciation of his efforts on behalf of their decimated team.

The Heathens had reached the KO Cup final and to add spice to the tie, the opponents they faced were their high-flying arch-rivals Wolverhampton. Wolves had also been forced to use guest riders due to injuries, notably to Ermolenko, and the team line-ups for both sides became a battle of wits.

Pratt, through necessity, had become a master in the art, and while Wolves supremo Chris Van Straaten fielded Brian Karger, Colin had Tatum and Jimmy Nilsen booked for the first leg at Monmore Green, and both performed admirably to give the Heathens an 8-point lead to take back to Dudley Wood for the second leg. Although Crossy had a bad match, Hancock, again, was superb, and was rapidly proving himself to be one of the hardest men to beat around the tricky Monmore circuit.

The Heathens kept up their League challenge, dispatching Reading with ease from Dudley Wood, Cross and Hancock both scoring 15-point maximums, and then five nights later, they faced Wolverhampton in the second leg of the KO Cup final at Cradley.

Meanwhile, Gundersen continued to improve. Once he was off the life-support system, his condition was analysed. Although doctors were reluctant to predict a full recovery, they did say that Erik would walk again and this became his new aim in life. The Heathens vowed to win the KO Cup and take it to Pinderfields Hospital to present it to Erik, and the second-leg match became a very emotional affair.

Cradley won the first battle by securing the services of Tatum for the match, despite the efforts of Van Straaten to get him to ride for Wolves. Pratt deliberated long and hard before deciding to track Shawn Moran as his second guest. Moran's ability was never in question, but Dudley Wood was by no means his favourite track, and his previous efforts as a Cradley guest had left a niggling doubt in the mind of the Cradley manager.

On 26 October, Wolves came to Dudley Wood with guest Jimmy Nilsen in the side, and the Swede top-scored for them with 10 points. His efforts were in vain, however, as the Heathens all fought valiantly to beat the Wolves by a mere 2 points to win the KO Cup for the fourth year in succession by 10 points on aggregate.

Moran came up trumps, scoring 14 points, and was ably supported by skipper Cross. Both guests Moran and Tatum were overwhelmed by the ovation that they received as Cradley collected the cup. The supporters at last had something to celebrate after the weeks of misery that they had endured – triumph over tragedy in their last home match of the season.

There followed an emotional scene when all the Heathens went up to Pinderfields Hospital to present the cup to Erik Gundersen. The event was covered by the media, and Erik made his first public appearance since his accident, being pictured in a wheelchair flanked by the team. The Heathens technically were still in the hunt for the League Championship with only 2 matches left, but they were tough tasks at Belle Vue and Oxford.

The recent form of Alan Grahame had been a cause of concern for Pratt, and as Cradley lost by 8 points to Belle Vue, the Heathens veteran failed to score, and Cradley's chances of the League Championship were gone. In contrast to the previous year, when Alan finished as Cradley's hero, Pratt branded Grahame as the villain of the piece, calling his efforts at Manchester 'pathetic'.

After being hit by the traditional end-of-season weather, the Heathens finally completed their fixtures at Oxford on 1 November, losing by 6 points to the Cheetahs. It gave Oxford the League Championship and put Cradley in third place behind Wolverhampton.

The Heathens found themselves at another milestone in their history. Gundersen officially announced his retirement from speedway, leaving some big boots to fill. He continued his recovery into the winter, eventually taking his first steps, but such were the extent of his injuries that doctors were talking in terms of years before he could be anything like the Erik of old. Typically, from his hospital bed, he desperately wanted to show his appreciation for the life-saving efforts of Pinderfields and launched an appeal fund, which raised thousands of pounds for the Leeds Infirmary.

Gundersen had been the inspiration behind the Cradley team since the departure of Penhall and had assumed the responsibility of the 'number one' role with dignity. He was a born leader – captain supreme for the Heathens and Denmark alike, and a team man through and through, who always gave his all for his beloved Heathens. He had joined the elite, a legend in his own lifetime, who always held his world titles with pride and humility. Erik had done it all and won them all, but he never lost touch with his adoring public and his fellow riders, and if the Heathens appeared at a National League track, he could often be found helping out the 'lesser lights' with their machinery and

1989 programme.

giving them tips and advice. It was no mistake that Pratt always paired the inexperienced riders such as Hancock with Erik upon their arrival at Dudley Wood. Gundersen was just as popular with his fellow professionals as he was with the fans, and to say that he would be missed was a great understatement. He was irreplaceable, and no rider of his standing had ever given greater service to a club than Erik did to Cradley Heath.

It is pure speculation how many years at the top fate had robbed him of, for at the time of that terrible disaster, he was still beating the best, with no signs of slowing up. He finished the season in fourth place in the BL averages with 10.00 points.

Ironically, for the first time since 1982, Gundersen had failed to top the Heathens' averages. That honour belonged to Jan O. Pedersen, who finished second only to Nielsen in the BL averages with 10.39 points. It had been a marvellous year for Pedersen, who had looked a fair bet to clean up until his accident at Monmore Green. He had become the biggest draw in the sport, and understandably fancied his chances in the World Championship, but his season had ended in despair just a few short days before Munich.

Simon Cross had been terrific. He had ridden when lesser mortals would not have done, for Crossy was made of stern stuff and refused to let a spate of injuries prevent him from leading the Heathens until the end of the season. He took over the role of skipper with pride, and rode through the pain barrier to finish seventh in the BL averages with 9.32 points.

Gert Handberg had shown what he was capable of in '89 by winning the Under-21 World Championship, but Erik's accident had left its mark on young Gert, and perhaps hampered his progress at the latter part of the season. Handberg finished with a 6.36-point average. Alan Grahame had begun the season well, but faded badly at the end. He was the only Heathen to take part in every match and averaged 6.25 points.

Greg Hancock had not been an overnight sensation, arriving at Dudley Wood with an injured shoulder, but he began to settle down and became a team-man supreme. Such was his admiration for Gundersen that after Bradford he contemplated retirement, but Erik persuaded him to continue, and continue he did – like a man inspired. Following Erik's accident, no one responded to the cause more so than Hancock did, as along with Cross, he became the backbone of the Cradley team. But for Greg's slow start, he would have vastly improved on his 5.97 average.

John Bostin finished at the bottom of the Heathens' scorers with just 2.96 points per match, but he had won the match for Cradley at Bradford, keeping them in the hunt for the League, and one could ask no more than that from a reserve.

It had been an emotional season for the Heathens. They had once again won the KO Cup, but had lost their greatest ever rider. Pratt did remarkably well under duress. He had held the team together whilst at the mercy of guest riders. In their quest to win something for their injured skipper, Cradley generated a team spirit so strong that even the guests, with a couple of exceptions, seemed to be emotionally charged when they joined the Heathens in battle. Even so, Colin must have heaved a sigh of relief when the season was over and done with, but his winter task was a daunting one – to find a replacement for one of the best riders that the sport had ever seen.

14

A CATALOGUE OF CATASTROPHES
1990

Pratt played his close season cards close to his chest in the winter months. The points limit had remained at 46 points, and although the Heathens had finished on 49.87 points, Gundersen's average would have to be taken from that. Colin seemed pretty keen on acquiring the services of Andy Galvin from National League Hackney or Leigh Adams from Poole. Adams had been the sensation of the NL in '89, and Ivan Mauger had already branded the young Australian a future World Champion, but even so, Poole's asking price of £25,000 seemed excessive considering Leigh's limited experience. It was certainly too rich for Derek Pugh's pocket, and ultimately, Adams signed for Swindon. Pratt was exploring all the options, and Alan Grahame, who was pushing Colin for a decision as to his future at Dudley Wood, was forced to wait as the Cradley manager contacted Mikael Blixt and then Billy Hamill.

Cradley were hit in the pocket when King's Lynn announced that they would not be renewing their loan arrangement for Lance King, no doubt hoping that they would be allowed to use the reformed Michael Lee in their line-up. As it was, their request was turned down, and Lee was left on the sidelines for another twelve months, but by the time the matter was resolved, it was too late to fit King into a British League outfit.

One by one, the Heathens squad was revealed. Pedersen, Cross, Hancock and Handberg were all offered new contracts, and after looking a doubtful starter, Grahame joined them. Pedersen had the plate removed from his arm a few weeks before the start of the season and declared himself fully fit. Pratt completed the American connection by signing 19-year-old Billy Hamill as a replacement for Erik, and decided to award the reserve spot to the most impressive junior on practice day. With the squad all but settled, there was a last-minute hiccup when Pedersen decided to chance his arm and make pay demands on the club that they were unable to meet. Fortunately a compromise was reached and he signed on the dotted line on the eve of the season.

Gundersen had continued to improve during the winter, and although far from fit, he had moved back to his Tamworth home with wife Helle. He pledged his continued allegiance to the Heathens, offering to help in any way possible. His services were put to good use, even before the first match. Hancock had lost his landlord when King had failed to find a BL placing, and Erik offered to put him up for the season. Not only that, but he extended the offer to Hamill, giving them both the facilities of his workshop.

On practice day, 22-year-old Mark Robinson was given the number seven shirt. Mark was a local Cradley lad and an ex-member of the track staff, and already had one successful season under his belt as a Cradley junior. A huge crowd saw the Cradley riders go through their paces on practice day, but they were unable to get a first look at Hamill, who had yet to arrive on these shores. When he did, Billy 'The Kid' Hamill proved to be typical of the American riders – self-confident, flash, silver-tongued and totally likeable. He was already a star on the USA circuit, and expressed a desire to do well in the BL, which was just as well considering the amount of faith that Pratt had placed in him.

The 1990 season got off to the best possible start at Dudley Wood, as thousands turned out to see Erik Gundersen take a lap of honour in an open-back truck, prior to the match. Although he looked pale and fragile, his spirit was still as bright as ever and the wonderful ovation that he received visibly moved him. Unfortunately that was the end of the celebrations for the Cradley fans on that particular night.

Jan O. Pedersen had expressed a desire to be captain of the Heathens and so had Simon Cross. Pratt was faced with a dilemma. Pedersen had a more laid-back approach that could be good for the riders, but who could fault Simon's performance as skipper when he had taken over from Gundersen less that a year ago? The matter was still unresolved by the first match on 17 March, and following his lap of honour, Gundersen was named as non-riding captain for the night as the Heathens faced King's Lynn in a challenge match. Cross was robbed of a maximum by engine trouble and Pedersen scored well after a shaky start but, apart from Hancock, the rest were disappointing, and the Stars won the match by 2 points. Hamill finished third in all of his four outings and looked promising, scoring paid 6 points.

Pratt, disgusted by most of his team's efforts to get out of the gate, immediately ordered a further practice for the following Monday morning. It was an indication of what was in store for Cradley when Handberg fell during the practice and damaged his hand, putting him out of the team for two weeks.

The following Saturday night at Dudley Wood, Pratt elected to use rider replacement for Gert as Cradley faced Bradford in the first Gold Cup match, but with only Alan Grahame performing on the night, the tactic was unsuccessful. Cross and Pedersen failed to win a race as the Dukes won by 8 points. Hamill emerged from the match with some credit and, although he missed the official practice, he was certainly getting some now, as Colin ordered all of the riders back on Monday morning for another session.

The Heathens responded with a marvellous performance at Oxford, forcing a draw in the first leg of the Premiership. Pratt took no chances and booked the sensational BL newcomer Mark Loram as a guest rider for Handberg, and the young King's Lynn rider showed his appreciation by scoring 10 points from the reserve berth. Pedersen and Cross were both superb, each beating Hans Nielsen and scoring a 4-2 in the last heat over the 'Main Dane' to save the match.

The return leg took place the following evening at Dudley Wood and Cradley made no mistakes, winning by 10 points to take their first trophy of 1990. The match got off to a cracking start, as Pedersen and Hancock scored a 5-1 over World Champion

Nielsen. Hans was also forced into second place by Cross in a subsequent race, which was started four times in all, Cross leading Nielsen on each occasion.

Handberg returned on the first Saturday in April, but he struggled at home as the Heathens easily beat Belle Vue. It was a tremendous team effort with Hancock and Grahame proving especially impressive, but Cradley lost Robinson in his second outing when he crashed into Shawn Moran after the race and damaged his shoulder.

The Heathens continued their Gold Cup campaign at Wolverhampton, when a majestic 15-point maximum from Pedersen led them to a draw with their deadly rivals. The match climaxed with one of the most exciting races ever seen at Monmore Green when, in heat 15, Pedersen and Cross needed a 5-1 to draw the match. They faced Wolves' guest Jimmy Nilsen and American favourite Ronnie Correy, who had both scored well. The Wolves fans began to celebrate as Nilsen shot from the tapes, but their celebrations were premature as first Cross swept past him on the third lap and then Pedersen did the same on the final bend. Oh joy! David Haynes had been called up from the juniors to replace Robinson and even though he, Grahame and Handberg failed to score, 14 points from track specialist Hancock saved the day.

Greg was riding better than ever, but even so, he was content to allow the more forthcoming Hamill to take the spotlight. Billy was, after all is said and done, in the team 'proper' while Hancock was operating from the reserve berth. But whereas Hamill was returning 5 or 6 points per match, Greg had scored double figures in his last three outings.

Billy had to pull out of Cradley's next fixture at Bradford with flu, and only Cross performed as the Dukes stormed to a massive 63-27 win. Hamill returned, with Robinson, in the middle of the month, when the Heathens thrashed Coventry on Bank Holiday Monday morning, before winning by 10 points at Brandon in the evening.

When they were 'on song', Cradley were an impressive outfit. Cross was riding phenomenally well and Pedersen was back to his best. Handberg and Grahame were filling the middle-order scoring and, considering the few matches that Hamill had ridden, he had been impressive and looked to be a winner. Hancock was at that time the ace in the pack, being the best reserve in the country, and although Robinson was finding life difficult in his debut season, he never gave up trying.

The Heathens went top of the northern section of the Gold Cup when they swept aside Wolverhampton at Dudley Wood. The match almost marked maximums for Cradley's Yanks. Hamill dropped only 1 point in four outings and Hancock dropped 1 point in six outings, but Pedersen made no mistakes, taking the full 15 points and even equalling the track record. He was at it again a few nights later at Cradley, once more recording 61.2 seconds in the first heat, as another fabulous all-round performance saw the Heathens crush Belle Vue in their first League match of the season.

At the end of April, Pedersen and Cross took first and second places in the Coalite Classic at Bradford, the home of the 1990 World Final. Both riders had also featured prominently in the England *v.* Denmark Test series during the month. The Danes were somewhat depleted after losing Knudsen and Gundersen, and consequently failed to win any of the three matches, but Janno did average 13 points a match. The man of the series, however, was Simon Cross. He top-scored for England with an incredible 16.67

Cradley Heath, 1990. From left to right, back row: Mark Robinson, Billy Hamill, Gert Handberg, Alan Grahame, Derek Pugh (promoter). Front row: Greg Hancock, Simon Cross, Jan O. Pedersen, Erik Gundersen. (Hipkiss)

average and beat Nielsen in every match, and one wondered if Crossy could be a surprise contender for the World Championship at Odsal. To make the month one of the most successful in Simon's career, after consulting Gundersen, Pratt decided to make Crossy the Heathens' skipper.

A puncture for Cross in the last heat cost Cradley the League points at Coventry as the Bees won by 2 points. After being 6 points down at Brandon after heat 13, sensationally Robinson followed Hancock home in heat 14, holding out Czechoslovakia's top rider Roman Matousek to score a 5-1 to keep the Heathens in the match before Crossy's misfortune.

Cradley continued their impressive League form as Reading failed to make any impression on them at Dudley Wood, but two nights later at Smallmead the Racers gained their revenge as the Heathens suffered a multitude of misfortunes and lost 33-57.

The Heathens needed to win their last Gold Cup match at Belle Vue to qualify for the final, but were denied by just 1 point, in one of the most incredible matches ever seen. Mechanical failures, falls and some disputable refereeing decisions turned the meeting into a long-drawn-out affair, in which three heats had only two finishers and riders continually fell on what proved to be a very difficult track. Unfortunately, Hamill came out of the mêlée rather the worse for wear, and was unable to take his place at King's Lynn the following evening. His absence cost Cradley the match, as replacement Dave Mullet scored only 1 point and the Stars won the match 48-42.

As Billy returned for the Heathens next match at Oxford, Pedersen was missing, injured on the Continent, and Cradley used rider replacement but lost the match by 14 points. Cross again proved master of Nielsen on two occasions, and although Hans was still a mighty force to be reckoned with, it began to look as though his 'reign of terror' might be over. He openly admitted that he was missing Gundersen, and found it harder to get motivated without Erik constantly 'snapping at his heels'. Nielsen was, however, superb the following night at Dudley Wood as, even with Pedersen back in the side, Cradley were unable to hold the Cheetahs and slumped to an 8-point defeat, their fifth in succession.

On Bank Holiday Monday morning, the Heathens stopped the rot when they easily beat high-flying Swindon at Dudley Wood, and only failed to win at Blunsdon in the evening by just 2 points in what proved to be an incident-packed match. The Robins lost Jimmy Nilsen in his third outing, following a brush with the over-zealous Simon Cross, but Cradley had their share of bad luck with Pedersen suffering an engine failure, Cross and Handberg being excluded, and Handberg and Hamill having to pull out of one race each.

The Heathens had a surprise individual trophy winner towards the end of the month, when Billy Hamill shocked the speedway world by winning the Peter Craven Memorial Trophy at Belle Vue with a magnificent display of riding. Meanwhile, over in Denmark, Pedersen won the Gold Bar meeting with one of the most breathtaking displays of speedway skill and determination that has ever been captured on camera. In an eight-

man, eight-lap final, he came from last place to pick his way through the star-studded field, and won the race (Crossy finished third).

May saw much activity in the World Championship rounds. Cross qualified from the British Semi-final at Dudley Wood by finishing second behind Gary Havelock, but Grahame failed at the first fence. In the British Final later in the month at Coventry, Cross was again runner-up, this time to Kelvin Tatum, but he was easily through to the Commonwealth Final.

In Scandinavia, Pedersen became the new Danish Champion, finishing 1 point in front of Nielsen and breaking the Holsted track record twice. Gert Handberg was robbed of a qualifying place when he finished ahead of John Jorgensen, only to be told that the

Mark Robinson. (Hall)

Coventry fall guy was being seeded through by the DMU at Gert's expense. The youngster was devastated but, despite protests from Colin Pratt, the DMU stood by their decision and Handberg was out of the competition.

Janno continued his quest for world supremacy by winning the Scandinavian title in Sweden at the start of June. Because of riders' absences and two rain-offs, the Heathens did not compete in another League match until the end of June, but meanwhile, the World Championship action continued. At Long Beach, California, Hancock rode his heart out to top-score jointly with Hamill, Rick Miller and Shawn Moran in the American round. In the subsequent run-off, Greg fell and Miller, who was some fifteen lengths behind him, ran straight into him, causing some questions to be asked in the pits. The news was bad. Hancock had sustained a broken arm, and although he attempted to have some sort of support constructed to enable him to ride in the Overseas Final, his season was effectively over.

Cross continued to get closer, finishing on the rostrum behind Tatum and Martin Dugard in the Commonwealth Final at Belle Vue, but in the Overseas Final at Coventry at the end of the month he had an uncomfortable passage, just scraping the last qualifying spot. Hamill was not so lucky: he had returned to England with a thoroughly disappointed Hancock and maybe it was his lack of experience or the big occasion that saw him score only 4 points and make his exit from the Championship.

The Heathens returned to League action at Wolverhampton without Hancock, Handberg and Robinson. Gert had injured his hand and was replaced by Sean Wilson, but juniors David Haynes and Gary Frankham replaced the other two riders and, with both failing to score, Cradley lost by 4 points. Sam Ermolenko had made his comeback from the terrible injuries he had sustained almost twelve months earlier, but he looked ill at ease and scored only 3 points.

The score was reversed at Dudley Wood the following evening as Handberg and Robinson both returned, and Per Jonsson proved to be a more than adequate guest for Hancock. In the matter of 24 hours, Sam Ermolenko was back to his brilliant best, top-scoring for Wolves with 12 points! Sam revelled in his role as the arch-villain at Dudley Wood. It was another incident-packed classic match that saw Grahame score five heat wins from the reserve berth. Cross hit the fence in his second outing and retired from the meeting badly winded, and Handberg retired after his third race, but the Heathens still had enough in reserve to beat the Wolves.

Cradley began July using rider replacement for Hancock at Belle Vue and put up a spirited performance, losing by only 4 points, but the following evening at Dudley Wood, with Pedersen suffering from flu and Hamill having a nightmare match, Reading took the League points and left the Heathens at the bottom of the League table. Two nights later at Smallmead, Cradley took swift revenge, putting on a tremendous display and beating Reading by 2 points. It was their first away win in the League, and Cross, Pedersen and Handberg all rode their hearts out.

With the League Championship looking well out of their grasp, the Heathens had to look once again to the KO Cup to provide any success from the season. They began their defence at Dudley Wood in the middle of July against Bradford, and their four-year reign as champions looked to be in danger as the Dukes forced a draw. Three nights later, Cradley were out of the competition, losing by 18 points in the return leg at Odsal. They were without Mark Robinson, who had damaged his shoulder, and also Billy Hamill, who was suffering from an injured knee, but the body blow was that Hamill would be out of the team for a number of weeks. It was only mid-July, and already the Heathens were poised to have their worst season for many a year. They were out of the KO Cup, the Gold Cup and the League Championship, so all that the fans had to look forward to was the World Championship assault by Cross and Pedersen.

If morale was flagging, then skipper Cross did his best to restore it by winning the Golden Hammer at Dudley Wood. Nielsen, Pedersen, Doncaster and the like all became his victims as he threaded his way through the all-star field to take the trophy for the first time. It was one of Simon's greatest performances, but what we didn't know at the time was that it was his last of the season. Cross had once again been chosen, with Kelvin Tatum, to represent England in the World Pairs Championship, and they had both been superb, winning the semi-final in Austria. The final took place in West Germany on 21 July and England's main rivals would undoubtedly be Denmark, who, although having lost Gundersen, had a first-rate replacement in Pedersen, who was to partner Nielsen.

For the past few years, the meeting had featured six-man races, supposedly to make the event more exciting, but this had proved to be very unpopular with the riders. They had no complaints at a track such as Pardubice in Czechoslovakia, which was a large track with wide sweeping bends, but most of the venues that had been chosen for the World Pairs Finals were considered by the competitors to be unsuitable. Bearing this in mind, the FIM announced that the 1990 final would be the last one with six-man races – but this was too late for Simon Cross.

Crossy and Tatum contested the first race against the USA and New Zealand, and as the riders fought to sort themselves out coming out of the first bend, the inevitable 'jam' occurred. Simon ran out of track, and he and his bike skated across the apex of the bend. It was the type of fall witnessed a hundred times in a season, with the rider normally getting up and dusting himself off, but it soon became obvious that Crossy was badly injured. He was taken to hospital, where it was discovered that he had cracked two vertebrae in his back. He was operated upon and given the good news that he would walk again, but the bad news that followed was that his speedway was over for probably eighteen months. Tatum was forced to contest the meeting on his own, and inevitably the Danes won the event for the sixth successive year.

Pratt was left looking at half a team. Hancock, Hamill and Cross were all injured, and he found himself, once again, at the mercy of the guest system, which he would almost certainly have to use for the rest of the season. To his credit, Colin did try to find a replacement for his skipper. Lance King, who was still in America, was approached but he was committed to work in the film industry and was unable to help Cradley in their hour of need. Peter Ravn, who had been transfer-listed by Belle Vue, was also considered but was not signed. Finally, Pratt contacted Swedish hotshot Henrik Gustafsson, only to discover that the young Scandinavian had already been approached by every other promoter in the British League and was not interested in coming to England. So the guests would come thick and fast. It was not as though Pratt was a great supporter of the guest system, and everyone in speedway was well aware of its

Simon Cross. (Hipkiss)

shortcomings, but in the case of the Heathens, if the guest system had not been available then they would have had to shut down mid-season.

Cross was, of course, out of the Inter-Continental Final in Denmark and Pedersen remained the only Heathen left in the hunt for the World Championship, and he booked his place in the final by finishing in fourth place in Denmark behind Shawn Moran, Per Jonsson and Hans Nielsen. The World Final was to be held at Odsal, a track that certainly held no fears for Janno. It was a circuit that riders could overtake on and, as passing was Pedersen's forte, he was reckoned to be in with a great chance of lifting the title. The Cradley fans were certainly looking to him to provide them with something to celebrate in those dark days.

After almost a month without a fixture, the Heathens returned to action at Monmore Green in mid-August to contest the first leg of the Dudley/Wolves Trophy, and Pratt had booked Kelvin Tatum and Bobby Ott as Cradley's guests. No doubt influenced by Cradley's dilemma, Hamill had decided to return and he put off his knee operation until the winter. Heavy rain had left the track surface saturated and, although the match got under way after a half-hour delay, it certainly wasn't a night for taking risks. After a third place and an engine failure, Pedersen saw fit to retire from the meeting, no doubt mindful of the consequences of last year's corresponding fixture. His loss was too much to overcome, and the Heathens lost the match 50-39.

Two nights later for the return leg at Dudley Wood, Pratt picked his guests wisely, Tatum and Jimmy Nilsen being drafted into the squad. They had a mountain to climb

Billy Hamill. (Hall)

to overcome the 11-point deficit. Pedersen had his wish granted and became the new Heathens skipper, and he led his team marvellously, dropping only 1 point to the aggressive Ermolenko. As a titanic battle developed, Cradley began chipping away at Wolves' lead, and went into the last heat needing a 5-1 to regain the trophy. Tatum, who by now was familiar with the importance that both sets of supporters placed on this trophy, was clearly caught up in the cup final atmosphere, and heat 15 saw him at his brilliant best. He lined up with Pedersen, Ermolenko and Wolves guest Sean Wilson and when Wilson made the gate, it looked as though Wolves were going to hang on to the trophy. But the Heathens would not be denied as first Tatum and then Pedersen overtook him to cross the line to a deafening ovation. The trophy was presented by a very stiff Simon Cross, who looked most uncomfortable, but at least he was walking and was the first to acknowledge that he was lucky not to be partially paralysed.

It was the last celebration of 1990 for the Heathens' supporters. Pedersen did not win the World Championship final – in fact, he never rode in it. The following day, just twelve days before the World Final, it seemed like a sick joke when the news was released that Jan Pedersen had fallen when walking at a go-kart meeting in Birmingham and had broken his arm in the same place as previously. Not only was he out of the World Final but he was out of speedway for the rest of the year. The World Final favourite was devastated. His World Championship dream had, once again, become a nightmare.

For Colin Pratt, the whole season had been a nightmare, and what must his thoughts have been as he watched his team being decimated before his very eyes? At the time of their respective injuries, Cross was lying fourth in the BL averages and Pedersen second, proof that they were among the best riders in the world, and now he had neither.

When guests Troy Butler and Martin Dugard failed to make an impact the following Saturday at Cradley Heath, the Heathens were unable to hold a rampant Belle Vue side, despite a magnificent performance from Handberg. The match was significant for what should have been the final appearance of Chris Morton at Dudley Wood. He planned to retire at the end of the season and ironically he scored his first ever 15-point maximum at Cradley.

Simon Wigg proved to be an excellent guest as the Heathens entertained King's Lynn and rattled off a superb 18-point maximum and, with Handberg supporting well, Cradley won 53-37. The Cradley jinx would not let go, however, and guest Tony Olsen was involved in a horrific crash in which he broke his thigh and elbow.

The much sought-after captaincy was up for grabs, but whereas everybody initially wanted the job, now Pratt couldn't get any takers for the position considering the fate that had befallen the last two skippers. It wasn't surprising, so fearless Colin appointed himself as captain for the rest of the season.

Bank Holiday Monday saw home and away fixtures against Coventry, with Cradley staging the morning match, and Pratt was obliged to book three guests in order to put out a team. His first choice was a shrewd move. He called up 'maximum man' Chris Morton. Chris' team-mate Bobby Ott was also booked, but Colin's third choice was controversial – he called up Sam Ermolenko. There was to be no maximum for Morton on this occasion, although he battled typically hard to score 9 points from five rides. Ott looked particularly impressive, winning two races, but he fell and retired in another two races and it effectively lost Cradley the match as they lost by 4 points. Handberg was again a revelation from the reserve berth, scoring paid 12 points, but Ermolenko let himself down badly, scoring only 2 points. The evening match was a surprise draw, thanks to the endeavours of Grahame, Handberg and Hamill, although Gary Havelock was a useful guest.

On 1 September, Per Jonsson became the shock winner of the World Championship at Odsal Stadium. Nielsen didn't even make the rostrum, finishing fourth behind Shawn Moran and the young Australian Todd Wiltshire, who was having his first season in the British League. It was a meeting that had some brilliant racing and far more overtaking than many previous World Finals – a testimony to some fine track preparation; it was a track that would have suited Jan Pedersen down to the ground.

Gert Handberg made the most of a lull in proceedings by taking off to Spain on a camping holiday, but even when abroad the Cradley gremlin got him and he had his van broken into and his passport stolen. Handberg enjoyed the type of relationship with engines that one enjoys with one's mother-in-law. He had blown God knows how many in the last eighteen months, but on the way back from Dover, Gert progressed to four-wheeled vehicles and blew up the one in his van!

September began with a heavy defeat at Belle Vue, but at Dudley Wood, Championship contenders Wolves were dealt a blow when the Heathens thrashed them 53-37. It was a match that seemed to be heading Wolves' way until heat 9 when Sam '2 points' Ermolenko ran into Alan Grahame and got himself excluded for his pains. The re-run began a spate of 5-1s that won the match for Cradley. 'Our Kelvin' was yet again a superb guest, dropping only 1 point to Sudden Sam in six outings.

Todd Wiltshire was also a big hit at Dudley Wood and he made his guest debut when the Heathens scored their biggest win of the season over visitors Bradford. His co-guest Jimmy Nilsen, as always, did himself credit, but it looked as though after two unbeaten rides Handberg was going to be the man of the match. That was until he tangled with Andy Smith and was taken to hospital with a foot injury. The Heathens were forced to do battle at Oxford without Cross, Pedersen, Hancock and Handberg. Pratt brought in

161

David Haynes to partner Robinson at reserve, booked Nilsen and Marvyn Cox as guests, and used rider replacement at number two. Cradley, largely due to their guests, managed to make a fight of it, and lost by only 6 points, Robinson scoring 6 well-earned points.

The middle of September found the Heathens fielding only three of their own riders when they played host to Oxford. Grahame, Hamill and Robinson were the only Heathens that were not injured (that is if you can count Hamill, of course, who was riding with a dodgy knee). Pratt booked three guests from Belle Vue, Chris Morton (who was making his third 'last' appearance at Dudley Wood) and the Moran brothers, and he gave the young Wolverhampton rider Wayne Carter a guest spot at reserve. Cradley, not surprisingly, had a disjointed look about them, and had no answer to Nielsen, Wigg and Dugard who all helped themselves to double figures as the Cheetahs stormed to a 51-39 win.

Hamill had beaten Hans Nielsen in the match and was becoming immensely popular at Cradley. He had made a big impact in his first season and, had he been fully fit, would no doubt have done even better. The Americans seemed to be quite impressed with him, so much so that they named him as reserve for the World Team Cup final at Prague. He was given two outings and finished second in both, helping the USA to only their second win in the event as they finished 3 points in front of defending champions England. Tommy Knudsen had made a comeback to the sport a couple of weeks earlier, and the Danes were so short of riders that they included Tommy in their squad. How things change!

The first match in October at Wolverhampton heralded the return of Handberg and Hancock, and one wondered if Greg could find his old flair on his favourite track, Monmore Green. The answer was no. He looked completely out of touch and struggled all night, scoring only 1 point. Handberg fared little better, and even with Tatum and Sean Wilson in as guests, the Heathens failed to make an impact on the Wolves and lost the match 36-54, Hamill being Cradley's only success.

The Heathens were back to a three-guest situation at Bradford when Hamill was forced to return to the States. Out of Neil Collins, Mark Loram and Leigh Adams, only Loram performed, but with Handberg returning to form Cradley were unlucky to lose by just 4 points. Hancock looked as though he was getting it back together when he won a race, but in heat 11 he was leading when the strain on his arm became too much and he crashed.

One began to fear for Colin Pratt's health when it was reported that Billy Hamill had been involved in a car crash in America and had suffered whiplash. He had not been kept in hospital, but he would miss the next three meetings for the Heathens. There were only three weeks of the 1990 season left, and nobody was looking forward to the end of it more than Colin Pratt was. For the last two years he had spent the winter months carefully forming a potentially successful team, only to watch helplessly as one by one his riders were struck down by injury. The only redeeming feature of the shambles was that even though Pratt had been forced to use the same guests many times over, and the Cradley fans were seeing the same riders week in and week out, they had stayed with him and support had not dropped significantly.

Such were the averages of Cross and Pedersen that no less than the World Champion Per Jonsson lined up with the Heathens, alongside third-placed man Todd Wiltshire and Peter Ravn when Cradley played host to Bradford. All three gave a good account of themselves as the Heathens won the match by 6 points. Although Handberg was at his best, top-scoring with 13 points, it was Mark Robinson who got the biggest cheer of the night when he beat England international Gary Havelock in heat 4.

Tommy Knudsen made his return to Dudley Wood with Coventry in Cradley's next match, and although he seemed a little rusty he gave the Bees the inspiration to come out on top 49-41. The remaining Heathens – Handberg, Grahame, Hancock and Robinson – were beginning to look demoralised, and whereas Hancock had been Cradley's inspiration twelve months ago, he was certainly not in any condition to be so this year as he struggled along, far from physically fit. Cradley lost by only 4 points at King's Lynn, thanks to a magnificent performance from guest Marvyn Cox, who was given staunch support by Alan Grahame, but the result saw the two teams exchange places in the League and the Heathens were now rock bottom.

Two nights later, Hamill returned to score 10 points as Cradley pulled off a surprise win at Swindon. Kelly Moran put in one of his better guest performances, and Wolves' Ronnie Correy showed that he had more scruples than some of his colleagues, as he fought for every one of his 10 points. Handberg was once again the star of the night, riding at his peak and scoring 16 points. He had another fine night at Bradford, but his 12 points, despite an engine failure, were not enough to save Cradley from a 10-point defeat.

1990 programme.

Jonsson proved once more to be a reliable guest, along with Jeremy Doncaster, as the Heathens beat visitors King's Lynn, and when the World Champion beat Dennis Lofqvist for the bonus point, the teams' positions were once more reversed and Cradley hauled themselves above the Stars in the League table. In their last League match of the season at Dudley Wood, 36-year-old Alan Grahame rolled back the years and defied the rain to put on a vintage performance and score a faultless 15-point maximum against Swindon to lead the Heathens to a 6-point win.

The curtain came down at Dudley Wood on the last night of October, when the Heathens faced Wolverhampton in a challenge match. It turned out to be the usual thrilling all-out war, but early on it looked as though Cradley were about to storm their deadly rivals, until Ermolenko staged a mini-comeback, winning three races in succession. Cradley fought back through Handberg, Grahame, Hamill and guest Tatum, and won the match 50-40. In the last race, Ermolenko slid to the floor, to great applause, and when he picked himself up and continued the race with a succession of wheelies, he was greeted with cheers and jeers alike. It was one of those lighter notes that had been few and far between in a season of hell for the Heathens. They finally finished above Coventry and King's Lynn in the League, seventh out of nine teams. The year belonged to Reading, who had won the League Championship and the KO Cup and boasted the World Champion Per Jonsson.

Hans Nielsen had again topped the BL Riders averages for the sixth successive season, but although he was still the most consistent rider in the BL, his dominance of the sport seemed to be on the wane. But just in case anyone thought that he was about to become easy pickings, he finished off the year by winning the British League Riders Championship. He had also written himself into the Cradley match programme again by setting a new track record of 60.7 seconds in the Golden Hammer.

Pedersen had been right behind him in the averages with 9.25 points at the time of his accident, and remained so until the end of the season. It had been a season of heartbreak for Janno. He did everything right and was on the crest of a wave on the eve of the World Championship, looking a good bet to take Nielsen's crown.

On the other hand, nobody would have put money on Simon Cross not taking the title. It looked as though it was going to be Crossy's year. He was riding better than ever, and had beaten Nielsen probably more times than any other rider during the season. At the time of his accident, he was arguably the best rider in the world. He was England's star in the Test series against the Danes, before a season that promised so much for him ended in disaster one night in West Germany, and now his career hung in the balance. Simon finished fourth in the BL averages with just over 9 points.

Billy Hamill had been a success. He had finished third in the Heathens averages with 6.82 points, and would have undoubtedly done much better, but for his dodgy knee. The confidence and ability that he displayed for one so young earmarked him as a star of the future.

Alan Grahame averaged 6.39 points per match, and on the odd occasion he rode as well as he had ever done in his career. He had bought a motorcycle shop in Birmingham during the season and was planning to build up his business in the winter before continuing his career in the National League, but he didn't seem so sure of his speedway plans following his 15-point maximum against Swindon. Alan was again Cradley's only 'ever-present' during 1990.

Gert Handberg showed what he could really do when he wasn't blowing up engines. After an early injury, his confidence slumped and, at one time, Pratt was pointing the finger at him as a possible candidate for replacement, but the end of the season saw the best of Handberg, when he frequently top-scored for makeshift Cradley outfits. But for a slow start, Gert's 6.13-point average would have been greatly improved.

Greg Hancock started the season as he finished the previous one, and looked as though he would finish the year amongst the top scorers, but it was not to be. He was a Heathen through and through, and returned to the sport after injury, prematurely, to make up the numbers. It proved to be an unwise move on Greg's part, and he struggled, as his average fell to 5.51 points. Mark Robinson had his share of niggling injuries, but his effort was never at fault. His wins over Matousek at Coventry and Havelock at Cradley brought the crowd to their feet. Mark averaged 2.56 points.

Erik Gundersen had failed to find a niche at Cradley. He began the season by being present at every match that it was possible for him to attend. He played landlord to Hancock and Hamill all though the season, and the help and encouragement that he gave to both would stand them in good stead for the rest of their careers, but Erik was not present at many of the later matches. He was still treated like a king on his visits to Dudley Wood, and rightly so as the man was a living legend, but he took much more of a 'low key' role in the sport than many expected him to. Perhaps Erik was not a very good spectator, or perhaps the devastation of the team got to him, but at the end of the 'season from hell', one got the feeling that Dudley Wood would not see much more of Erik Gundersen.

15

JANNO GETS HIS JUST REWARD
1991

The 1991 season marked a milestone in British speedway, as the amalgamation of the British League and the National League took place to form the Sunbrite League Divisions One and Two. The existing teams from the old British League welcomed Wimbledon, Berwick, Ipswich and Poole to their ranks, and the top and bottom teams were to be promoted and relegated respectively. The points limit for the new league was set at 40 points and master of the numbers game Colin Pratt was obliged to build the 1991 Heathens within that limit. His task was made easier by the fact that Simon Cross would not be competing in '91 as he was still recovering from the back injuries that almost ended his career. Pedersen had spent the winter nursing his broken arm and, after declaring himself fit, he became the first squad member to sign as early as February. Janno was raring to go. He had missed out in the last two World Finals and fancied his chances this season.

Pratt set about building his team around last year's top five. This gave him a total of 34.10 points, leaving 5.9 points for the two reserves. Enter 18-year-old Scott Smith, a self-employed jeweller from Sheffield. The ex-Sheffield team mascot had spent over £3,000 in the winter getting his bikes in shape and certainly seemed keen enough. Loanee Wayne Garratt was recalled from Division Two side Arena Essex, and along with Hamill, Hancock, Grahame and Handberg, joined Pedersen to form what looked to be a strong team that could possibly challenge for the League Championship that year. Billy Hamill gave an early indication of things to come when he qualified for the Overseas Final by finishing fourth in the American Final at the beginning of March. Greg Hancock was, however, not so fortunate, crashing out in the same round, Rick Miller being the eventual winner.

Practice day at Dudley Wood was rained off and Pedersen, showing his enthusiasm for the oncoming campaign, flew off to Austria for four days' practice. He returned and asked Colin to make him the Heathens' captain for the 1991 season.

Dudley Wood opened its doors on Wednesday 20 March, the opening fixture being a challenge match against Swindon. The Robins were without Leigh Adams, but even taking that into account, the Heathens looked a formidable outfit. Pedersen led the Cradley scorechart with paid 13 points, Hamill paid 12 (he fell in his last race), Handberg 11, Hancock 8, Grahame 6, Garratt 6 and Scott Smith 3.

Before the League competition could take place there was the matter of the Gold Cup to contest. Cradley were placed in the Northern section and played hosts to reigning champions Bradford in their next match. The champions were slaughtered 59-31 as Handberg led the field with paid 14 and Pedersen, Grahame and Hamill all scored 10. Pratt looked as though he had made a shrewd signing in young Wayne Garratt as he again shone, scoring 7 points. The following Saturday, Poole ran the Heathens close at Dudley Wood, losing by only 4 points in a challenge match.

Bank Holiday Monday morning saw Cradley in Gold Cup action against Coventry. Greg Hancock had been injured in Germany the previous day, when he had sustained a badly bruised shin. Mark Robinson, who had been left out of the team when Garratt had been signed, took his place. As if to prove a point, Mark had an excellent meeting, scoring paid 9 points, and with Janno recording his first 15-point maximum, the Bees were eclipsed 48-42. That evening saw the return leg at Brandon, the Heathens' first away match. The scores were reversed as Robinson failed to score and Pedersen could only muster 8 points. Billy Hamill came to the rescue with 14 points but failed to beat evergreen Tommy Knudsen in the run-off for the bonus point.

Have bike, must travel, and on 12 April Cradley had a fair bit of travelling to do – all the way up to Berwick in fact. It was a long way to go for a Gold Cup match that was to be rained off after only 4 heats. The next night, the Black Country boys were back at

Cradley Heath, 1991. From left to right: Gert Handberg, Billy Hamill, Greg Hancock, Jan O. Pedersen, Wayne Garratt, Alan Grahame, Colin Pratt (manager). Kneeling: Scott Smith, Mark Robinson. (Hall)

Dudley Wood to face local rivals Wolverhampton in another cup match. The Wolves were yet to win a match in the competition, but they were a good team on paper and were being led by Sam Ermolenko, who was showing some vintage form. With Hancock back in the side, the Cradley supporters looked forward to hammering the old enemy, but it was not to be. Janno and Billy scored 11 and 10 points respectively but the rest of the boys had a poor night and the Heathens went down by 8 points, the difference being that the Wolves reserves scored paid 16 points whilst Cradley's mustered only 3.

Wayne Garratt had not been able to maintain his early form and Scott Smith was finding the pace a little too hot. Garratt was a classy rider who could really look the business, but he was not into contact sports and when his opponents closed up on him, he was easy to move over. Smithy, on the other hand, was a 'fire and brimstone' rider, all too keen to take a chance, but his lack of experience was telling in these early days.

A pattern was emerging: Pedersen, as expected, usually top-scored for Cradley and more often than not Billy Hamill was up there with him. The American seemed set to have a fine season. Grahame and Hancock were inconsistent, as was Handberg, and these three seemed to hold the key to the success the Heathens would achieve in 1991.

The following Saturday, Belle Vue visited Dudley Wood and lost by 6 points in a cup match marked by an amazing incident. In heat 4, Wayne Garratt was leading the Aces' Neil Collins when the Belle Vue man ran into him when trying to overtake. Both men

Mark Robinson and Jan O. Pedersen. (Hall)

Alan Grahame, Greg Hancock, Simon Cross. (Hall)

were brought down and Collins was first on his feet, He ran over to the felled Cradley rider who was about to get to his feet when Collins appeared to push him. This type of behaviour was not uncommon to Neil, but he was about to receive his comeuppance, as Wayne punched him to the ground, jumped on top of him and repeatedly rained blows upon him until track staff pulled him off his stricken victim. The referee immediately imposed a £50 fine on Garratt, and the young Heathen responded by producing his best performance so far with 9 points. The incident was far from over, however, and Wayne was reported to the Speedway Control Board.

One week later, Oxford visited Cradley, but with their main man Hans Nielsen away on the Continent and Billy Hamill on duty in the USA, the fixture was a challenge match, which Cradley easily won. Two away matches at Bradford and Wolverhampton saw the Heathens lose cup points despite spirited performances from Hamill and Pedersen.

Sunday 5 May saw Dudley Wood stage a British Semi-final and, although not riding at his best in the team, Alan Grahame was aided by Eric Gundersen in the pits and the Dane inspired Big Al to finish as runner-up to Poole's Steve Schofield. The 8th was a milestone in the club's history – the Eric Gundersen farewell meeting. Eric was leaving England for his native Denmark, but he wanted to say goodbye to his hundreds of fans in his own way – on the track. The meeting was a three-team event between Cradley, Wolves and Coventry, which Cradley won, but that was almost insignificant as thousands turned out to pay homage to one of speedway's legends.

Jan O. Pedersen – World Champion. (Hall)

Before racing took place, an expectant crowd watched the pit gate when *Simply the Best* began to filter over the public address system, and suddenly there he was in his white leathers, sitting unaided on a speedway bike. Gingerly he rolled down the ramp onto the track and the stadium went ballistic. The man who had been one of the fastest that the sport had ever seen coasted slowly around the track like a child on his first bike ride without stabilisers. He waved to the crowd and every time he let go of the handlebars to do so his bike wobbled and our hearts leapt to our mouths. But this was Eric – just as brave now as when he took chance after chance to score hundreds of points for Cradley over the years.

He did two emotion-packed laps with the other Heathens riding a respectful distance behind him, and by the time he finished, there was not a dry eye in the house. And then he was gone. Gone, but not forgotten. Never ever forgotten.

Cradley continued their Gold Cup campaign, winning at Belle Vue and losing at Ipswich, and mid-month, Alan Grahame tumbled out of the World Final competition by scoring only 4 points in the British Final won by Bradford's Gary Havelock. Pedersen made no mistakes, however, becoming Danish Champion. Tommy Knudsen and Hans Nielsen chased him home, and Gert Handberg qualified for the next round in fifth place.

Big Al returned to his best form in a Gold Cup match at Dudley Wood with a paid maximum as the Heathens hit top form and Berwick were crushed 59-31. It was a fine all-round performance, but Scottie Smith stole the show in heat 11 when he held off Kelvin Tatum for four laps to follow Billy home for a 5-1.

Cradley began their League campaign on 18 May and they maintained their good form, thrashing Wimbledon at Dudley Wood 53-37. Pedersen, Hamill, Grahame and Hancock all gave impressive performances. One week later at home, the Heathens faced Ipswich in the KO Cup. Billy Hamill was absent, having been injured a few days before in Sweden, but the team never faltered and 8 points from Wayne Garratt helped them to a 50-39 win. The following Monday morning, still at home and still without Hamill, Cradley got off to a bad start against Swindon in the League, losing Garratt in heat 2 when he fell and injured his wrist ligaments, but they would not be denied and double-figure scores from Pedersen, Hancock, Grahame and Handberg helped the boys to a 52-37 win. The same night at Blunsdon, without Hamill and Garratt, Cradley inflicted the second defeat of the day on the Robins and won by 2 points.

June opened with a home League match against King's Lynn. Hamill was still out, but Garratt decided to give it a go but withdrew after one race. Cradley's top four were on fire, however, and the Stars found themselves on the end of a 57-32 defeat.

The next couple of weeks saw a decline in Alan Grahame's form and it showed in the results. Even though Hamill had returned, a 3-point League defeat at Reading was followed by a visit to Berwick, where a 10-point defeat finished off the Heathens' Gold Cup aspirations. However, their League form was good, and continued to be so when, two weeks later, Cradley were back at Berwick where they took further points at Berrington Lough, inflicting the northern team's first home defeat by 6 points and establishing themselves at the top of the League table.

Speedway was rocked in June as premier stadium Wimbledon closed its doors to the sport. The best solution anyone could come up with was to move the Dons to Arlington and so Wimbledon continued their season riding at Eastbourne.

Cradley continued the month contesting the HEAT four-team tournament, winning the qualifying rounds against Wolves, Belle Vue and Bradford, and losing to Ipswich in the final. It was also World Championship time again and in the Overseas Final at Odsal, Billy Hamill clinched second place behind Kelvin Tatum after a run-off with red-hot Sam Ermolenko, proving that the young American had developed into a truly world-class rider. In the Nordic Final, Janno too was runner-up, this time to Hans Nielsen, and Gert

1991 programme.

sneaked through to the next round in seventh place. The next stage was to be two semi-finals – one at Rovno, Russia, and the second one at Abensberg, Germany. Billy drew the short straw and was drawn at Rovno, whilst the other two Heathens were Germany-bound.

The end of the month saw Cradley thrash Reading at the Wood, with only the reserves failing to impress. Smithy looked in a different class to anyone else in the reserve league where he remained virtually unbeaten, led the averages, and had captained the Cradley Juniors to the top of that league, but apart from the odd performance when he would put the fear of God into some very accomplished opponents, he struggled. Wayne Garratt was a different kettle of fish. He had the ability – no doubt about it. It was very frustrating when he put on performances that belittled his obvious talent. However, the points acquired at Reading's expense found the Heathens 6 points clear of Ipswich and Wolverhampton.

July began with a home fixture in the BSPA Cup when Belle Vue were dispatched with ease. After the match, a lonely rider was to be seen speeding around the Dudley Wood circuit – Simon Cross was back in the saddle. Not such good news for Wayne Garratt though. He was summoned by the Speedway Control Board about the Collins affair, fined £900 and suspended for the rest of the season. The severity of the sentence shocked speedway and an incident that had got out of hand had taken Wayne's livelihood away from him for the next few months.

Cradley recalled Mark Robinson and continued their quest for the title at home against Oxford. Janno was missing with a viral infection, but despite a brilliant display from Cheetahs skipper Hans Nielsen, who dropped his only point in six rides to Hamill, the Heathens still won by 6 points. Wolverhampton were proving to be Cradley's main League rivals that year and had yet to be beaten in the League. That was until they came to Dudley Wood on 13 July and were trounced in a match that saw young Mark Robinson score paid 8 points. Sam Ermolenko was the star of the night, however, winning five races and dropping his only points when he fell in heat 9.

He made no such mistake at Cradley's next meeting, when he won the prestigious Golden Hammer from Handberg, Pedersen and Billy Hamill. Although Janno could only manage third place in the Hammer, he managed first place in the World Pairs final as he and Hans Nielsen carved up the opposition, with 14 points apiece, to take the Championship. Another world final was Janno's next target – the World Longtrack final. He finished third in that, but his involvement meant that he would miss the next two matches for Cradley.

Although Hancock, Hamill and Handberg battled gamely without him, the Heathens lost the League points at Belle Vue. Colin Pratt had been in this position before, when the League title had been within Cradley's grasp only to be lost at the end of the season, but this year he was determined to hold on to the leadership until the bitter end. He inspired his team to a 10-point win against Berwick at Dudley Wood the next night, with Grahame and Robinson responding with gritty performances.

The following Monday night looked a tough prospect – Wolves at Monmore Green. On a hot summer night, in front of the biggest crowd of the season, in an explosive atmosphere, this top-of-the-table clash was a cracker. Pedersen's Monmore bogey

struck again when he broke his nose in his third outing and retired from the meeting. Although Cradley were up against it, Hamill and Hancock led a spirited fight, but in the end the match was conceded by 3 points and Wolverhampton replaced Cradley Heath at the top of the League table – a bitter pill indeed for the Heathens to swallow.

A lacklustre performance without Pedersen at Poole saw the boys make an early exit from the BSPA Cup, but the first match in August saw them at their best, taking the points at Cowley where they beat Oxford 47-43 to keep the pressure on Wolves.

It was World Championship time again and Billy Hamill flew off to win the Russian Semi-final and book himself a place in his first World Final. In Germany, Janno finished behind Hans Nielsen and qualified comfortably, but poor old Gert Handberg missed out by just 1 point. At least Cradley would have two representatives in the Final.

The Heathens won their next two home League matches against Ipswich and Belle Vue and, as they did, Wayne Garratt received a letter from the Speedway Control Board informing him that he had been reprieved, so back in he came at Robinson's expense. So, what about Simon Cross? Well, he had got fed up with hanging about and had signed for Second Division Middlesbrough, and on 15 August he made his debut, scoring a creditable paid 10 points. Three days later he was back at Dudley Wood, riding in his own testimonial. This was never expected, but he was found a place, however – riding for the Swedish Select. Simon once again impressed, scoring 9 points.

The end of August meant Bank Holiday Monday, and Bank Holiday Monday meant the Dudley/Wolves Trophy, the most bitterly contested trophy in speedway. Ermolenko was out with a cracked knee: could Wolverhampton possibly regain the trophy without him? Not a bloody chance! Cradley slaughtered them on the morning and slaughtered them again in the evening to retain the trophy. Life was sweet.

A nightmare League match at Poole ended the month. Smith fell and brought down Grahame, Hamill fell and was excluded and so did Garratt. Even so the Heathens forced the Pirates to a last-heat decider, only to lose by 3 points and still trail the Wolves in the League table with two matches in hand. At this stage of the season, Pedersen led the Heathens' averages with 10.27 (he was third in the League averages behind Ermolenko and Nielsen) and the others were as follows: Hamill 9.29, Hancock 8.47, Handberg 8.33, Grahame 7.3, Robinson 4.46, Smith 2.87, Garratt 1.91.

On 31 August 1991, Jan O. Pedersen took his rightful place in the history books by becoming the World Speedway Champion. Never the best gater in the world, he produced five perfect starts to take the title with a 15-point maximum. At his best, Janno was the best – maybe the best of all time. What he could do on a speedway bike was breathtaking. There was nobody, but nobody, who could withstand his persistent assault when he was on song. Janno joined Cradley's elite and deservedly became their third World Champion. He made his comeback to England two days later at Reading for a KO Cup semi-final match, but was unable to ride due to a stomach complaint. He managed a lap of honour before the track doctor sent him home. Without him, Cradley's American dynamic duo took the reins and held the Racers to a mere 3-point win to bring to Dudley Wood five days later. Before the return leg got under way, a now-fit Pedersen received a rapturous welcome home and the Heathens moved into their tenth KO Cup final with an easy 11-point win. Pedersen was beset by machine problems all night, and Hancock stole the thunder with a superb 15-point maximum.

Janno added a third World Championship to his collection that year by scoring a 15-point maximum and leading Denmark to a win in the World Team Cup final. What a year it had been for him, but it was not over yet. We all wanted him to lead Cradley to victory in the KO Cup final and the Sunbrite League Championship.

A victory against Poole at Dudley Wood kept the pressure on but, in the last match

of the month, a draw at King's Lynn robbed the Heathens of a vital point, Bradford crept into second place, and it all started to go wrong. It was déjà vu for Colin Pratt as news came through from Denmark that Gert Handberg had injured his knee and was out for the rest of the season. He was replaced by junior Antony Boyd at Ipswich, and when Hamill crashed and withdrew, Pedersen with 13 points was the only Heathen to score more than 6, and the championship was beginning to look beyond their reach.

Crossy, meanwhile, had broken his collarbone, but even so Pratt recalled him into the squad and, after fifteen months, Simon lined up at Dudley Wood to help the Heathens take on second-placed

Simon Cross's testimonial programme.

Bradford. Poor gating only allowed him 6 points, but Cradley's top three all scored double figures and the match was won 49-41, so a glimmer of hope still remained.

Three days later at Bradford, an upset looked on the cards as Cradley stormed into an early 12-point lead, but an uncharacteristically bad score by Hancock and, once again, poor reserves' scores allowed the Dukes to claw back the points to win the match 49-41. Pedersen beat Gary Havelock for the bonus point. Wolves, meanwhile, had completed their League programme with only three defeats in total. The League Championship was lost, Pratt had once again been denied, and at best Cradley were looking at the runners-up position and that meant winning their last three matches.

On 16 October, a jaded Heathens side beat Coventry at Dudley Wood 48-42, but two nights later, a 49-41 loss at Eastbourne saw their runners-up spot in jeopardy. However, there was still the matter of the KO Cup final to deal with against the team that had become the thorn in Cradley's side in the '91 season – Bradford. The following night saw the first leg take place at Odsal. Hancock, once again showing his dislike of the circuit, could only muster 4 points, and with Cross having three engine failures and failing to score, Cradley yielded 10 points in that first leg.

The end of the season was lunacy – three matches in as many days. There was a meaningless challenge match lost at Belle Vue, a lost League match at Coventry, which saw the Heathens finish in third place in the League, and the KO Cup final as the last meeting of the season on 27 October at Dudley Wood. A dull Sunday afternoon was an unlikely setting for the match, but it typified the Heathens' performance. Pedersen, Hamill and Hancock rode well, but lacked support. Bradford wanted it more and consistently outgated the Heathens to win the match by 4 points and lift the KO Cup. It was a disappointing end to the season. Colin Pratt was left wondering if he would ever win the League Championship and to ponder how much Handberg's injury had cost Cradley. Cross, to his credit, answered the call but was far from fit, and was unable to do anything like his best. Grahame, after some vintage performances, had finished the season with a whimper, and Garratt had been a disappointment. Smith tried his hardest, and although his scores were poor, he would surely come good in the future.

Hamill and Hancock had become world-class riders in 1991 – possibly the hottest prospects in speedway. Both represented their country on a regular basis and both had established themselves as the future of American speedway. Jan O. Pedersen had a wonderful year on a personal level, winning three world titles. It had only been what the most exciting rider in the world had deserved. Who would have thought that Gert Handberg would have had such a bearing on the 1991 season? He finished fourth in the Heathens averages, but undoubtedly his injuries cost the Heathens dearly. When he sustained them, Cradley had eight matches left and were still in with a chance of the League Championship and the KO Cup. As it happens, without him, they won neither.

16

NO RESPITE FROM INJURIES
1992

The proposed relegation and promotion of last year came, as expected, to nothing, and the only change League-wise was that Berwick decided to move down to Division Two whilst Arena Essex joined the teams in Division One. Billy Hamill had spent part of the winter playing ice-hockey for the Los Angeles Sabres, and Simon Cross had a successful winter riding in Australia. Before signing for their British clubs, most of the top riders were signing for overseas clubs in Denmark, Sweden and especially Poland where speedway was the biggest spectator sport in the country, some matches boasting attendances of 15,000 spectators. Cradley's top five from 1991 were amongst these.

The shape of the 1992 squad was rarely in doubt, although supremo Colin Pratt, back for his ninth season at Dudley Wood, took his traditional 'vow of silence' during the close season. The points limit for 1992 was set at 47 points, and Pratt was accused by his fellow promoters of 'playing the numbers game' by getting Cross in the team with a 6-point average, following his short spell with Second Division Middlesbrough. Colin knew he was within the rules, he had spent the last ten years manipulating numbers prior to the opening of a new season, so his peers' objections fell on deaf ears.

The top four – Pedersen, Hancock, Hamill and Handberg – were reinstated, and Crossy was signed as captain, and things were looking decidedly dodgy for Cradley stalwart Alan Grahame. A move to Second Division Long Eaton seemed to be on the cards. Big Al was philosophical about the situation, no doubt thinking that, at his age, there would be some easy pickings in the lower division. In the event Grahame, after an incredible fourteen years as a Heathen, joined Stoke Potters. Pratt decided to stick with Scott Smith, and Mark Robinson was signed again, and with young Justin Walker just waiting for a chance, Wayne Garratt found himself first out in the cold and then in the Newcastle Diamonds team, also in Division Two.

The eve of the season saw the Cradley manager locked in a battle with Pedersen over finances. As new World Champion, Janno argued that he was worth a lot more money, and he probably was, but Pratt countered that the club could not afford to meet the Dane's demands and stuck to his guns. As Britain slumped into recession and the impending season grew closer, it became a war of nerves, neither man giving an inch. Pedersen claimed that he could make a living riding on the Continent, but, virtually as the tapes went up on the first match, Janno, maybe influenced by the fact that it was his testimonial year at Cradley, signed on the dotted line and Pratt completed a fearsome looking line-up.

On 21 March, the gates at Dudley Wood opened on another season of speedway at Cradley Heath. Miserable weather saw a miserable Heathens side lose a challenge match to Reading by 2 points. Hancock and Hamill were quickly back in the groove, both giving brilliant performances, but the others were a very mediocre bunch, Pedersen, for all his demands, managing only 5 points. In the return leg the following night, he showed somewhat better form, scoring 10 points, but once again young Hancock was the team's top scorer. Cradley again lost, only by 3 points, but the star of the two matches was undoubtedly Reading's flying Swede, Per Jonsson. Janno quickly answered his critics with a blistering 15-point maximum at Swindon, where the Heathens won a further challenge match by 4 points.

Cradley's Gold Cup campaign began in the first week of April at Dudley Wood, when not even a vintage 17-point performance by 'the Professor' Hans Nielsen could save Oxford from a 10-point defeat. Top-scoring Pedersen was the only Heathen to beat him.

The following Friday they visited Belle Vue, and the Aces fell victim to a fabulous Cradley team effort. Pedersen rattled off his second 15-point maximum, and for a change, Cradley's advantage was at reserve, Smith and Robinson scoring 4 and paid 7 points respectively. The return Gold Cup match the following night at Dudley Wood saw Janno notch up yet another five-ride maximum, and he was already looking a good bet to retain his World Title. Crossy, improving with every match, dropped only 1 point to the opposition, as did Hancock and Hamill, and Gert did his bit with paid 9 points. Cradley won the match 58-32.

Two nights later saw the Heathens' first visit of 1992 to Monmore Green in the Gold Cup. In the first race, Charlie Ermolenko clipped the back wheel of Simon Cross' bike, sending the Heathen crashing into the barrier and demolishing 30 yards of safety fence. Cross was rushed to hospital and, on a diabolical track, Cradley battled valiantly, but Wolverhampton's Americans, Sam Ermolenko and Ronnie Correy, led the Wolves to a 4-point victory. Cradley's Americans, Hamill and Hancock, were just as impressive and rode brilliantly for the Heathens, but Pedersen once again showed his lack of enthusiasm for these competitive matches at Monmore, scoring only 7 points.

Cross was back at Dudley Wood for Cradley's first League match against Eastbourne, but, some five nights after his crash, was still complaining of headaches. He still managed to score paid 9 points, but the star of the night was World Champion Jan O. Pedersen, who helped himself to another 15-point maximum. Billy Hamill had an unhappy night, with machine problems and also a last-ride crash, especially as mentor Bruce Penhall was beside him and team-mate Hancock in the pits. Bruce, as always, was a tremendously popular visitor to Cradley, always taking time to mingle with his many fans. Such was the case for most ex-Heathens. A couple of years later, I was speaking to Roy Trigg who was here on holiday from his home in New Zealand. Roy, a particularly modest man, could not believe that anyone could even remember him, let alone give him the reception that they did during his visit to Dudley Wood.

Maximums from Pedersen, Handberg and Cross were the order of the day, as King's Lynn were trounced at Cradley, with the Heathens racing to their third League win,

Cradley Heath, 1992. From left to right: Gert Handberg, Andy Grahame, Billy Hamill, Simon Cross, Scott Smith, Andy Phillips, Greg Hancock. (Hall)

and they were at it again the next night when they came away from Arena Essex with the points.

In the middle of the month, Cross rode in the British Quarter-final at Exeter, and had scored 10 points from four rides when a crash involving Andy Galvin held up the meeting. With repairs to the safety fence taking place, the 10 p.m. curfew was reached with no further racing taking place, and a decision was reached by the SCB that the meeting would have to be re-run. Back at Dudley Wood on Monday morning, 24 April, however, Cradley's Gold Cup campaign suffered a blow when visitors Coventry stole the match. It was an awful match for the Heathens as Pedersen and an on-form Scott Smith suffered engine failures and Gert Handberg fell in one race, but, worst of all, Simon Cross fell in his second outing, and was back in Russells Hall Hospital with a cracked kneecap. The evening return match saw the Bees complete the double by only 6 points. Although Pedersen, Hamill and Hancock never gave up, you can't replace a rider like Simon Cross with junior Anthony Boyd and get away with it.

On the other hand, things were going well for another Cradley rider. Scott Smith, now known as 'Scud', was the surprise winner of the British Under-21 final at Long Eaton, with Mark Loram and Joe Screen taking second and third places.

Without Crossy, Cradley began the KO Cup competition, and maximum men Pedersen, Hamill and Hancock thrashed Poole Pirates at Dudley Wood. Smithy celebrated his victory with a fighting paid 9 points. The next day, Sunday 26 April, saw the Jan Pedersen Testimonial Meeting, a pairs event won by Ermolenko and Correy from Hamill and Hancock.

The following day saw Cross take matters into his own hands, defy doctors, remove his plaster, compete in the British Quarter-final re-run at Exeter – and win the bloody thing with a 15-point maximum! However, the Semi-final was only six days later, albeit at Dudley Wood, and Simon fell in his first race, aggravated his injured knee, and was forced to withdraw from the meeting and the World Championship competition.

Two engine failures by Hamill when leading possibly cost Cradley the match at Bradford, and also ended any ambitions they might have had in the Gold Cup. Pedersen began May with a win in the Danish Gold Bar Meeting, but that was to be his final success of the season. In a meeting in Viborg, Denmark, he fell and became the third Cradley rider to break his back in as many years. His season was over, and with it, the defence of his World Championship, and maybe his career. It was an awful blow for the Heathens, although they did not have a match until the 23 May, but with Mark Robinson also injured in a rained-off match some two weeks earlier, they had no time to regroup. As Colin Pratt put it, 'You can't replace the World Champion.'

Greg Hancock was also experiencing difficulties with his World Championship campaign. The AMA had decided not to run an American round of the Championship and instead nominated five riders to ride in the Overseas Final – Ermolenko, Correy, Hamill, Rick Miller and Mike Faria – no Greg. It was a ludicrous decision, and one that cost the AMA a lot of credibility in speedway circles. Bruce Penhall even offered to stage and pay for an American round, but the decision stood and Hancock was out. One could only hope that this instance would be remembered when he was riding his heart out with great success for his country. Scott Smith found the pace a bit too much

The spectacular Scott Smith. (Hipkiss)

in the Under-21 World Championship, where he managed only 6 points, Joe Screen taking the title.

Using rider replacement and Anthony Boyd, Cradley lost in the Gold Cup at home to Wolverhampton, Hamill and Hancock bearing the brunt, and Cross still not fully fit. At this point, the Heathens headed the League table and the Juniors were also top of the Junior League, courtesy of Justin Walker, but, unless a good replacement was found for Janno, there was only one direction in which Cradley was going to go. However, a further League victory against Poole at Dudley Wood kept them up there.

The first match of June saw the Heathens move through to the next round of the KO Cup on aggregate by conceding 8 points at Poole, but Cross was again taken to hospital when he fell in his second outing and sustained concussion. Certain Cradley riders, Hamill and Hancock included, are known for fighting harder when the chips are down, and Handberg joined them at Dudley Wood with his finest ever performance for the club, scoring an 18-point maximum to beat Bradford in the Gold Cup.

Handberg's next meeting was the Nordic Final in Norway, won by Sweden's Tony Rickardsson, but Gert did enough to qualify and was on his way to the World Semi-finals. No such luck for Hans Nielsen, however. In the same event that had ended Pedersen's season, Hans had broken a collarbone, and his injuries proved too much for him as he scored only 6 points and went tumbling out of the competition.

While Gert was away, Cradley rode their final Gold Cup meeting at Oxford, but without him, despite brilliant performances from Hancock and Hamill, the Cheetahs moved into second place in the Northern Section, the Heathens being relegated to third.

Cradley next entertained Wolverhampton in the first leg of the Midland Clubcall Trophy. With Handberg yet to return, Robinson still injured, and guest Dean Barker scoring only 5 points, gritty performances from Crossy and the two Yanks were not enough. Wolves refused to be denied and took a 6-point lead into the second leg, courtesy of Ermolenko and Correy.

As if that wasn't bad enough, the Heathens' season then took a real nosedive. Billy Hamill not only crashed out of the World Championship in the Overseas Final, but he also crashed into the fence, breaking his wrist and dislocating his shoulder – approximately six weeks out of action was the estimate. Mark Robinson then announced his retirement.

Gert Handberg returned in time for a League match at Dudley Wood against a

Scott Smith. (Hall)

Andy Grahame. (Hall)

strong Reading outfit. Justin Walker was drafted in at the bottom end of the Cradley team, and a new signing was made in time for the match. Bobby Schwartz had turned up at Eastbourne, which left Andy Grahame out in the cold, so Pratt pounced and signed the Birmingham man. Although now a journeyman and probably past his best, Andy, younger brother of Alan, had on many occasions especially for Oxford ridden like a World Champion at Dudley Wood, beating the best that Cradley had to offer. If he could recapture some of that form, then he would prove to be an inspired signing by Colin. He made his debut with 6 points as the rampant Racers won the match by 5 points. Scott Smith crashed in his first race and he joined the injured list. In the return leg at Smallmead, Mark Meredith was called in for Smithy, but was out of his league. Crossy and Hancock rode splendidly, and Grahame fared a little better, scoring paid 9 points, but what of young Handberg? Gert was involved in a horrific crash in his second outing, broke his jaw and also ended up on the injured list, which now had almost as many riders on it as there were on the teamsheet. Reading, led by the awesome Per Jonsson, took full advantage of the Heathens' plight and inflicted a crushing defeat.

Colin Pratt had never made a secret of his desire to win the League, but his main ambition at that time became to keep as many of his team on their feet and out of hospital. But he never wavered, and swooped to sign 23-year-old ex-Wolves rider Andy Phillips from Poole to join Walker at reserve, and with Pedersen, Hamill and Handberg out, Cradley were allowed a guest facility.

Oxford were the next League visitors to Dudley Wood at the beginning of July and a rampant Greg Hancock beat Hans Nielsen three times. A never-say-die performance from Simon Cross, and 8 useful points from Grahame, saw the Heathens take a 10-point victory. Phillips won his first race and added another point to debut with 4. Smith returned, scoring two paid 3 points. The next night, Cradley were in Scotland to ride against Glasgow in the BSPA Cup, and although Grahame gave his best performance in Heathens colours so far, scoring 11 points, guest Freddie Schott's 4 points let the side down and the result was a 2-point defeat for the injury-ravaged Heathens.

Mid-July saw Greg Hancock at reserve for the USA in the World Pairs Championship. Sam Ermolenko was in devastating form, but team-mate Ronnie Correy was replaced four times by Greg, who only dropped 1 point. Let's hope the AMA appreciated Greg's

Andy Phillips. (Hipkiss)

11 points, winning the title for America! Shortly afterwards, the Golden Hammer rolled around, but it was a poor show by the Cradley riders, Andy Grahame being the best with 9 points. Ermolenko won the event from Per Jonsson.

Gert Handberg made his comeback on 24 July at Arena Essex in a KO Cup match, only to fall in his first outing, aggravate his broken jaw and rejoin Cradley's injured list, and the Heathens found themselves with an 8-point deficit to overcome in the home return. The next night at Dudley Wood saw Cradley blow a 10-point lead and turn it into a 10-point defeat at the hands of Bradford, with Jimmy Nilsen proving to be an unfortunate choice of guest, scoring only 4 points. The Heathens began to slip down the League table. A draw at Monmore in the second leg of the Clubcall Trophy saw the Wolves win the event, but Cradley's ex-Wolves riders, Grahame and Phillips, both did well, scoring 10 points and paid 11 points respectively.

In the last match of July, Handberg made a triumphant return to Dudley Wood to knock Arena out of the KO Cup with a sizzling paid 16 points. He inspired the Heathens to one of their biggest wins of the season, the top four all scoring double figures. This began an incredible couple of weeks for Handberg that saw him win the Champion of Champions Trophy, win the Danish Championship, and score a 15-point maximum to win the German World Championship semi-final from Sam Ermolenko and Tommy Knudsen. However, he came in for a roasting from Colin Pratt in the Heathens' next match at Ipswich. Although they came away with a League point, thanks to the timely return of Billy Hamill, Gert only managed to score 3 points and Pratt was swift to criticise the Dane, along with Smith and Phillips, for their poor displays.

The end of August saw Handberg, much to many people's surprise, take third place in the World Final in Wroclaw, Poland. The Brits at last had something to celebrate, when Gary Havelock kept his head to win the meeting from Per Jonsson and become the first Englishman to win the title since Michael Lee in 1981. However, there was a downside to the occasion. Reigning World Champion Jan O. Pedersen had not even been officially invited to the meeting to hand over the trophy and was bitterly disappointed in the FIM. Pedersen rightly felt like the forgotten man of speedway, and for one yet to decide whether or not to continue in the sport, his omission from the proceedings may have been a deciding factor.

The last Monday in the month was the Bank Holiday – Dudley/Wolves Trophy time. By the time the tapes went up on the morning leg at Dudley Wood, Handberg was still stranded at Dover. However, this was serious stuff – never a meeting for the faint-hearted – and Andy Phillips rode like a champion against his former club to score paid 13 points from five rides and lead Cradley to a 50-38 win. Handberg made it to Monmore for the evening return, but scored only 1 point. But Hamill and Hancock relished their visits to Wolverhampton and liked nothing better to get the better of Sam and Ronnie, and while Greg was marvellous, scoring paid 12 from 15, Billy was even better, grabbing the full 15. There was one wonderful moment in the final heat when Billy was the intended victim of the dreaded Ermolenko/Correy scissors movement. He avoided them, and both Wolves riders crashed into one another, Correy being excluded – wonderful stuff. Anyway, Phillips was once again magic, scoring 10 points, and the Heathens won the match 47-41 to retain the trophy.

The beginning of September found the boys back in League action at Poole, and just as Cradley threatened to upset the Pirates' fine home run, an engine failure by Handberg, whilst leading partner Andy Phillips, sent him crashing into the fence in the penultimate race. Poole sewed up the match in the last heat, when Cox and Schofield led a shaken Handberg and Cross home. Hamill and Hancock managed only 4 points each, and Pratt criticised his riders, saying that they had taken on too many Continental meetings.

The Heathens struggled to beat Coventry in their next home match, and found themselves in ninth place in the League. Old rivals Wolves headed the table, ahead of

Greg Hancock leads Ronnie Correy. (Hipkiss)

Belle Vue. The second-placed team were far too good for the Heathens in their next match at Belle Vue. Led by a fabulous maximum from young whiz-kid Joe Screen, the Aces romped home 55-35, Hancock and Hamill scoring 24 points between them. It didn't help, however, when Handberg crashed in his first race, damaged his ankle and took no further part in the meeting. He was absent from the team the following night at Dudley Wood, but, using rider replacement, Cradley swept to their biggest win of the season, beating a hapless Arena Essex 59-31 in a League match in which only Scott Smith failed to score double figures.

The Heathens had many black days in 1992, but none more so than Sunday 13 September, when Wayne Garratt crashed at Newcastle. He was rushed to the hospital and underwent emergency brain surgery after which he was put on a life-support machine. He fought for his life for the next two weeks before he finally passed away. Cradley had lost another son, and it was a brutal reminder to all speedway fans of the lengths these boys go to to entertain them.

Beginning with the Arena match, Cradley hit a patch of form that took them through the month. Wolverhampton failed at Dudley Wood as Phillips scored his second successive paid 12 points. A weakened Coventry side couldn't hold the Heathens at Brandon, and Cradley won a last-heat decider at Wolverhampton in a typically competitive match, but Cradley were still only in sixth position in the League. Strangely enough, through Cradley's purple patch, Grahame had hit a patch of bad form, scoring only 13 points in his last three matches, but Crossy, Handberg and the Yanks kept the team rolling.

1992 programme.

Jan O. Pedersen's testimonial programme.

America became the World Team Cup Champions in Kumla, Sweden, led by Ermolenko with 10 points, but he wouldn't have done it without the help of Greg and Billy, who scored 11 and 10 points respectively. The USA also white-washed England 3-0 in a Test match series that saw the Cradley duo score heavily. Simon Cross was rewarded for his determined riding with an England recall in the final match and scored 8 points.

The Heathens began October with a disastrous match at Reading in the KO Cup, losing 55-35, Hancock scoring almost half of the team's total points. Pratt stormed out of Smallmead calling his team's performance 'pathetic'. A couple of nights later at Cowley, after a few well-chosen words by Colin, the Heathens picked up the pace to share the points at Oxford. Although probably past his best, Nielsen was still a mighty force to be reckoned with, as demonstrated by the fact that he still led the League averages alongside Sam Ermolenko. Greg was Cradley's best, lying in tenth place. He represented the Heathens in the British League Riders Championship but scored only 4 points in the event, which was won by young Joe Screen from Per Jonsson and World Champion Gary Havelock. The next night, Cradley hit the depths against a determined Poole side at Dudley Wood, Hancock being the only rider to score more than 7 points. The 51-39 win kept the Pirates in the League title race, and put the Heathens right out of it.

One week later, after some more verbals from Pratt, they easily beat Ipswich at Dudley Wood and beat Eastbourne at Arlington 55-35! As so often happens, Andy Grahame returned to his old track and scored his only maximum of the season. A visit to Bradford was a different matter, however, as only Hancock performed and the Heathens lost 52-38. The third week in October saw Cradley with a mountain to climb in their KO Cup semi-final return at Dudley Wood against Reading. In a match that saw Phillips and Smithy in nasty crashes, Andy Grahame ended the season one week early with a broken collarbone. However, Reading were focused and, not only did they move into the final, but they won the match by 1 point.

Justin Walker deputised for Andy in Cradley's last home League match against a disappointing Belle Vue. Justin had just won the Division One Reserve Riders Championship at Poole, but he managed only 1 point in the Heathens' 52-38 win. The

Heathens won their last League match at King Lynn, led by a super 14 points from skipper Simon Cross, but it was all a bit too late and Cradley finished the season in fourth place, just above Wolverhampton. Reading, Bradford and Poole occupied the first three places.

A disappointing season came to a disappointing end on 31 October, when Wolves won the last meeting of 1992 at Dudley Wood. Hamill, Hancock and Smith tried hard in this challenge fixture, but the rest were a motley crew, and Wolverhampton deserved their 6-point win. All things considered, 1992 was a commendable performance from a team that constantly had to battle against injuries as well as opponents, but it must have been a disappointment for Pratt who knew that, at the beginning of the season, he had the potential League Champions at Dudley Wood.

Jan O. Pedersen ended the season recovered from his operation, but with a question mark over his future in the sport. He made his best-ever start to a season, and was on top form when he was stricken by injury. As World Champion, he lost out on a fortune that would have undoubtedly come his way in the 1992 season, and his disgraceful rebuff by World Championship officials still lingered with him. Janno's official average for the 1992 term was 11.37.

Greg Hancock had a fantastic year. Overshadowed by Hamill the previous year, he reversed the roles in '92 to become the top Heathen following Pedersen's exit, and finished seventh in the League averages with 9.65. He was voted top Heathen by the supporters. Billy Hamill lost a bit of impetus during the year, and although disappointed to have missed out on the World Championship through injury, he showed time and time again what a great speedway talent he is. Billy averaged 8.64.

Simon Cross had a torrid year, so much so that in the last match he hinted at retirement. But, battered and bruised, and still in pain from his dreadful back injury sustained in 1990, Crossy never faltered. He was inspirational when the chips were down (and they were down very frequently in 1992) and he played a true captain's role. Simon averaged 7.91.

Gert Handberg – what an enigma he was. He was the shock of the World Final, taking third place, and at times, for Cradley, he rode like the third-best rider in the world, but not often enough for Colin Pratt, and Gert, on more than one occasion, found himself on the wrong end of a tongue-lashing from the team manager. Gert averaged 7.4.

Andy Grahame had big shoes to fill at Cradley. He arrived as Eastbourne's top-scorer with a new lease of life, but he proved to be a shadow of his former self. Andy averaged 6.33. Scott Smith improved a little on the previous season and he was now British Under-21 Champion, but that was to be the highlight of the season in which he averaged 3.79 points. Andy Phillips was by and large a success, brought in late on with his confidence at a low ebb. He improved steadily and went through a purple patch that saw him up with the top-scorers, but injury caused him to struggle at the end of the season. Andy averaged 4.17 points.

At the end of 1992, many questions were left unanswered. Would Pedersen make a comeback? Would Cross retire? Would Pratt ever win the League? Hancock was the only rider to escape injury in 1992. The others were all missing at some time or other – but poor Wayne Garratt was missing forever.

17

NO RESPITE FROM INJURIES II
1993

The close season was a winter of bitter discontent for, as recession hit Britain, the Speedway Control Board announced new pay rates that most riders found totally unacceptable. Hans Nielsen led the way by announcing that he would not be returning to Britain for the 1993 season, and riders rushed to book their places in the Continental teams in Poland, Sweden and Denmark. Following Hans' announcement, Oxford announced that they were closing, but relented a few weeks later and opted to ride in the Second Division. Nielsen also relented before the start of the season and signed for Coventry.

Jan O. Pedersen announced that he was not yet ready to make a comeback and would sit out the 1993 term. That was a bad enough start for Colin Pratt, but worse was to follow. Billy Hamill had decided that the pay rates in Britain were not worth returning for. He could make enough money riding in America and on the Continent – so count him out. Although they complained, Greg Hancock returned and so did Andy Grahame, and Simon Cross was also persuaded to give it another go. When Oxford had announced their closure, Pratt had moved quickly to sign the promising 21-year-old Dane, Morten Andersen.

As the season approached, it was revealed that this year there were to be eight-man teams and matches would be ridden over eighteen heats. This left room for 39-year-old Alan Grahame to return, as Stoke had folded in the winter. Swindon joined Oxford in the Second Division, which left eleven teams to ride each other four times in the League – no Gold Cup that year.

As D-Day approached, Pratt was told by Wolverhampton that if he wanted Andy Phillips in the Heathens' line-up, then he would have to buy him. Instead, he pencilled in Justin Walker and Anthony Boyd. Scott Smith claimed that the new rates would cut his earnings by fifty per cent and therefore it was not worth riding any more, but Pratt wanted him in the side and found him sponsors. Smithy signed, and Gert Handberg completed the Heathens' 1993 line-up.

On 20 March, Cradley got off to a bad start, losing their home leg of the Clubcall Trophy by 2 points to Wolverhampton. Hancock found his form immediately and Scott Smith was very impressive with paid 9 points, but apart from the other reserve, Anthony Boyd, the other Heathens were disappointing – Andy Grahame 6, Handberg

Cradley Heath, 1993. From left to right: Morton Andersen, Anthony Boyd, Simon Cross, Scott Smith, Gert Handberg, Alan Grahame. Kneeling: Greg Hancock, Andy Grahame. (Hipkiss)

4, Andersen 5, Cross 6 and Alan Grahame 7. A 6-point defeat in the return leg at Monmore was no surprise, and Cradley's lack of a third heat-leader was evident, even at this early stage.

The Heathens' League programme opened on the last Saturday in March when they faced Poole. Although Cradley won the match by 4 points, they looked fragile, and with only Hancock, Cross, and to a lesser extent, Handberg performing, their success that year already seemed as if it would be limited.

In the first match of April at Eastbourne, despite 15 points from Hancock and a battling paid 10 points from Smithy, Cradley were outclassed. In the return at Dudley Wood, the Heathens won by 8 points, but one couldn't see the likelihood of many bonus points in 1993. A defeat at Dudley Wood at the hands of Coventry and a right going-over at Belle Vue saw Pratt hit the roof. Hancock was beyond criticism, scoring a wonderful 17 points at Belle Vue, and young Smithy was riding out of his skin, but the rest came in for it.

Scott won three races in the next match at Dudley Wood, when Cradley narrowly beat Arena Essex. This put him in the team proper, deservedly so, and Alan Grahame found himself alongside the struggling Anthony Boyd at reserve. Hancock was looking in a different class from the rest of the team, which of course he was, and Simon Cross was doing his best to support him. Morten Andersen was proving to be a real racer, but occasionally his inexperience let him down and Gert Handberg was, as always, up and down. It didn't look as though the Grahame brothers were in for a renaissance, and Cradley trundled on. At the end of April, the boys lost heavily at Bradford and after being told by their manager that 'heads would roll', they immediately responded with an away win at Ipswich and an easy home win in the return.

As the World Championship got underway, the Dudley Wood British Semi-final saw Andy Grahame finish third behind Gary Havelock and Andy Smith. In a very creditable fourth place was Colin Pratt's young son Troy, who was making a name for himself at Arena Essex. Simon Cross made an early exit from the competition, scoring only 6 points.

Defeats at Wolverhampton and Arena followed, and while Alan Grahame was getting much better scores at reserve, Smithy was finding the points hard to come by in the number two spot. He also lost his British Under-21 title when he managed only seventh position, as Joe Screen stole the show, followed by Carl Stonehewer.

On 8 May 'No Respite II' began. Despite a stunning 18-point maximum from Greg (who trailed only Ermolenko and Nielsen in the League averages), Cradley lost to Reading at Dudley Wood. However, not only did they lose the match, they lost Alan Grahame with facial injuries and Simon Cross with back and internal injuries, and as the couple lay in adjacent beds at Russells Hall Hospital, they must have wondered how the hell the Heathens would cope in their oncoming fixtures.

Cradley used rider replacement for Crossy, and Justin Walker was brought in for Big Al, but in their next match, a defeat at Poole, Scott Smith found himself in the local

Alan and Andy Grahame. (Hipkiss)

hospital with concussion after a heat 11 crash. However, Scud was made of stern stuff and three nights later he was the talk of Dudley Wood, beating red-hot Swede Henryk Gustafsson twice, as the Heathens beat King's Lynn 57-51. He could not repeat the performance the following night at Saddlebow Road in the return as Greg Hancock took on the Stars virtually on his own and Cradley were thrashed 69-39.

On the World Final front, Andy Grahame crashed out at the British Final stage, but it was better news for Greg, who was nominated as one of the five riders to be seeded through to the Overseas Final, alongside Hamill, Ermolenko, Correy and Bobby Ott. Grahame sustained leg injuries in the British Final and had missed the match at King's Lynn. He made it back for a KO Cup match at Belle Vue, but was forced to retire after one race and the Heathens lost by 10 points. The return leg at Dudley Wood was reckoned to be the best match seen there for years. Cradley, staring defeat in the face, won three of the last four heats 5-1 to pull back the deficit and draw the tie, only to have to do it all again. Only Andersen failed to impress, and young Smithy helped himself to paid 15 points.

With both the Grahame brothers and Simon Cross still out, the Heathens were allowed a guest rider for their match against League leaders Wolves at Dudley Wood, and Pratt managed to get one of the hottest properties in Britain, young Joe Screen, but his 4 points did little to help fine performances from Handberg and Hancock. What did help, though, was a brilliant showing from Smith. He had dropped back down to reserve and revelled in the position, top-scoring with 15 points. However, Wolves still took the match by 2 points.

The second week in June saw the return of Billy Hamill to Britain to contest the Overseas Final at Coventry. At last Pratt had him where he wanted him – back in England. Martin Dugard won the Final, but Greg easily qualified in fourth place, as did Billy in sixth position. In the Nordic Final in Finland, Gert Handberg took the last qualifying place. Pratt persisted. He found Billy new sponsors, and, at last, the American relented – he was back in the Heathens. He admitted to being apprehensive about facing the Cradley fans after his absence, but on 26 June the prodigal son was welcomed back big-time. He responded with paid 15 points against Bradford, in a match

Morton Andersen. (Hipkiss)

190

Anthony Boyd. (Hall)

that saw Andy Grahame return, but when the jinx hits Cradley, it hits hard, and Hancock crashed in his fourth outing damaging his knee ligaments. The Dukes took full advantage of the situation and won the match by 3 points.

Alan Grahame had recovered from his injuries and was set to take his place in the team, but Hamill was back and there was no berth available, and Alan found himself on loan to Second Division Oxford. The Heathens were allowed a guest facility for Hancock, but a lively Martin Dugard could not save them at Reading. Ronnie Correy also did a good job on the first leg of the re-run KO Cup match against Belle Vue, the Heathens winning the home match by 10 points. Craig Boyce was a brilliant guest for the next two matches, a home win against Arena-Essex and the return KO Cup match at Belle Vue, but the latter was a disaster. After building up a 6-point lead at the halfway stage, Cradley first of all lost Handberg with a broken wrist, and then Hamill with a chipped bone in his wrist. Subsequently the match was lost 59-47, and the Heathens were out of the Cup.

A very strange-looking Heathens team faced Poole at Dudley Wood, with no Cross, no Hancock, no Hamill, two guests – Leigh Adams and Freddie Schott – three reserves – Boyd, Smith and Walker – and Andy Grahame and Morten Andersen. Smithy shone, scored paid 14 points, and led the Heathens to a 6-point win.

Hancock made his return in time for the Golden Hammer on 21 July but struggled, scoring only 6 points, the surprise winner being Wolves' Peter Karlsson. Greg fared much better a week later, scoring double figures along with Grahame, Andersen, Smith and returnee Billy Hamill, to beat Belle Vue at Cradley Heath, but the Heathens still had only two teams between them and the bottom of the table.

The World Championship semi-final at Lonigo saw Hans Nielsen back on top form, winning the meeting, but only after a run-off with Billy Hamill, and with Hancock only 1 point behind them, Cradley's two Americans were safely through to the final.

The Heathens' best performance of the year without Cross and Handberg saw them trounce Ipswich at Dudley Wood 74-34 at the beginning of August, before losing at Arena, but Billy was riding as well as ever and Morten Andersen had hit a rich vein of form. Their good form took a nose-dive one week later, however, when Belle Vue took the points at Dudley Wood. And then Simon Cross returned. He made his comeback in a challenge match against Wolverhampton at Dudley Wood in an old-fashioned

Farewell Alan Grahame. (Hall)

thirteen-heat formula match. Simon was understandably cautious and managed only 3 points as the Heathens lost the match 33-45. Cradley had no answer to Ermolenko and Correy, who were both unbeaten on the night. These two would also be in the World Final, which was just one week away.

On 29 August in Pocking, Germany, Sam Ermolenko deservedly became 1993 World Champion. He led the League averages, his team led the British Speedway League, and he was very much the man of the moment. Billy Hamill finished tenth, and Greg Hancock, who seemed totally over-awed by the occasion, finished in last place.

Sam made his return to Britain at Dudley Wood on Bank Holiday Monday for the first leg of the Dudley/Wolves Trophy, but it was Cradley who took the honours, winning by 6 points. Sam was beaten only by Greg Hancock, but in the evening match, Hancock, Hamill and Morten Andersen all took his scalp, as the Heathens shocked home and away supporters alike with a power-performance that saw them take the match 62-45 and retain the trophy once again. The matches also featured the return of Gert Handberg, who seemed out of sorts.

Andersen was absent with food poisoning for the first match of September at Dudley Wood, and with Cross and Handberg still struggling, Cradley were unable to hold Hans Nielsen and his Coventry Bees, and they sank to the bottom of the League.

The team was back at full strength, however, and a trip to Bradford showed what they were capable of when Hamill and Hancock led them to a 60-48 victory over the stunned Dukes. The following week at Dudley Wood, Cradley dented Wolverhampton's title hopes, winning the match by 4 points. Ermolenko gave a World Champion performance with an awesome 18-point maximum. The Heathens had little to celebrate, however, losing Andersen in a heat 7 crash. He sustained a badly bruised shoulder and ankle, and was out for the next two matches. There seemed to be no end to it as Simon Cross crashed at Poole and badly gashed his head. Cradley were already using rider replacement for Andersen, and although they battled gamely, the task proved too much for them as they were eclipsed by 8 points.

In their next match at Dudley Wood, Cradley faced an up-hill task against title-chasing Eastbourne. Cross and Andersen were already out and, to make matters worse, Handberg had been recalled to Denmark. Hancock responded with a flawless 15-point maximum and Billy scored the same from 6 rides, but the night belonged to Scott Smith with 14 points, leading the Heathens to a 56-52 win. On the international front, Greg and Billy combined with Sammy and Bobby Ott to win the World Team Cup final for America.

Back on the home front, Heathens talked of retirement. Crossy had mentioned it weeks ago – he had been walking wounded for three years now, and there seemed no end to it. He said that 1993 would be his last year in the sport. Scott Smith complained that he just couldn't make it pay and would be better off with a regular job, as did Andy Grahame. Andy was working four days a week in brother Alan's motorcycle shop to subsidise his speedway earnings. He argued that, apart from the reserves, he was the lowest paid rider in the team, and that when he was at Wimbledon, he was paid £35 per point, at Eastbourne £40 per point, but with the new pay scales at Cradley, he was paid only £25 per point, so, unless things changed, Cradley would not be seeing him in 1994.

Simon Cross and Morten Andersen both returned for a match at Monmore Green on 27 October, but the Dane fell in his first ride and aggravated his injuries, keeping him on the sidelines. Hamill and Hancock attempted to take on the League leaders virtually on their own but it was, of course, beyond them, and Wolves coasted to a comfortable win.

Narrow losses at Coventry and Ipswich saw Cradley lose three matches in one week, but typically, with Andersen still out and Hamill away in America, Cross and Smith came good at Dudley Wood in the first match of October to beat Reading and move the Heathens off the bottom of the League table. Hamill and Andersen returned for the next match at Belle Vue which put Cradley back at full strength. With the match already lost, and riding in the rain under hazardous conditions, Hancock fell in his last outing. The diagnosis was not good, he dislocated his elbow, and Cradley's number one rider was out for the two remaining weeks of the season. Once again the Heathens were allowed a guest facility, but it was of little consequence. They won their last two home League matches and lost their last four away matches, losing Morten Andersen and Scott Smith on the way and both riders finished the season on the injured list.

Cradley were not the only team left licking their wounds at the end of 1993. World Champion Sam Ermolenko was left nursing a broken leg, and his injuries had ultimately cost Wolves the League title, Belle Vue pipping them at the post.

1993 programme.

However, the Heathens finished well and truly at the bottom of the League in what had been a disastrous season. Their injury record was second to none. As regards the supporters, it had not been a season for the faint-hearted, one best forgotten in fact.

Greg Hancock had a fantastic year. He established himself among the elite in 1993, and only Ermolenko, Per Jonsson and Nielsen finished above him in the League Riders averages. He must have been bitterly disappointed with his first World Final performance, but there was no doubt whatsoever that he would appear in future Finals. Greg averaged 9.85 points.

Billy Hamill once again proved his class in 1993. All too many times he was left with Hancock to fight a two-man battle against the opposition, but Billy never faltered and was developing into one of the most competitive riders in the sport. Billy finished eighth in the League Riders averages with 8.99 points.

Simon Cross finished another season battered and bruised – it was to be his last, he assured us – he couldn't go on living like this. The skipper gave his all in 1993, and then some more, but the well had run dry. Simon averaged 6.22 points.

Gert Handberg continued to frustrate Colin Pratt throughout the season. One wondered how long the Cradley manager would persevere with the Dane. In any case, Handberg left Dudley Wood at the end of the season with no intention of returning to the British League. Gert averaged 6.15 points. Scott Smith improved in leaps and bounds, and often proved to be a match-winner for Cradley, but now his future seemed to be uncertain. Scott averaged 5.95 points.

Morten Andersen proved to be a big hit with the supporters with his determined riding, but too often his enthusiasm got the better of him resulting in injuries. However, Morton looked a good prospect for the future and averaged 5.84 points. Andy Grahame's form continued to slip, and for a lot of the season he appeared to be going through the motions. He, along with Handberg, took the brunt of most of Pratt's verbal onslaughts, and his prospects at Dudley Wood looked grim. Andy averaged 5.2 points.

Justin Walker and Anthony Boyd did everything that Pratt could have asked of them. Sometimes, through injury, thrown in hopelessly out of their depth, they kept their heads down and got on with it, both scoring well on occasions. They averaged 4.56 and 3.22 points respectively.

And what of Pedersen? He had played his cards close to his chest all season, not giving an answer as to his future intentions. He had kept himself busy saloon car racing in Denmark and had met with some success, but he was putting off making his decision until he had seen this doctor, or that doctor, or until he had his pins out – and so it went on. Anyway, just before Christmas, he partly revealed his plans. He may ride again – he may not, but if he did, it would not be for Cradley or any other League club. Pedersen was quitting British speedway for good!

If there had been any hope at all in the traumatic 1993 season, it had been that Janno would return to lead the Heathens to greater things in the future, but, for the supporters, a miserable winter followed a miserable season. Cradley had lost another World Champion – one of the most entertaining riders the sport had ever seen.

18

THE EXORCIST
1994

As early as February, Dudley Wood's owners Derek and Nora Pugh announced their retirement and leased out the speedway rights to a new promotion company, headed by a local businessman, Les Pottinger, who was no stranger to Cradley Heath speedway, and ex-Heathen Mike Gardner. The fans were told that it was 'business as usual' at Dudley Wood.

Colin Pratt dusted himself off and prepared for another term at Cradley which, for his health's sake, he hoped would be better than the last one. He immediately set about recruiting new blood, his target being the young unsigned American Chris Manchester and he went to meet him at the airport as he flew in with Billy Hamill. He was told that Chris had all but signed for Wolverhampton, but in the end it was Belle Vue who acquired his services.

The new points limit was set at 44, there was a return to seven-man teams, and matches were to be contested over sixteen heats. With better pay rates on offer, Hamill was the first to sign, followed by Morten Andersen. Scott Smith had re-kindled his enthusiasm during the winter and announced that he was raring to go. Andy Grahame had found himself a full-time job in the close season working in engineering, but his boss was a speedway fan and agreed to give him time off to ride, so he too was signed up. Pratt brought in 25-year-old David Clarke from Second Division Oxford. Dave had ridden some good matches at Dudley Wood for Coventry a few years ago, and he looked a good bet at reserve.

Greg Hancock was made the new captain of the side, but with days to go before the start of the new season and Handberg not wanting to return, Colin was still short of a third heat-leader. Suddenly, Simon Cross had a complete turn around and promptly announced an end to his retirement, whereby he completed the Cradley seven. So late had Crossy left it, that he had not even had a practice ride, and his equipment was far from being ready for the opening meeting of the season. However, he announced that in 1994, we would see a new Simon Cross, a much cooler Simon Cross who would take things in his stride, would not get upset and would enjoy his racing. He added that although he would 'give it everything he had', he would not be trying to go through gaps that were not bigger than his handlebars! Not much of a change then by the time the gates re-opened in 1994 to a bumper crowd – and Wolverhampton in the Clubcall Trophy.

Sam Ermolenko got straight into the groove, the World Champion scoring a 15-point maximum, but it was not enough to prevent the Heathens from winning the first leg, albeit by only 2 points. Greg, as expected, led the scorers with 11, Morten Andersen 10, Billy Hamill 7, Scott Smith 7, Andy Grahame 6, Dave Clarke 4, and finally Cross paid for his late preparation, scoring only 4 points. Two nights later, Sam was at it again, scoring another 15-point max. and leading the Wolves to their first trophy of the season, at Cradley's expense.

The League campaign got underway at Dudley Wood on 23 March, when visitors Belle Vue were hammered 69-27. Every one of the Heathens scored a bagful of points, and it was nice to see Crossy sort himself out and score paid 12 points. Things were different at Bradford, however, when world-record signing Joe Screen led the Dukes to a 16-point win. Only Hancock shone on a night that saw Hamill blow two engines and put himself £3,000 out of pocket.

On 28 March, Scott Smith won the British Quarter-final at Exeter, but Andy Grahame became the Heathens' first casualty, falling in his first race and breaking two bones in his wrist. Cradley used rider replacement for him at Dudley Wood, as Coventry were subjected to a power display from Smithy at reserve, scoring paid 13 points. Hans Nielsen had announced that this was to be his final year in British speedway, but he still had a lot to offer, and, scoring 17 points, he was beaten only by Billy Hamill, as Cradley beat the Bees 52-44.

A rainy Sunday saw the Heathens visit a strong Eastbourne side, and on a rain-soaked Arlington circuit, Cradley showed little heart for the match. It was abandoned after 13 heats but the 53-25 result, in the Eagles' favour, stood. A similar fate awaited the next match at Dudley Wood, which was rained off after 12 heats, and again the 43-29 score against Poole stood, moving the Heathens up to third place in the League behind Wolves and Reading.

Hancock and Hamill had settled quickly – they were, after all, world-class riders – but Morten Andersen was already looking a bit special in the early stages of '94. He had almost an 8-point average, and, with Crossy still trying to sort himself out, Mort seemed favourite to take the third heat-leader spot. Dave Clarke had also got off to a good start and was proving to be a very solid number seven, whilst it seemed only a matter of time before Scott would leave him behind and move into the team proper. He had begun the year riding out of his skin and had quickly established himself as the best reserve in the League.

Cross, meanwhile, felt that he was letting down the team and practised behind closed doors at Dudley Wood. The result was third place in the British Semi-final at Monmore Green, behind Joe Screen and Mark Loram, and his first maximum for two years against Ipswich in the KO Cup at Cradley. Simon was not so fortunate in the return leg KO Cup match at Ipswich, however, and was taken to hospital following a crash in which he injured his leg. It was the second ambulance to be used in the match. Morten Andersen was waiting for Crossy at the hospital. He had crashed in his first outing and had badly gashed his arm. Scott Smith had also fallen and had aggravated the collarbone injury that he had sustained at the end of the '93 campaign. Pratt shuddered. Could it all be happening again? He already had Grahame out and was now looking at the prospect of having only three men left, only four weeks into the season. Cradley understandably lost heavily at Ipswich, but the massive lead they had established in the first leg was enough to take them through to the next round of the KO Cup.

Cross took his injuries in his stride (he said he would – remember?) and declared himself fit for the next League match at Coventry two nights later. With Andersen, Smith and Grahame out, Pratt restructured the side to use rider replacement for Mort and call in guest Rene Madsen. Anthony Boyd was recalled at reserve, but the task proved too great. Cross pushed back the pain barrier to score paid 13 points, and Hamill and Hancock put on their usual splendid display, even pairing up to score a 5-1 over Nielsen in heat 13, but the Bees won 52-43.

Andersen and Smith rejoined the squad at Dudley Wood on 30 April for a League match against Arena-Essex. But there was little cause for celebration, as Cradley officially became the unluckiest team in speedway history, having three riders stretchered off in the opening heat of a disastrous encounter. Andersen, still with stitches in his arm, lifted on the first bend and collided with Hamill, sending both riders into the fence and on their way to hospital. They were replaced by reserves Smith and Clarke in the re-run, but Clarke fell, broke his ankle and went off to join Morten and Billy in Russells Hall. The night belonged to Scott Smith, already riding against doctors' advice, and in pain he took seven rides to score paid 15 points and earn himself an accolade from an appreciative crowd. Crossy and Hancock were both brilliant, scoring 13 points apiece, but it was an impossible task and Arena won the match 55-40.

Sunday 1 May saw Andy Smith win the British Final from Joe Screen at Brandon. Simon Cross qualified from the meeting in sixth place, but he refused to get excited about his prospects in the World Final competition – he was being cool.

Reading superstar Swedish Per Jonsson, after failing to agree terms with Reading, had spent the beginning of the season in his homeland, but by the time Cradley had got to Reading at the start of May, so had Per. He swept to a faultless 15-point maximum as a decimated Heathens were beaten by 20 points. The team had a strange look about it with Hamill, Grahame, Andersen, Clarke and Smith missing. Martin Dugard was a fine guest, but Lawrence Hare, Steve Ledwidth and Craig Taylor all found the task a little beyond them. The team was in dire straits and Pratt acted swiftly. He signed Swedish Peter Nahlin to replace Andy Grahame. Nahlin was a Swindon asset, but when they had moved down into the Second Division, he had stayed in Sweden. The man was a former Under-21 World Champion, and his ability was beyond question. Andy Grahame was about to return when Peter was signed, so he suddenly found himself alongside brother Alan at Second Division Oxford, who were incidentally being managed by Jan O. Pedersen.

Cradley had one more match before Nahlin's arrival, the return against Reading at Dudley Wood. Andersen had returned to Denmark, Clarke would probably be out for the rest of the season, and Hamill and Smith were both still injured. However, with Mark Loram and Ryan Sullivan riding well as guests, and Hancock and Cross riding their hearts out, the depleted home team were victors by 52-44.

The Cradley curse was impartial, it was indifferent to age or nationality. Its only criterion was that you were connected to Cradley Heath speedway, in which case, you were fair game. But it had developed over the last two years, and it now had greater

Cradley Heath, 1994. From left to right: Mike Gardner, Jonathan Forsgren, Greg Hancock, Peter Nahlin, Simon Cross, Billy Hamill. Kneeling: Scott Smith, Lance Sealey. (Hipkiss)

powers – it could stretch overseas! Before he had the chance to make his debut, Peter Nahlin broke his collarbone in Sweden. Pratt was gutted, the Cradley riders were gutted, the supporters were gutted and Nahlin was gutted. The Swede arranged to have laser treatment on his injury and promised to be at Dudley Wood as soon as it was humanly possible.

The Heathens continued their KO Cup programme at Arena-Essex in the second week of May when Andersen and Hamill returned. Justin Walker had been recalled to the team and rider replacement was used for Peter Nahlin. Morten still looked a little delicate, but managed 9 points, however, Hamill came storming back to top-score with 16 points. Hancock, as always, gave staunch support, but Cradley were forced to concede 8 points. Smith returned in the reserve berth with a magnificent paid 11 points from 4 rides in the return leg at Dudley Wood, and a rock-solid Cradley team performance saw the Hammers crushed 59-24.

It was World Championship round time in mid-May, and, in Ventura, USA, Greg became the new American Champion, with Billy claiming the runner-up spot, both easily qualifying for the Overseas Final. No such luck for Crossy, however. He fell in his third outing in the British Final, damaged his knee and withdrew from the meeting. His challenge was over but, to the new-look Simon Cross, it was 'just one of those things'.

Peter Nahlin made his League debut at Ipswich on 26 May and scored a very impressive paid 12 points, and he made the difference as Cradley managed a draw at Foxhall Heath. Had the Heathens turned the corner? Had they laid the curse to rest? Of course not! Morten Andersen packed it in his kitbag and returned to Denmark to ride in the Danish World Championship rounds. Morten broke his arm and his season was over. Colin Pratt was at his wits' end. The season had developed into a battle between him and the Cradley curse, so Pratty decided to deal it a double blow. First of all, he looked once again to Sweden and signed up highly rated 20-year-old Jonathan Forsgren. He then looked to Lye, Stourbridge, where he signed the Revd David Woodhouse to perform an exorcism at the Dudley Wood stadium! That should get the little blighter. In the event, Mr Woodhouse did not perform an exorcism but he did bless the track for the slightly deranged Cradley manager.

While they were awaiting Forsgren's arrival, the Heathens beat Bradford at Dudley Wood before their next home fixture, which was a meaningless challenge match against a League Select side. Jonathan made his debut at reserve, scoring paid 3 points.

Sunday 12 June was Overseas Final time at Brandon, with Cradley's two Americans both competing. Sam Ermolenko became the 1994 Overseas Champion, with Greg Hancock in second place. Billy had an uncomfortable time, but even so, snatched the final qualifying place.

The Heathens were on top form for King's Lynn's visit to Dudley Wood. Mark Loram was the only opponent to give any resistance to a rampant Cradley side who thoroughly deserved their 20-point win. It's worth noting the scorers – Hamill paid 13, Hancock 12, Cross paid 12, Forsgren 6, Walker 0, and Peter Nahlin a stunning 15-point maximum.

Nahlin had quickly forged a friendship with Simon Cross. They were both golf fanatics, but their real forte was as a duo on the track. They were paired together and quickly became one of the most prolific pairings in the League. In the return at Saddlebow Road, King's Lynn proved to be much tougher opponents, and with Billy Hamill having an uncharacteristically bad night, the Stars won by 10 points.

In the middle of June, speedway received a terrible blow. 'Top of the League Averages' Per Jonsson crashed in Poland, sustaining neck and back injuries. It was a bad one – Erik Gundersen all over again – but Per was not so lucky, and was to spend the rest

Justin Walker. (Hall)

199

of his life in a wheelchair. Jonsson was a class act through and through. The top Swede already had one World Championship under his belt and looked a safe bet to gain more. It could be said that he was at his peak when he was so cruelly robbed of his career – almost his life. It was a shocking reminder of the risks these boys take.

June saw Cradley involved in the League four-team tournament, and they rode like demons, winning all four of their legs at Coventry, Belle Vue, Dudley Wood and Wolverhampton to take the Northern Section of the competition easily.

The Heathens seemed to be stuck in ninth place in the League, and frankly, barring miracles, the Championship was already looking beyond them, and so the KO Cup became their prime goal. Their next opponents in the competition were Coventry, and the two teams met in the semi-final at Dudley Wood on 2 July. Despite some stout opposition from Hans Nielsen and John Jorgensen, Cradley, due to a brilliant display from their top four, gained a 14-point lead to take to Brandon in the return leg.

One week later saw the staging of the first World Championship semi-final in Prague, which featured both Greg and Billy. The Pole Tomasz Gollob won the meeting from Sweden's Tony Rickardsson. Greg and Billy both tied for the last qualifying place. In a run-off, Hancock beat Hamill – Greg was through to the Final, Billy was reserve.

Cradley's recent run of fine form ran into a brick wall at Dudley Wood, against arch-enemies Wolves on 13 July. Forsgren showed what he was capable of, scoring paid 11 points, but the only other Heathen on top form was Peter Nahlin. However, in his fifth outing, the Swede broke a chain and was thrown into the fence, breaking two bones in his hand and badly gashing his chin. Led by Sam Ermolenko and Peter Karlsson,

Morton Andersen. (Hall)

New co-promoters Les Pottinger and Mike Gardner. (Hipkiss)

Wolverhampton took full advantage of the Heathens' bad luck and took the match by 2 points. Pratt had an appointment with a certain Reverend in Lye – he wanted his money back!

Three nights later and it was the return leg of the cup semi-final at Coventry – without Nahlin. This time it was the Bees who experienced bad luck as, during the course of the match, Andy Smith was taken to hospital, followed a short time later by Nielsen. 19 points from Hamill, paid 13 from Hancock, and paid 13 from Cross put Cradley into the KO Cup final.

Wednesday 20 July was Golden Hammer night and the 1994 Champion was fast-rising Mark Loram. Greg Hancock finished in third place behind Garry Havelock and Billy took fifth, behind Sam Ermolenko.

Cradley did well at Arena-Essex, considering that they were without Nahlin and Cross but, despite brilliant performances from the two Americans, they were forced to concede the match by 6 points. Cross returned to the team the next night at Bradford and made the difference, but with Forsgren crashing in his first outing and taking no further part, the match was lost by a whisker, and the Heathens moved down to bottom-but-one place in the League. Cradley helped themselves to 3 League points by beating Ipswich at Dudley Wood, but although Hamill, Hancock and Cross were all performing heroically, Nahlin was being missed. Their last home match in July was a disappointment, Cradley losing narrowly to a Bradford side led by a red-hot Joe Screen and Jimmy Nilsen.

Peter Nahlin returned to Dudley Wood on 7 August in a League match against Arena-Essex, and dropped just 1 point to the opposition in five rides, as did Cross and

Hancock, but the Heathens' 10-point win would no doubt would have been greater had Forsgren not been missing with a foot injury sustained in the Nordic Under-21 Championship. The next day was the four-team finals at Peterborough, the Northern leg of which had been totally dominated by Cradley. With each rider having only 3 rides each, the Heathens put out their top four guns, Nahlin dropped only 1 point, Cross dropped only 2, but Hamill and Hancock both had a nightmare meeting, scoring 3 and 2 points respectively, and Cradley finished in second spot behind Poole.

For their third meeting in as many days, the Heathens visited Belle Vue for a bottom-of-the-table clash. Without Forsgren, the tail-end of the team looked weak with Walker and Boyd, but the top five looked formidable, and they proved to be so, beating the Aces on their own turf by 2 points and moving up a place to overtake Ipswich in the League table.

Two weeks later at Vojens, Denmark, Tony Rickardsson became the winner of the last ever one-day World Final, from Hans Nielsen and Craig Boyce. Billy failed to get a ride, but Greg had a marvellous night, winning three races and finishing fourth. The event was now to be replaced by the Grand Prix series.

The Heathens were at Smallmead, Reading, on 22 August and Forsgren made his return, scoring paid 9 points and helping Cradley to an 8-point win. The end of the month saw Crossy get a recall to the England squad to face America, but 'Mr Laid-back' rejected the offer on the grounds that the national team would be better served by younger riders. Young Lance Sealey from Reading Juniors was brought in at reserve to replace Justin Walker who had injured a shoulder, but he could muster only a single point at Dudley Wood as a solid-looking Cradley crushed the King's Lynn Stars. He repeated this score on Bank Holiday Monday morning in the Dudley Wolves Trophy at Cradley Heath, but the Heathens maintained their good run. With the top four riding well and Cross and Nahlin back together, Wolves found themselves with an 18-point deficit to make up in the second leg that night. With Cradley in this sort of form, it was too much for Wolverhampton. There was salt rubbed in wounds as the Heathens won at Monmore by 2 points and retained the trophy.

Even with Peter Nahlin away in Sweden, Ipswich were no match for the Heathens at Dudley Wood. Their next match was a tough one at League leaders Poole on 7 September. Nahlin returned, but gave by far his worst showing of the season, scoring only 4 points, and lacking support from Smith, Forsgren and Sealey, Cradley were defeated 50-34.

Due to postponements, the next match was not until 21 September at Dudley Wood. It would be a dress rehearsal for the KO Cup final, for Cradley's opponents in the final, Eastbourne, were the visitors. Cradley's top four were too strong for the Eagles and the match was comfortably won by 12 points, but the more cautious would note that the usually immaculate Martin Dugard had scored only 3 points, and that was unlikely to happen in the final.

Wolverhampton almost upset the applecart at Dudley Wood in the Heathens' next match. Halfway though the fixture, Cradley were 10 points clear, but then the rain came and washed away their spirit. Wolves began to claw back and, as Ermolenko revelled in the wet conditions, the home team struggled to win by just 1 point. Forsgren took a tumble in his final ride and was badly shaken up. For the return League match at Monmore, Green Ermolenko was absent, and so was Hancock, so it was reckoned to be even-stevens, but the Heathens were also without Forsgren. Nahlin was tremendous, storming to an 18-point maximum, but with Walker and Sealey scoring only 2 points between them, the result, incredibly, was the same as at Dudley Wood – Wolves 48 Cradley 47. Maximum man Nahlin could not catch Peter Karlsson in the run-off for the bonus point.

The first match in October saw bottom-of-the-League Belle Vue come calling, and they stunned Cradley with a tremendous performance that made a laughing stock of their lowly League position. Dave Clarke made a surprise return to replace Cradley's injured Swedish reserve, but he failed to score, and with Cross having an off-night, the Aces, led by a flying Jason Lyons, pinched the match by 2 points. The Heathens failed to win their next home match when a determined Coventry went into the final heat 4 points up. The brilliant pairing of Nahlin and Cross saved the day with a 5-1 against Brian Andersson and Hans Nielsen and the points were shared. No doubt about it, Cradley were missing Forsgren at reserve. When he returned three nights later, on 8 October, so did the Heathens' form, and they stormed to a 61-35 against Reading, Cross and Hancock both recording maximums and Jonathan scoring paid 9 points from four rides.

Cradley's next match was at Brandon. Hamill and Forsgren were super, but with Hancock having a poor night, the Bees were comfortable 10-point winners. Forsgren fell in his last outing and again sustained injuries that would keep him out of the next fixture. After the match, Nahlin flew home to Sweden for treatment on his injured

Dave Clarke. (Hipkiss)

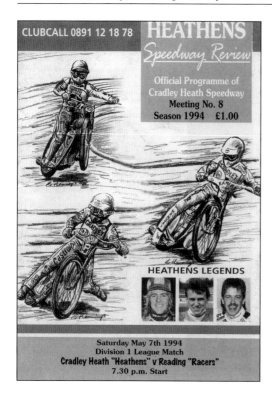

1994 programme.

shoulder. Without him and Forsgren, the Heathens struggled to hold table-toppers Poole at Dudley Wood and were forced to settle for a draw. Hancock, Hamill and Cross all rode well, and Dave Clarke, in for Forsgren, did well also to score paid 6 points, but Sealey failed to score, and Smith, who was going through a quiet period, scored just 5 points.

As usual, Cradley found themselves heading rapidly toward the end of the season with a pile-up of fixtures. On 21 October, they lost at Arena-Essex, even with the Swedes back in the team, and two days later, on Sunday 23rd, they faced Eastbourne in the first leg of the KO Cup at Arlington. The Eagles were rampant. Martin Dugard made no mistakes this time and led his team with a 15-point maximum, and with Dean Barker and Stefan Danno each scoring paid 14 points, the Heathens were in trouble – 22 points worth of trouble in fact, one hell of a deficit to pull back. Apart from Greg Hancock, and to a lesser extent Nahlin, the team just didn't do well, and they faced a mountain to climb at Dudley Wood if they were to achieve anything in 1994. The very next night, they won at Wolverhampton in the first leg of the Willow Print Trophy by 3 points.

On 27 October, with time running out, Cradley lost at Ipswich. The 29th saw the return leg of the Willow Trophy rained off at Dudley Wood – and there was no time left to re-stage it. On the 30th, the Heathens lost their last League match at King's Lynn and finished ninth out of eleven. The KO Cup final return leg at Cradley Heath was held on 31 October. Cradley won the match but by only 2 points, giving the cup to Eastbourne. They were led by the skipper, Cross, who scored a brilliant paid 17 points out of a possible 18. Hamill supported well with 14, Nahlin 9, Hancock picked the wrong night to have a 'bad un' scoring 7, Forsgren 4, Smith 1 and Sealey 0.

Apart from the KO Cup final, Greg had another fabulous year, topped by his fourth place in the World Championship. His club average for '94 was 9.27 points. Peter Nahlin had been a huge success at Cradley, he breathed life into the team and virtually resurrected Simon Cross' career. The immensely popular Swede won the Cradley Rider of the Year Award and averaged 8.76 points.

Billy Hamill was so often the backbone of the Heathens' outfit. He was just as comfortable riding at the away tracks as he was at Dudley Wood. He was bitterly disappointed not to be in the World Championship Final, but still had a tremendous year, averaging 8.43 points. Simon Cross rattled up hoards of points, never giving up, and proving on many occasions to be the Heathens' match-winner. Simon averaged 7.70 points.

Morten Andersen had begun the season like an express train and looked as though he would be a right handful in 1994, but injuries got the better of him, a broken arm being the killer blow. Morten averaged 7.29 points. Smithy certainly had his moments in 1994, but they tended to be in the first half of the year. He was now in the team proper, and understandably found the points harder to come by. As the season progressed, he found himself battered from pillar to post, and ended the year jaded in comparison to his lively start. The aching Scott Smith averaged 5.03.

Young Johnny Forsgren was great. He put in some fine performances on tracks that he had never seen before, but often his enthusiasm got the better of his ability, and he too was the victim of many crashes. Jonathan averaged 4.41 points. Dave Clarke could have been a match-winner for Cradley at reserve but his season got off to the worse possible start. However, he was back before the end, riding in a handful of matches and picking up points even though he was far from match-fit. David averaged 3.76 points. Justin Walker was in and out of the team like a yo-yo but, to his credit, never refused when asked to cover for an injured rider. Justin averaged 1.81 points. Both Lance Sealey and Anthony Boyd were there too often just to make up the numbers, and found life in the First Division at this stage of their careers a little too demanding.

Even though it had been another poor season for Cradley, despite a very disappointing final match, spirits were much higher than at the end of the previous year. New sensation Peter Nahlin was saying that he wanted to ride for Cradley for the rest of his career – and so was Forsgren, and there was young Andersen too. Cross had already told Pratty that he wanted to return next year.

Due to new blood in the team, there was an air of expectancy about Dudley Wood. Mainly due to the demise of the Grahames, the average age of the team had plummeted. Let me say at this time that nobody had served the club better than Alan Grahame over the many years he spent with Cradley, but he had been sent to graze in the pastures of Division Two and was quite happy to do so. Everything looked set for a much rosier future.

That is until a press release on 24 November read 'Cradley Heath Speedway to close'. Cradley Heath Speedway was given notice to quit Dudley Wood Stadium by the owners, Cradley Heath Greyhound Stadium Limited, the reason being that 'Speedway was not viable'. A dumbfounded and shocked Les Pottinger disclosed that during the 1994 season he had paid the owners £40,000, which seemed to him to make it viable. And so it began, a winter of protests outside the stadium, thousands of petition forms, letters to the Council, letters to the Government, meetings between the promoters and the supporters, and so forth. A committee was formed and a strike fund set up – Cradley Heath Speedway was not going to take this lying down.

19

THE FINAL YEAR
1995

Mike Gardner was the first to jump ship, as early as December 1994, when he announced that business commitments would not allow him to remain with the club. In the same month, a meeting of the supporters was held at Quarry Bank Labour Club, so that Pottinger and Pratt could give an update on the situation. Over 500 fans turned up, and many more were turned away. The situation was this. Cradley Heath Speedway wanted to buy the stadium, but the owners did not want to sell. Derek Pugh owned only one third of Dudley Wood Stadium. The other two thirds were owned by the Bridgewater family, who quickly became the villains of the piece. George Bridgewater had built the stadium in the 1930s, but upon his death, his son Noel and daughters Judy and Susan were the inheritors.

Swedish Sven Heiding had been appointed a Cradley director, and together with Pottinger he set about looking for a site upon which to build a new stadium, but, he informed the supporters, they were few and far between in the Black Country. Many such meetings were held in the winter with local councillors and the like getting up and having their five minutes of fame, but February arrived and the Heathens did not have a home. The Cradley riders were understandably getting nervous.

The winter speedway news was that in 1995, there would be one big League with twenty-one teams, and the points limit would be 40. This meant major restructuring for many teams, especially the ones which had previously been in Division Two. Riders were at a premium, and, if they ran at all, Cradley would have to drop some of theirs. Peter Nahlin would certainly be re-called to Swindon. Uncertain of his future, Morten Andersen signed for King's Lynn.

A consortium had been formed – Cradley Leisure Limited, led by local businessman Ken Williams. He made an appointment with the owners at the end of February to put a bid in for the stadium. He was unsuccessful, but there was good news: he had struck a deal for the 1995 season, but only for the 1995 season, he warned. Cradley were back in business! Immediately, Colin Pratt set about forming his squad, with only a couple of weeks until the tapes went up on the new season.

The first signing was 16-year-old John Wilson from Ilkeston. John had had some second-half rides in 1994 and looked to be a good prospect for the future. For his other reserve, Pratt signed young Steve Knott on loan from Sheffield.

For the rest of the squad, he looked to the old guard – Hancock, Hamill, Cross and Smith. Forsgren was contacted and he was only too keen, but he had injured his leg whilst training and would have to miss out on the start of the season – but they all signed, and, at the last minute, Pratt had a team to ride in 1995 at Dudley Wood. Steve Knott was the first Heathen in action when he finished as runner-up to Justin Elkins in the British Under-21 semi-final at Mildenhall.

Dudley Wood opened on 25 March with the annual Clubcall Trophy against Wolverhampton. Thousands packed into the stadium for a night that many thought would never happen. Hamill immediately hit top form, being beaten only once by Sam Ermolenko. Hancock scored paid 12, Smith paid 11, Cross paid 9, Dave Clarke, brought in to cover for Forsgren, paid 3, Wilson 2, and Knott 4. Cradley won the first leg by 6 points. On the following Monday night at Monmore, once again the Heathens proved too strong for the Wolves, winning by 5 points and gaining their first piece of silverware of the season.

Their last match of March was an away visit to Ipswich in their first League match of the season. Hamill, Hancock and Cross all settled in quickly and scored well, and a battling Cradley only just lost the match by a single point. The big three rode well in the return two nights later at Dudley Wood, but lacking virtually any support, they found themselves an incredible 16 points behind after just seven heats, courtesy of Jeremy Doncaster and Chris Louis. Mr Pratt had a few inspirational words with his boys and an amazing comeback got underway, but the Witches grimly hung on to win the match by 2 points.

Cradley Heath, 1995. From left to right, back row: Scott Smith, Billy Hamill, Steve Knott, Jonathan Forsgren. Front row: Simon Cross, Greg Hancock, John Wilson. (Hipkiss)

On 8 April, Cradley entertained one of the new teams in the League, Peterborough, but the Panthers lacked a rider of the same class as Hancock or Hamill and the Americans went through the card unbeaten to lead the Heathens to a comfortable victory. The next night at Arlington, Cross was absent on longtrack duty. Cradley were still without Forsgren at this stage, so when John Wilson crashed out of the meeting in his first race, the odds were stacked against the Heathens. Even so, they rode doggedly to hold Eastbourne to just a 7-point win.

Simon returned to lead Cradley to two home victories against Reading and Coventry, before the Heathens headed North to another of the new teams to the League, Edinburgh. Forsgren had returned and debuted with paid 4 points, Hamill scored a blinding maximum, but a couple of engine failures by Hancock proved to be costly, the Monarchs winning the match 50-46.

Sheffield and Glasgow offered little resistance at Dudley Wood and both were dispatched with ease, as Cradley moved into seventh place in the League. Hamill and Hancock were joint third in the League riders averages, with almost 11 points, bettered by only Peter Karlsson and Joe Screen. Crossy regularly scored double figures, but Scott Smith was inconsistent. The two young reserves were proving to be a lively pair. Wilson was rarely point-less and was putting in some gutsy performances, but Stevie Knott had shown himself to be a real battler, fighting for every point and scoring a fair few into the bargain.

A loss at Reading was followed by a big win over King's Lynn at Dudley Wood, but the win was marred. In Morten Andersen's first outing for the Stars, he sustained bad neck and back injuries. The ex-Heathen eventually recovered, but was told that another crash could prove fatal. His speedway career was over, and it must be said that during his short spell at Cradley he had become immensely popular with the fans.

The middle of May saw a revolution in speedway, as the Grand Prix Series finally began. Billy and Greg were both involved in the inaugural year, and from the form that they were showing in the League, both expected to do well. The first Grand Prix was held in

Steve Knott. (Hall)

Wroclaw, Poland, and was won by non-League rider Tomasz Gollob from non-League rider Hans Nielsen. Hancock finished in eleventh place, with Billy fifteenth. It was not a good start for the Americans, but with another four rounds to go, they were not too despondent.

Cradley's first away success was a sweet moment, for it was at Monmore Green. Wolverhampton had the same problem as the Heathens – a top-heavy team – and whilst Ermolenko and Peter Karlsson were unquestionably world-class riders, they lacked a Simon Cross to complete their heat-leader trio. It was the usual nail-biting, dramatic, classic speedway match that one had come to expect from these two bitter rivals, and Cradley stole it by just 2 points.

Hancock and Hamill were in a different class from every other rider at Belle Vue when they both recorded maximums to lead the Heathens to victory at the Manchester track, but the Black Country outfit slipped up in their next match against Swindon on Bank Holiday Monday morning at Dudley Wood. Cradley went into the last heat 4 points down, but with Hamill and Hancock representing them, a draw seemed to be on the cards. However, it was not to be, as Peter Nahlin split the pairing and the match was lost. That same night at Blundstone, the Robins won the return by 10 points.

Johnny Forsgren made a cautious start when he returned and, in the main, he blew hot and cold, but a handful of good scores now saw him challenging Smithy for fourth place in the team averages. The Heathens were blowing hot and cold too, but the fans were pouring into Dudley Wood by the thousands, as if they sensed that they were not going to see speedway at Cradley Heath for much longer.

Cradley saw out the month of May with an away win at Long Eaton and began June with a 2-point defeat at Middlesbrough. Hamill and Hancock once again both scored maximums, this time at Glasgow, where the Heathens lost by a single point in the first leg of the KO Cup competition.

League points were taken at Poole, despite an impressive performance from young Pirate Jason Crump. The Aussie was just as impressive at Dudley Wood a few nights later, but Cradley put in a great all-round performance to win the match by 14 points and move up into sixth place in the League. The Heathens were given a fright by a very determined Glasgow Tigers at Cradley in the return leg of the KO Cup fixture, but won the meeting 59-53 and moved into the next round of the competition.

The next round of the Grand Prix was at Neustadt, Austria, on 17 June, and this time Greg and Billy knew what to expect. Billy continued his fabulous year by winning the meeting from Tony Rickardsson and Hans Nielsen. Hancock also improved on his last showing, finishing in seventh place. Surprisingly, Cradley only had the League Fours competition to compete in before it was Grand Prix time again, this time in Abensberg. Tommy Knudsen was the surprise winner, with Billy finishing in third place and Greg back in eleventh. Billy moved into third place in the Grand Prix table.

The Golden Hammer was a walkover for the Americans, but the trouble was that the winner was not a Heathen, it was Sam Ermolenko, closely followed by Greg and Billy. Hancock had a superb July on the individual front, gaining revenge over Sam by winning the Olympique at Wolverhampton and also collecting the Silver Jubilee Trophy at Peterborough.

Jonathan Forsgren. (Hall)

Hull were beaten visitors at Dudley Wood and the Heathens then held them to a draw in the away fixture to move into fourth place in the League behind Bradford, Eastbourne and Swindon. A successful month was completed with an away win at King's Lynn, a home win against top-of-the-League Bradford, a 4-point defeat at Glasgow, and a move into the quarter-finals of the KO Cup after defeating Oxford on aggregate. Everything in the garden continued to be rosy, as Cradley picked up their second trophy of the season, winning the Fours Championship final at Peterborough at the beginning of August, and they followed this with a win over Belle Vue at Dudley Wood.

White-hot Hamill had moved into second place in the League Riders averages with a super 10.75 points, bettered only by Joe Screen. Hancock was only red-hot, in seventh place with 10.23 and Cross was nineteenth with 8.96. Forsgren had moved above Smith (5.62 and 5.18), and Knott and Wilson averaged 3.93 and 2.61 respectively.

The beginning of August brought the fourth Grand Prix at Linköping, and that man Tommy Knudsen did it again! He would no doubt have been in with a chance of the Championship but for the first two rounds that, through injury, saw him score just 2 points in each. Tony Rickardsson, Greg Hancock and Grand Prix leader Hans Nielsen followed him home on the night. Billy Hamill could manage only ninth place, and slipped to fourth place overall. Sheffield were saved only by reserve Rene Aas, as Cradley's American dynamic duo powered to another pair of maximums at Owlerton, but without Forsgren, the Heathens' tail-end was weak, and the Tigers scraped home by 2 points.

Friday 18 August saw Cradley at Belle Vue for the first leg of the KO Cup semi-final. Hamill was his usual fantastic self, dropping only 1 point and scoring 17, Hancock and Cross backed him admirably, but the rest were a sorry bunch. Forsgren had two falls and failed to score, as did Smith, Knott scored 3, Wilson 1, and the Heathens found themselves with 11 points to make up the following night at Dudley Wood. It got off to a bad start as Cradley lost Knott when he crashed in his first outing, and Cross also crashed in his last race. Forsgren and Smith fared a little better than the previous night, but not even 14 points from Hancock and a faultless 15-point maximum from Hamill could save Cradley from losing the match by 8 points, thereby ending their KO Cup run.

As Billy scored another maximum at Oxford, he moved into top spot in the League Riders averages, and staked his claim to be possibly the best rider in the world at that particular moment, but the Heathens, especially away from home, had become a team split into two: Hamill, Hancock, Cross – and the rest. And that was the case at Cowley when they lost by 5 points. It only took one of the top three to have a bad night, which they rarely did, and Cradley struggled. Crossy had one against Arena-Essex at Dudley Wood, but, fortunately Forsgren and Smith raised their game to cover him and the Heathens won the match 50-46.

The end of August heralded the Dudley/Wolves Trophy. The matches were usually bruising affairs, and this one was no different. The speedway world shook their heads in disbelief at the passion with which this particular trophy was ridden for, year in and year out. They argued that it wasn't a matter of life and death; no, it was more important than that – it was the Dudley/Wolves Trophy.

Ermolenko became the first casualty, having to withdraw from the meeting after two brilliant heat wins. He suffered a damaged ankle after Smith had taken him into the fence. Smith himself crashed twice during the turbulent encounter, as did John Wilson, but nevertheless, Cradley took a 4-point advantage to Monmore Green that night. With no time to recover, Ermolenko and Wilson did not make the return leg. Dave Clarke stood in for Wilson, and Sam's brother Charlie stood in for him, scoring 10 points. Again, it turned into a brutal affair, this time Forsgren became the first casualty in heat 1 when he fell and broke his wrist. He was missed, but a 15-point maximum by Billy held the Wolves to a mere 2-point win, and the Heathens retained the trophy.

Exeter were no match for a rampant Cradley at Dudley Wood. Crossy scored a brilliant 18-point maximum, and Smithy scored 11 points. The Scud had found his best form of the season in the last few weeks, and he revealed the reason – religion. Scotty had found religion. Well, the track had been blessed!

On 6 September, Hans Nielsen won the fifth Grand Prix in front of his own countrymen in Vojens, Denmark. He won the meeting from Sam Ermolenko and Tony Rickardsson. Billy finished in seventh place and Greg in sixth.

The Heathens' next match was a toughie – a visit to Bradford. The Dukes were unbeaten at home all season and were the team that sat between Cradley and top-of-the-League Eastbourne. Using rider replacement for Forsgren and led by

Billy Hamill. (Hall)

a vintage 16 points from Crossy, Bradford were toppled by just 2 points and the Heathens replaced them at second place in the League. The Yanks, of course, gave Simon solid support, but the difference was Smithy, digging in and scoring paid 11 points. The Cradley demolition machine trundled on to Exeter and crushed them 56-39, and again Cross rolled back the years to score an 18-point maximum. Enthusiasm was high, both in the team and on the terraces, but the end of the season was nearing, and Cradley were looking at the prospect of their precious team being homeless at the end of it.

Mid-September, Forsgren returned to score paid 10 points, which, combined with a couple of maximums from the Americans, was too much for Long Eaton to handle at Dudley Wood. At Brandon the following night, the Heathens looked in the early stages as though they were going to pull it off, but Coventry rallied and stormed back to an 8-point win. Eastbourne were now 14 points clear of Cradley and looked unassailable.

Saturday 30 September brought the final Grand Prix of the season – the British Grand Prix. A special stadium had been built for the event in Hackney, the London Stadium. Greg Hancock became the first-ever British Grand Prix winner, beating Sam Ermolenko and Mark Loram in the final. Hamill finished in fifth place, just ahead of Nielsen, but it was enough for the Dane. Hans became the 1995 World Champion. He was followed by Rickardsson and Ermolenko, but in fourth and fifth place were Greg and Billy. They both did themselves proud. The future looked bright for the Cradley pair. They probably had not even reached their peak yet and, even though he was World Champion, Nielsen was past his.

Cradley moved out of September and into October with wins at Dudley Wood over Edinburgh and Middlesbrough, but a loss at Peterborough handed the League title to Eastbourne. The League Champions were the next visitors to Dudley Wood, and, as if to prove a point, the Heathens took them apart. They won their final League match at home against Oxford, but unfortunately, having completed their fixtures, their final League position was out of Cradley's control. Bradford had matches in hand, and the Heathens could only stand by and watch as the Dukes piled up the points to overtake the Heathens in the League and snatch the runners-up spot from under their noses.

It had still been a great year. Billy Hamill had been amazing; he had

OFFICIAL PROGRAMME OF CRADLEY HEATH SPEEDWAY £1.20

HEATHENS 1995

Speedway Review

Meeting No. 18
Saturday 15th July 1995 at 7.30 p.m.
British Premier League Match
Cradley 'Heathens' vs
Hull 'Vikings'

CLUBCALL 0891 12 18 78 • CLUBCALL 0891 12 18 78

1995 programme.

finished on top of the League averages with 10.86 points and 16 maximums. Fellow countryman Greg Hancock had been just as amazing. He had finished seventh in the League averages with 10.40 and 16 maximums. The pair were truly at the top of their profession. They had become part of the Cradley elite, who had started at the bottom and had risen to the very top. Dudley Wood had been a breeding ground of champions, and they were well and truly established as part of its folklore.

Simon Cross had a fantastic year; he did everything that could have been asked of him, and then much, much more. A lot of people thought that Simon hadn't got another season in him like his '94 season, but he came back with a bang to average 9.16 points. Cradley had a relatively injury-free season, but not for Johnny Forsgren, he had been in and out of the team like a yo-yo but always gave his best. John averaged 5.63.

Scott Smith took more knocks than Forsgren, but missed fewer matches. Battered and bruised, he still turned out, sometimes to his detriment, but Smithy did put in some fine performances, though inconsistency kept his average down to 5.46. Steve Knott had been a success. He averaged 4.0 points in his first season in the top speedway league in the world, which is no mean feat. John Wilson had also done well to average 2.02 points. He had proved himself to be a bonny battler and the supporters hoped that his future lay at Cradley Heath speedway – if Cradley Heath speedway had a future.

The last match at Dudley Wood was a challenge match between the Hancock Select and the Hamill Select. The outcome is inconsequential, the important thing is that that's what it was – the last match at Dudley Wood. As Hancock crossed the line in heat 16, there was a tear in many an eye on an emotion-charged night. During the season there had been many collections, discos, social functions and the like to raise funds to fight the enemy during the close season. Now the season was over, the fight to save Cradley Heath Speedway could begin in earnest.

At the beginning of 1995, the enemy was unknown, but by the end of 1995, it had revealed itself to be Barratt Homes – a formidable opponent indeed. The end of November bought about a significant event. Pratt jumped. He offered his resignation and it was accepted. The reason that this was so significant is that Colin was still on speaking terms with Derek Pugh, and this meant that Pratt probably had a clearer picture of the situation than anyone else, Pottinger and Heiding included. After twelve years and some awful times that would have seen many a man quit, he decided to throw in the towel. There could be only one reason – he saw no future for Cradley Heath Speedway, and he was rarely wrong.

So what would he do? Colin had a reputation for playing his cards close to his chest. He was never going to get a degree in public relations, and he knew it. But that was his style. He informed the public that he didn't even know if he would be involved in speedway any more, but the more astute suspected that he would turn up managing the new London Stadium, which was about to put in a League side for 1996, and in the event he did. Pratt had his critics, but what was he expected to do? He couldn't save Cradley. He was a speedway manager and he had to have a team to manage, otherwise – no job.

The Bridgewaters obviously wanted to sell the ground to the re-developers because they were a big company with big money, but there were certain obstacles to overcome before building could take place, and the Cradley Strike Force would make sure that every single one of them was addressed.

It was said that the ground was contaminated (that blessing couldn't have worked), and then there was the question of Dudley Wood being a sports ground, and therefore not eligible for development and so on and so forth. The battle raged, as plans were submitted and turned down and resubmitted and turned down again, but the tale has overrun.

Cross was next to jump, as early as December, not very far in fact, and he signed for Coventry Bees. Simon had adored being at Cradley – there was no doubt about that whatsoever. He had proved it time and time again, giving his all when he was in no fit condition to be on the track, and his move was an indication of how people on the inside felt the situation would turn out. At such a crucial time, the promoters were desperate to keep support for the club well and truly behind them, and so regularly held meetings to answer any questions and to keep the public updated as to what was happening. At such a meeting, held at a Brierley Hill Bingo Club in December, Plan C was revealed. Pottinger first of all informed a packed hall what had happened to Plans A and B. Plan A – Buy the stadium. Any bid that the promoters had put in had been turned down by the owners. Plan B – Find a suitable plot of land and build a new stadium. The Black Country had been searched extensively and no plot had yet been found. Sven Heiding told the supporters of Plan C – the only option that lay open to the club. Cradley were going to ride the 1996 season at Stoke or close down.

20
LOOMER ROAD
1996

The Loomer Road Stadium in Stoke was host to only a handful of Academy League Speedway meetings in 1995 and was in bad repair. Much work was to be carried out both on the track and the stadium in the close season in order to make it fit to stage First Division racing.

Jan O. Pedersen was appointed team manager and acted swiftly to secure the services of Hamill and Hancock. He bought in Swedish Dalle Anderson to replace Cross, Stuart Swales to replace Forsgren, Colin's son Troy Pratt to replace Smith, who had returned to Sheffield, and he retained Knott and Wilson as reserves. As regards the Cradley supporters, coaches would be laid on every week to transport them to Loomer Road.

Before the season began, there was dissent between the Stoke and Cradley supporters. The Stoke supporters didn't want the team who rode on their track to be called Cradley. It was a bit like the team playing at Molineux Football Stadium being called West Bromwich Albion, so to speak, and the Cradley supporters would be damned if their team was to be called Stoke, so the team was christened Cradley Heath and Stoke!

Work was still being carried out at Loomer Road when the season began, and it wasn't much to look at, but it was home to the Heathens in 1996, their final resting place as it were. Initially hopes were high – Hamill and Hancock began like greyhounds and didn't let up all season. Journeyman Les Collins was brought in after a few months to give the team a lift and he did an admirable job.

It was a relatively injury-free year for Cradley Stoke, and they finished in the top ten in the League, but attendances had declined. The Dudley/Wolves Trophy match, a phenomenal crowd-puller at Dudley Wood, attracted only 500 spectators, and Les Pottinger was losing money hand over fist. In fairness, the match was on Wednesday night, and for some the 100-mile round trip was just too much to manage.

Billy Hamill achieved his ambition and became World Speedway Champion. Hans Nielsen was runner-up and Greg Hancock finished in third place. Between them, the Americans ran riot in the League, taking the top two places in the League Riders averages. They had breathed new life into the sport, and with the advent of television covering speedway, they were both naturals on camera. Hamill and Hancock now stood at the very pinnacle of the sport, the most dynamic duo that speedway had ever seen.

By the end of the season, Pottinger was a beaten man. He had done what he said he would and had given the Heathens another season in the British League, but financially it had cost him. He was always on a loser and probably knew it. Once the early season furore had died down, it was inevitable that the Cradley contingent of supporters would dwindle – even Coventry was closer to Dudley Wood than Stoke was, and Wolves was a hell of a lot closer than that. Pottinger had relied on the people from Stoke giving their support, but that never really happened. However, you had to applaud old Les. Nobody had done more for the Heathens in their hour of need, and he proved himself to be one of a rare breed that put his money where his mouth was. But now he could do no more.

It was already obvious that another season at Loomer Road would be a financial disaster, so again the attentions turned to the owners of Dudley Wood Stadium. All through the 1996 season, the protests from the Cradley supporters never let up. Planning permission to build on the stadium had again been refused, but still Barratt Homes would not pull out. And then it got nasty. Noel Bridgewater, clearly frustrated at not being able to do what he wanted with his own plot of land, issued a chilling statement, the gist of which was, even if Barratt Homes did not purchase the land, Mr Bridgewater would never ever sell to Cradley Heath Speedway under any circumstances. There would never again be speedway at Dudley Wood. Derek Pugh whole-heartedly endorsed the statement.

It was all over. The supporters were up in arms, refusing to give up and determined to fight on. While they were doing so, the bulldozers drove into Dudley Wood Stadium.

EPILOGUE

8 November 2001

Dudley Wood Stadium lies derelict, the sound of the motorcycles and the smell of the fuel long gone. It has been flattened, it has been flooded, it has been burned, it has been many things – but not re-opened. Permission to re-develop has still not been granted. The owners remain steadfast in their refusal to sell to Cradley Heath Speedway.

London Speedway Stadium closed to speedway after only one season, and Colin Pratt moved back into the Midlands to manage Coventry. He signed Greg Hancock to the Brandon outfit and, that same year, Greg followed in Billy Hamill's footsteps and became the 1997 World Speedway Champion. Hamill found himself at Belle Vue, but the following year, Colin had signed him too, re-uniting him with Hancock.

At the time of writing, the sport is going through a renaissance, mainly due to Sky Sports taking a big interest, not only screening all the Grand Prix but a weekly League match also. How they would have enjoyed those Cradley-Wolves matches!

This is a strange tale, for it is a tale without any winners – only losers – and everybody lost. Derek Pugh and the Bridgewaters must have lost thousands of pounds in revenue from Cradley Heath Speedway. Barratt Homes has lost thousands of pounds in appeals and planning permissions that so far have been rejected and refused. Cradley Heath supporters have lost their beloved Heathens.

I stand in front of what was once Dudley Wood Stadium, derelict for some six years now. The cynic in me says that in the not-too-distant future, I shall be seeing a new development of houses there, and yet again a big corporation with big lawyers and big money will win another battle against the common man. However, the die-hards still exist, and to them such talk is heresy. They firmly believe that speedway will return to Dudley Wood – and God bless them for it.

In either case, the memories will always remain. As I stand there, many come flooding back:

> The smell of the fuel – it used to hit you about a quarter of a mile from the stadium, and it was utterly fantastic. On pre-season practice day you would approach the stadium taking bloody great whiffs of it up your nostrils. You hadn't had any for a least four months, and this would be your first fix of the year.

> My first boyhood hero – The White Ghost of Dudley Wood – Ivor Brown.

> The time Colin Pratt beat Ivan Mauger twice in the same night.

> The countless matches against Wolverhampton.

> Bruce Penhall becoming Cradley's first World Champion.

> Erik Gundersen's tragic accident and his farewell two laps of honour.

Wonderful, wonderful Dudley Wood Stadium. To be honest it was far from wonderful. It had changed little over the last twenty years, the management arguing that the money was spent on the riders, and nothing was left to spend on improvements to the stadium – but so what? It had been the home of the Heathens, and there was no better place to be on a Saturday night.

I leave the dereliction, and head for Cradley Heath town. A couple of hundred yards into my journey, I pass a brick-built bridge. It is the one which has painted on it 'Ivor is king'. Those were the days.

Peter Foster

THE HEATHENS THROUGH THE YEARS

(Averages shown in brackets)

1977   British League – 7th place   **(19 teams)**
        Dudley/Wolves Trophy Winners

TEAM: Anders Michanek (10.35), Bernt Persson (8.34), Steve Bastable (7.86), Bruce Cribb (capt.) (6.54), Bob Valentine (6.50), Dave Perks (6.00), Arthur Price (5.61), Nigel Wasley (0.57), Richie Caulwell (1.00), Phil Collins (4.57).

MANAGER: Dan McCormick

1978   British League – 5th place   **(19 teams)**
        Dudley/Wolves Trophy Winners

TEAM: Steve Bastable (9.52), Bruce Penhall (9.26), Alan Grahame (8.21), Kristian Praestbro (6.56), Bruce Cribb (capt.) (6.22), Phil Collins (5.44), Dave Perks (5.23), Pekka Hautamaji (5.22), Dave Shields (5.05), Arthur Price (3.68), John Hack (4.50), James Moore (3.00), Les Sawyer (2.29), Pip Lamb (0.00).

MANAGER: Bob Wasley

1979   British League – 3rd place   **(18 teams)**
        KO Cup Winners
        Inter-League Cup Winners
        Dudley/Wolves Trophy Winners
        Bobby Schwartz – American Champion

TEAM: Bruce Penhall (9.88), Alan Grahame (8.34), Phil Collins (7.85), Bobby Schwartz (7.84), Steve Bastable (capt.) (7.71), Kristian Praestbro (7.54), Eric Gundersen (7.35), Dave Perks (6.84), John Hack (4.77), Les Rumsey (4.76), Mike Sampson (4.71).

MANAGER: Bob Wasley

1980   British League – 5th place   **(17 teams)**
        KO Cup Winners
        Midland Cup Winners

Dudley/Wolves Trophy Winners
Bruce Penhall – American Champion

TEAM: Bruce Penhall (capt.) (10.35), Dave Perks (8.96), Alan Grahame (8.22), Phil Collins (8.16), Eric Gundersen (8.09), Ila Teromaa (4.94), Mike Sampson (4.42), John Hack (4.38), Derek Harrison (3.24), Craig Featherby (1.25), Paul Bosley (0.70).

MANAGER: Bob Wasley

1981   British League Champions   **(16 teams)**
Bruce Penhall – World Champion
Intercontinental Champion
American Champion
World Pairs Champion
Eric Gundersen – Midland Riders Champion

TEAM: Bruce Penhall (capt.) (11.08), Eric Gundersen (10.26), Alan Grahame (9.26), Phil Collins (7.26), Dave Shields (6.12), Bent Rasmussen (4.70), John McNeil (3.61), Dave Perks (2.67).

MANAGER: Peter Adams

1982   British League – Runners-up   **(15 teams)**
KO Cup Winners
League Cup Winners
Premiership Winners
Bruce Penhall – World Champion
Eric Gundersen – Midland Riders Champion

TEAM: Bruce Penhall (capt.) (10.74), Eric Gundersen (10.18), Alan Grahame (9.22), Phil Collins (7.30), Simon Wigg (6.67), Lance King (6.30), Ian Gledhill (3.45), Andy Reid (3.02), Wayne Jackson (3.00), Jan Verner (2.69), Bill Barratt (1.78), Simon Cross (3.37).

MANAGER: Peter Adams

1983   British League Champions   **(15 teams)**
KO Cup Winners
Midland Cup Winners
Phil Collins – Overseas Champion
Eric Gundersen – Midland Riders Champion
British League Riders Champion

TEAM: Eric Gundersen (capt.) (10.18), Simon Wigg (8.86), Lance King (8.74), Alan Grahame (8.69), Phil Collins (7.98), Peter Ravn (7.97), Jan O Pedersen (6.78), Simon Cross (6.00) Andy Reid (2.55), Dave Cheshire (2.33).

MANAGER: Peter Adams

| 1984 | British League – 3rd place | (16 teams) |

1984   British League – 3rd place   (16 teams)
         League Cup Winners
         Midland Cup Winners
         Premiership Winners
         Eric Gundersen – World Champion
            World Longtrack Champion
         Lance King – Overseas Champion
            Midland Riders Champion

TEAM: Eric Gundersen (capt.) (9.54), Lance King (8.65), Phil Collins (8.40), Alan Grahame (7.87), Simon Cross (7.27), Finn Jensen (5.08), Mike Wilding (1.96), Steve Collins (1.49), Bill Barrett (1.71).

MANAGER: Colin Pratt

1985   British League – 7th place   (11 teams)
         Premiership Winners
         Eric Gundersen – World Champion
            World Pairs Champion
            British League Riders Champion
         Lance King – Overseas Champion
            Midland Riders Champion

TEAM: Eric Gundersen (capt.) (10.38), Phil Collins (7.93). Jan O. Pedersen (7.90), Alan Grahame (7.36), Simon Cross (6.21), Finn Jensen (5.41), Kevin Smith (4.25), Steve Collins (1.22), Nigel Leaver (1.20).

MANAGER: Colin Pratt

1986   British League – Runners-up   (11 teams)
         League Cup Winners (shared)
         Dudley/Wolves Trophy Winners
         Eric Gundersen – World Longtrack Champion
            World Pairs Champion
            Intercontinental Champion

TEAM: Eric Gundersen (capt.) (11.03), Jan O. Pedersen (8.58), Phil Collins (7.80), Simon Cross (7.17), Steve Bastable (6.08), Nigel Leaver (3.74), Paul Fry (3.23), Paul Taylor (2.06), Wayne Garratt (0.67).

MANAGER: Colin Pratt

1987	British League – Runners-up	(12 teams)

> KO Cup Winners
> Midland Cup Winners
> British Trophy Winners
> Dudley/Wolves Trophy Winners
> *Eric Gundersen – Nordic Champion*
> > *World Pairs Champion*
> > *Intercontinental Champion*

TEAM: Eric Gundersen (capt.) (10.45), Jan O. Pedersen (9.60), Simon Cross (9.33), David Walsh (5.10), Alan Grahame (4.94), Jan Jakobsen (3.94), Dean Barker (3.79), Paul Fry (3.47), Wayne Garratt (0.67).

MANAGER: Colin Pratt

1988	British League – 3rd place	(11 teams)

> KO Cup Winners
> Premiership Winners
> Dudley/Wolves Trophy Winners
> *Eric Gundersen – World Champion*
> > *World Pairs Champion*
> *Simon Cross – Overseas Champion*
> *Jan O. Pedersen – Intercontinental Champion*
> > *Danish Champion*
> > *British League Riders Champion*

TEAM: Eric Gundersen (capt.) (10.06), Jan O. Pedersen (9.88), Simon Cross (8.22), Alan Grahame (6.92), Gert Handberg (5.10), David Walsh (4.50), Wayne Garratt (0.67), Justin Walker (4.00).

MANAGER: Colin Pratt

1989	British League – 3rd place	(9 teams)

> KO Cup Winners
> Premiership Winners

221

Eric Gundersen – Danish Champion
World Pairs Champion
Gert Handberg – World Under-21 Champion

TEAM: Jan O. Pedersen (9.94), Eric Gundersen (capt.) (9.53), Simon Cross (8.86), Gert Handberg (6.36), Alan Grahame (6.25), Greg Hancock (5.97), John Bostin (2.96), Justin Walker (2.19).

MANAGER: Colin Pratt

| 1990 | British League – 7th place | (9 teams) |

1990   British League – 7th place   (9 teams)
       Dudley/Wolves Trophy Winners
       Premiership Winners
       Jan O. Pedersen – Danish Champion
          World Pairs Champion
          Scandinavian Champion

TEAM: Jan O. Pedersen (9.25), Simon Cross (9.03), Billy Hamill (6.82), Alan Grahame (6.39), Gert Handberg (6.13), Greg Hancock (5.51), Mark Robinson (2.56), David Haynes (0.62).

MANAGER: Colin Pratt

1991   British League – 3rd place   (13 teams)
       Dudley/Wolves Trophy Winners
       Jan O. Pedersen – World Champion
          World Pairs Champion
          World Team Cup Champion
          Danish Champion

TEAM: Jan O. Pedersen (capt.) (9.58), Billy Hamill (8.96), Greg Hancock (7.97), Gert Handberg (7.87), Alan Grahame (6.82), Simon Cross (5.40), Mark Robinson (4.60), Wayne Garratt (3.58), Scott Smith (3.18), Mark Meredith (0.00), Anthony Boyd (0.00).

MANAGER: Colin Pratt

1992   British League – 4th place   (13 teams)
       Dudley/Wolves Trophy Winners
       Gert Handberg – Danish Champion
       Scott Smith – British Under-21 Champion

TEAM: Jan O. Pedersen (11.37), Greg Hancock (9.65), Billy Hamill (8.64), Simon Cross (capt.) (7.91), Gert Handberg (7.40), Andy Grahame (6.33), Andy Phillips (4.17), Scott Smith (3.79), Justin Walker (2.50), Mark Robinson (0.75).

MANAGER: Colin Pratt

1993 **British League – 11th place** **(11 teams)**
  Dudley/Wolves Trophy Winners

TEAM: Greg Hancock (9.85), Billy Hamill (8.99), Simon Cross (capt.) (6.22), Gert Handberg (6.15), Scott Smith (5.95), Morton Andersen (5.84), Andy Grahame (5.20), Alan Grahame (4.64), Justin Walker (4.56), Anthony Boyd (3.22).

MANAGER: Colin Pratt

1994 **British League – 9th place** **(11 teams)**
  Dudley/Wolves Trophy Winners

TEAM: Greg Hancock (capt.) (9.27), Peter Nahlin (8.76), Billy Hamill (8.43), Simon Cross (7.70), Morton Andersen (7.29), Scott Smith (5.03), Jonathan Forsgren (4.41), David Clarke (3.76), Justin Walker (1.81), Lance Sealey (1.49), Anthony Boyd (1.27).

MANAGER: Colin Pratt

1995 **British League – 3rd place** **(21 teams)**
  League Fours Champions
  Dudley/Wolves Trophy Winners

TEAM: Billy Hamill (10.86), Greg Hancock (capt.) (10.40), Simon Cross (9.16), Jonathan Forsgren (5.63), Scott Smith (5.46), Steve Knott (4.00), John Wilson (2.02).

MANAGER: Colin Pratt

THE DUDLEY WOOD STADIUM TRACK RECORD

TRACK LENGTH: 367 YARDS OR 338 METRES

DATE	TIME	HOLDER	DATE	TIME	HOLDER
21/06/47	81.6	Les Beaumont	30/04/63	70.4	Ivor Brown
28/06/47	81.4	Geoff Bennett	13/07/63	70.4	Norman Hunter
05/07/47	80.0	Cyril Roger	13/07/63	70.4	Ivor Brown
12/04/47	79.6	Geoff Bennett	20/07/63	68.2	Ivor Brown
06/09/47	79.6	Bob Fletcher	12/05/69	67.0	Eric Boocock
17/04/48	78.0	Alan Hunt	13/06/70	66.8	Jim Airey
14/05/48	75.6	Alan Hunt	20/06/70	66.2	Ole Olsen
30/07/48	75.6	Joe Bowkis			
08/10/48	74.6	Alf Bottoms	25/08/74	66.2	Dave Jessup
20/05/49	73.2	Alan Hunt	16/08/75	66.2	Ivan Mauger
26/08/49	72.8	Alan Hunt	04/10/76	66.0	John Boulger
07/10/49	72.8	Alan Hunt	01/04/77	65.9	Bernt Persson
25/04/50	72.2	Alan Hunt	06/07/77	65.4	Ole Olsen
29/04/50	72.2	Billy Bales	23/09/78	65.4	Steve Bastable
24/06/50	72.0	Alan Hunt	11/10/78	64.6	Steve Bastable
17/07/50	72.0	Alan Hunt	14/10/78	63.9	Steve Bastable
14/04/52	72.0	Harry Bastable	10/09/79	63.9	Bruce Penhall
18/04/52	71.4	Harry Bastable	21/06/80	63.9	Bruce Penhall
25/04/52	70.6	Bob Baker	23/07/80	63.4	Alan Grahame
25/07/52	69.8	Phil Malpass	04/07/81	62.9	Bruce Penhall
			27/07/83	62.3	Dennis Sigalos
Track closed until 1960			01/06/85	62.0	Phil Collins
			24/07/85	61.8	Erik Gundersen
23/07/60	73.4	Ross Gilbertson	18/10/86	61.5	Hans Nielsen
23/07/60	73.4	Harry Bastable	13/04/88	61.5	Hans Nielsen
20/08/60	71.6	Harry Bastable	09/07/88	61.5	Erik Gundersen
29/04/61	71.6	Reg Reeves	20/07/88	61.5	Simon Cross
17/07/61	71.6	Harry Bastable	06/09/89	61.2	Erik Gundersen
29/07/61	71.4	Ivor Brown	23/09/89	61.2	Kelvin Tatum
23/06/61	71.4	John Hart	18/07/90	60.7	Hans Nielsen

224